Think About These Things

Richard C. Boyd

Parson's Porch Books

Think About These Things
ISBN: Softcover 978-1-955581-81-3
Copyright © 2022 by Richard C. Boyd

All Scriptural references are taken from the New Revised Standard Version of the Bible unless noted otherwise.

Parson's Porch Books is an imprint of Parson's Porch *&* Company (PP*&*C) in Cleveland, Tennessee. PP*&*C is an innovative organization which raises money by publishing books of noted authors, representing all genres. Its face and voice is **David Russell Tullock** (dtullock@parsonsporch.com).

Parson's Porch *&* Company *turns books into bread & milk* by sharing its profits with the poor.

www.parsonsporch.com

Think About These Things

Contents

Come By Here. 9
Praying with Suction 10
Humming 11
Weeds and Lillies 12
Rivers of Living Waters 14
Ring The Bells That Still Can Ring 16
Our Kind of People 17
Earth's Crammed With Heaven 19
God-shaped Vacuum 20
On Grace and Gratitude 22
Murmuring 24
Choosing the Best Road 26
Rocks 28
Clouds 30
Birds 32
Brooding 34
Nevertheless 36
On Standing 38
Hold Your Horses 40
Goodbye 42
Ubiquity 43
Shadow 45
Mind 47
Single-minded 49
Pass 51
Drawing Upon What is Known to be True 53
Strength Alongside 55
"Rent Space" in Our Minds 58
On Being Shaped 60
Living With Fear 62
Thanksgiving 65
Advent 67
Waiting 69
Stars 71
Stories 73
Gifts 75
On Feeding 77
Cold Water 80
Gladness 83
Awake 86
Seeing Clearly 88
Coming Clean 90
A Room Called Remember 92

Seeking the Welfare of Others..94
With Wings Like Eagles...96
Gethsemane..99
Easter (1)..102
Redemption...105
Weeds..108
Tending...110
Smile...113
Seasons...116
Propensity...118
Precious..120
Journey...122
Pleasure..124
Lagniappe...126
Locusts..128
Hidden..130
Unlikely Story...132
Denial...135
Blessing...137
Gradually, then Suddenly...139
Consequences...141
Awe and Wonder..143
Rest...145
Hills..147
Labor...149
Sorrow..151
Laughter..153
All In The Same Boat...155
Trouble...157
On Giants and Grasshoppers..159
Dreams...161
Remembering..164
Thanksgiving (2)...166
Bread..169
Daily Bread...172
Now/Not Yet...174
Christmas..176
Light in the Darkness...180
Keeping Christmas..183
Beginnings..185
Eyes..187
Hands...189
Way...191
Sounds..194
Whispers...197

Coming Home..199
Fear..201
He Leadeth Me...204
Face...207
Blessing...209
Palm Sunday...211
Easter (2)..213
Shadows..216
Water...218
Breath..220
Sit...222
Secret...224
Sufficient...226

Come By Here.

Holy Week. In ordinary times, it stands out for us – Palm Sunday, Maundy Thursday, Good Friday, Easter Egg Hunt, Easter worship on Easter Day. But it takes a special action of thought and mind for it to stand out if we are all staying separate in our homes. We will have an Easter service on Facebook at 11:00 AM this Sunday (Croatan Presbyterian Church), but the other remembrances and celebrations will have to wait until next year. Is it necessary, however, that this is to our detriment? I don't think so.

One of the wonderful things about our religious faith is the fact that everywhere we go, God is there with us. Listen to the Psalmist in Psalm 139 (vss. 7-12):

> *"Where can I go from your spirit? Or where can I flee from your presence?*
> *If I ascend to heaven, you are there; if I make my bed in Sheol, you are there.*
> *If I take the wings of the morning and settle at the farthest limits of the sea,*
> *even there your hand shall lead me,*
> *and your right hand shall hold me fast.*
> *If I say, "Surely the darkness shall cover me, and the light around me become night,"*
> *even the darkness is not dark to you;*
> *the night is as bright as the day, for darkness is as light to you."*

One of the comments I remember from my youth pertaining to the nearness of God was the expression "God who is as near as hand and face." That's pretty near! So often we tend to want God to be "out there" where we can see him active in our lives. But the truth is that God is as near as "hand and face." It's a way of saying he is close by. Very close by, like the Psalmist says. Like the camp song "Kum Bah Yah" ("Come By Here") points to. Like a sincere awareness of the risen Lord in our lives reveals. Like the words from "Taps" convey: "All is well, safely rest, God is nigh."

So, as we go through this very different Holy Week separated in our homes, but not in our sense of community, let us remember that God is near, very near, to each of us.

Praying with Suction

As we go through the series of days now strung together in a kind of sameness, I wonder if each of us has found our praying during this time suffering from a sense of sameness as well. Of course, that will vary from person to person, but for me, it can become kind of repetitive unless I invoke some helpful thoughts about how to pray.

I mentioned in a sermon or two several years ago that one helpful thought to assist in praying with our hearts focused on God was the notion of "praying with suction!" A rather unusual application of terms for praying, don't you think? But it can be helpful. For, you see, to pray with suction is to pray in a manner of "taking in" visions, words, pictures, stories, and music that draw us into the presence of God. So, when one prays and begins with, say, a parable of Jesus in the forefront of the mind, one might draw from the parable words and images to help shape the prayer. One is "sucking in" images and ideas from the parable. Take the Prodigal Son parable, for example. After reading it and listening to what God might be saying through it, one might begin to pray: *"Father God . . . and I call you Father this night because you have presented yourself to me in this parable as a father just as you have in many ways throughout my life. I see you as one who opens doors to take me in even in those times when I have shut the door to you. And I see your nature as that of a God who welcomes the stranger, receives the penitent, seeks the confused, and offers comfort to the grieving. Like a Father. So help me move into the days to come as a grateful son, filled with the desire to serve and honor you."* I think this is praying with suction – drawing into my prayer elements, thoughts, and words from the Scripture that help me to form my prayer and my desire to honor God. Of course, words, images, and other elements may be drawn from just about any area of our lives, sucking in the pictures and images and words to help us form our prayer to God. Try it during these repetitive days.

By the way, Kim Hardison once told me that observing me at our church dinners could be described as "eating with suction." I wonder what she meant by that?

Humming

This morning I woke up humming. That doesn't happen every day for me, but it did today. I was humming a song we usually sing at the time of Advent – "There's A Song In The Air." It has a simple, delightful tune which makes it quite hummable. But I wonder why that song for this morning? We're nowhere near Advent. I cannot recall anything that crossed my path in the last several weeks that even brought Advent or Christmas to mind, so where did that tune come from at this particular time?

I suppose one must be versed in the workings of the subconscious mind to find any reason for my association with this song at this time. Since I am not so versed, I'll just enjoy the tune and go on into my day, or so I thought. Our minds, thankfully, don't work quite like that, however. One just doesn't click a thought off and go on. The thought lingers, grows tentacles, and runs around into other areas of one's mind. That "Song In The Air" I was humming metamorphosized into thoughts about other songs and about songs in general. Very soon after I was aware of humming that Advent tune, my mind stumbled into to the words of Psalm 96 which I remembered begins Like this: *"O sing to the Lord a new song: sing to the Lord, all the earth."* Isn't it wonderful how the mind can work? In short order I had moved from a song hanging lazily in the air to a new song to be sung to the Lord by the whole earth. Talk about taking a giant leap! I went from my own air space to the whole earth as celestial choir. I'm glad a mind can do that! I'm glad it can move from the mundane to the magnificent in a blink of an eye. I do believe that that's how we catch a sense of God with us.

I miss singing with our church. Among its many other blessings, singing together the songs of faith take us from the mundane to the magnificent continually. Listening to Bonny's musical pieces that we have placed on our Facebook page can do that, too. And if we start tapping our feet and humming along to the tunes the Oliver family have given us on our Facebook page, we can easily leave the ordinary and move into a place with a beat, a smile, and a sense of life together. That's part of the magnificent, too.

Maybe we can make better use of the time we have with this shut-down as we hum, whistle, sing, and listen to the songs of the earth and the songs which draw us to God. Pastor Rich

> *O sing to the Lord a new song;*
> *sing to the Lord, all the earth.*
> *Sing to the Lord, bless his name;*
> *tell of his salvation from day to day.*
> *Declare his glory among the nations,*
> *his marvelous works among all the **peoples.***
> --Psalm 96:1-3

Weeds and Lilies

I'm glad I'm not in charge! That is, I'm glad I'm not in charge of some of the bigger and better things of life. Like how our garden and yard grow! This spring I have found that if you put 100 pounds of 10-10-10 fertilizer all over one's yard, that all over one's yard things will grow. And I mean grow! I'm hoping that tomorrow I can get out there with the weed-eater and the clippers and the rake and what-not and trim her up. With all the recent rain, I've never seen such a profusion of green – a verdant cathedral of trees, shrubs, flowers, and such. Did I forget to mention the weeds? Yes, all that lushness and weeds, too! It shouldn't surprise me that there are weeds, though. It's part of life.

I am reminded that Jesus once told a parable about weeds which, of course, means that weeds aren't all that new. In Matthew 13: 24-27 we find this: *He put before them another parable: "The kingdom of heaven may be compared to someone who sowed good seed in his field; but while everybody was asleep, an enemy came and sowed weeds among the wheat, and then went away. So when the plants came up and bore grain, then the weeds appeared as well. And the slaves of the householder came and said to him, 'Master, did you not sow good seed in your field? Where, then, did these weeds come from?"*

I've asked that question myself. While Jesus is using this parable to explain how evil exists alongside of what is sown good, I find it comforting to know that my weeds weren't sent just to me by some special provision but have been sprouting up for thousands of years. So, tomorrow, I'll harvest them in order for the garden to flourish – at least for a while.

While we're talking about this, let me also remember another statement of Jesus: *"Consider the lilies of the field, how they grow; they neither toil nor spin, yet I tell you, even Solomon in all his glory was not clothed like one of these."* He sure got that right! Fertilizer or no fertilizer, the garden and yard is growing. Susie's lilies are outstanding. And I'm so glad! I'm glad because I can see that what is around us is designed to grow. Yes, we might have a role in managing it some, but it does it on its own (or, rather, it does it because that's the way of God. Indeed, it grows because of the energy of God. Praise him!).

So, tomorrow, I shall be happily at it – managing the weeds, promoting and trimming the plants, shrubs, flowers, and trees. And it will be good because God made it that way!

> *For the beauty of the earth,*
> *For the beauty of the skies,*
> *For the love which from our birth*
> *Over and around us lies,*
> *Lord of all, to thee we raise*
> *This our hymn of grateful praise.*

For the joy of human eye,
For the heart and mind's delight,
For the mystic harmony
Linking sense to sound and sight,
Lord of all, to thee we raise
This our hymn of grateful praise.
                    -Folliott S. Pterpoint, 1864

Rivers of Living Waters

I'm a bit river-headed right now. By that I mean that during this shut-down with time on my hands, my mind wanders, like a river, all over the place. It goes to places I haven't visited in years. It runs over shallows where I recall incidents and words of little worth. And it runs deep and sure over great thoughts and words of significance. In some moments, I even go to places that make me laugh, and I suspect I'm not the only one. And, for the most part, I am enjoying the meandering. Sometimes I'm standing on the bank watching the water go by. At other times, I'm on some broad rocks in the midst of the stream. And sometimes, believe it or not, I let the river take me into deep water where I flow along with the stream. Wherever I am and wherever I go, a river runs through it. Oh, the places I've gone, the scenes I've reviewed, the journey it has presented to me!

Right now, I'm perched on the riverbank reviewing it all. And, like many before me, I have thought how much a river running through time and landscape is an apt picture of some important parts of life. There is the river of creation that connects us all, with the evolution of the ages moving us ever onward through time. There is the river of history, told and retold as preface to the future. There is the river of family which connects us ethnically, culturally, and genetically. Perhaps, though, the river that runs through it all from the beginning of creation to the present and on to the interminable future is what is called in the Bible *"the river of living waters"* (Jeremiah 17:13). It's a theme that, like its namesake, runs throughout the Biblical story.

The story of the streams of flowing water reveals the history of humankind in the Bible as well as God's continual presence to nourish his creation both physically and spiritually. Remember that river that went out from the Garden in Genesis – it watered the garden and was parted to water the earth. In the Psalms, we hear that God's people shall *"be abundantly satisfied with the fatness of your house; and you shall make them drink of the river of your pleasure"* (Psalm 36:8). Jeremiah morns over the faithlessness of Judah as their destruction and captivity neared stating plaintively these mournful words: *"O hope of Israel! O Lord! All who forsake you shall be put to shame; those who turn away from you shall be recorded in the underworld, for they have forsaken the fountain of living water, the Lord."*

The Psalmist, like most of the Old Testament writers, understands that there are those who live in God's ways and those who do not. Only the righteous partake in the godly flow of the river of life. Listen to the Psalmist in Psalm 1: *Happy are those who do not follow the advice of the wicked, or take the path that sinners tread, or sit in the seat of scoffers; but their delight is in the law of the Lord, and on his law they meditate day and night. They are like trees planted by streams of water, which yield their fruit in it season and their leaves do not wither. In all that they do, they prosper.*

The river of life flows through history and our lives. The Bible uses the metaphor to show that God's nourishing water ever flows through time and history, through Israel and the church, through each life. Some recognize that living water and drink of it; some do not. Some recognize God's grace given in his Son and are baptized with that water. But just as the Bible begins with the river flowing out to cover the world, so it ends with the river. In Revelation 22 we find: *Then the angel showed me the river of the water of life, bright as crystal, flowing from the throne of God and of the Lamb through the middle of the street of the city. On either side of the river is the tree of life. . . .*

I really am more than a bit river-headed right now. For in the midst of this coronavirus and all its dangers and confusions, that river of living waters flows right on, and like the rafters on the Nolichucky, I aim to flow right on as well.

Ring The Bells That Still Can Ring

Leonard Cohen has written numerous lyrics to wonderful songs prior to his recent death. One song, <u>Anthem</u>, which deals with the imperfection of the real world and our expectations of it, offers what appears to be an explanation as to what those imperfections represent. The lyrics begin: *"The birds they sang at the break of day/ start again/ I heard them say/ Don't dwell on what has passed away or what is yet to be. . . ."* With several images that paint a similar picture to those words, Cohen ties them together with his beautiful refrain: *"Ring the bells that still can ring/ forget your perfect offering/ There is a crack in everything/ That's how the light gets in. . . ."*

One doesn't have to go far into each day's events to see the cracks in many things – continuing and increasing coronavirus, attempts to stifle the press, the killing of unarmed citizens, voter-suppression attempts, and the politization of the country – to name a few. Can light come from these cracks and others?

In the Christian community, we're in the light business. We listen to our Lord who tells us over and over not to be anxious, not to worry about what is not before us or about insignificant things. We hear his assurances that there is no darkness that can put out God's light, and that the people who walk in darkness can see a great light. And, we are the folks who are to find the light in the cracks so that we can learn, can repair, can re-think, can find hope, and can live on in the full expectation that goodness can and will come as we stay the course. So, yes, we should "ring the bells that still can ring." We must recognize that there is "no perfect offering." And we live on as the people who seek the light that shines through the "crack in everything." Sound utopian? Perhaps. But it allows us to move positively into the future, following our Lord. Paul describes our way quite well in Philippians 4:6: *The Lord is near. Do not be anxious about anything, but in everything by prayer and supplication with thanksgiving let your requests be made known to God.* Light shines through the cracks in everything, so we ring on with the bells we still can ring.

Our Kind of People

After I had finished my second Master's Degree at Union Theological Seminary in Richmond, VA, I was awaiting the imminent birth of my first child. Being through with school and the baby still several weeks away, I joined some fellow seminarians and took work for a transfer and storage company in the meantime. One day, a fellow seminarian and I had taken a truck load of household furniture and goods to a customer's new home 100 miles away from Richmond. My friend and I spent the day hauling in the furniture and goods as well as assembling things like beds, the swingset, and other items. The wife of this family was there to tell us where to place items. She had her 4 year-old son with her, a delightful young boy who spent most of the day hanging around us and talking with us. His mother called him away for lunch at mid-day. When he came back to where we were upstairs assembling some beds, he was chatting away when he stopped and looked at us asking, "What kind of people are you?" We told him that we were just regular people like most and so forth. Then he made a comment I have never forgotten. He said, "Mother says that you are not our kind of people." That took us aback for a moment. It appeared that since we were in workmen's outfits doing yeoman work for minimum pay ($2.00 an hour, by the way; it was 1970.), that we were not the same kind of people as the mother felt she and her family were.

"Not our kind of people." In a nutshell, this is the root problem we are facing in our society right now. It's not new. It's been there since the founding of the nation. And while many define "our kind of people" in different ways, there is little doubt that this has been a foundational problem regarding race in our society. When others are seen as "not our kind of people," it is easier to criticize them. It is easier to misunderstand them. It is easier to exclude them without much thought. And it is certainly easier to pretend that they are not there until something intrudes into our paths. There is also little doubt that racial prejudice, social ostracism, and hatred of others based on race or ethnicity is the original sin of our society. We have been dealing with it ever since the first African slaves were brought to this country. And perhaps no place is it seen more clearly than in those terrible cases where law enforcement jumped too quickly and sometimes too harshly to using their guns or other means to subdue with deadly results.

Avoiding the "us and them" arguments which polarize rather than help, there is no doubt that we have got to address this "not our kind of people" issue facing us. Most thinking and caring people are just tired of it. Most law enforcement folks are as well. And Christian people? Christian people have marching orders from the Lord himself to welcome the stranger, make a place for the outsider, to offer hospitality to all, and to see each other regardless of differences as brothers and sisters. Christian people of all citizens of our society are the ones who insist on God's justice and fairness in all concerns. There is no other way for Christian people. That's why when we see continued murder and injury to minorities in the name of the law or in the name of "not our kind of people" we must speak out and support those afflicted as well as advocate clearly for the corrections needed in our society. The prophet Micah (6:6-8) has said it well for us and to us three thousand years ago:

> *"With what shall I come before the Lord, and bow myself before God on high?*
> *Shall I come before him with burnt offerings, with calves a year old?*
> *Will the Lord be pleased with thousands of rams, with ten thousands of rivers of oil?*
> *Shall I give my first born for my transgression, the fruit of my body for the sin of my soul?*
> *He has told you, O mortal, what is good: and what does the Lord require of you*
> *But to do justice, and to love kindness, and to walk humbly with your God?*

This, of course, means that everyone is "our kind of people."

Earth's Crammed With Heaven

Elizabeth Barrett Browning is well-known and respected for some 600 letters she wrote to her husband prior to and during their marriage. From her writings many wonderful insights have sprung forth. One quotation has been of interest and delight to me through the years and I share it with you now as a part of our devotional together.

> *Earth's crammed with heaven,*
> *And every common bush afire with God,*
> *But only he who sees takes off his shoes;*
> *The rest sit round and pluck blackberries.*

She is sharing a perspective that transforms moments into times of wonder and insight (delight, too, often). If "earth is crammed with heaven," then the very place we live, the very things we see, and the very lives we live among others can and do reveal a bit of that which comes from above. In other words, God is imminent (known in our present surroundings and lives), not transcendent alone (above and beyond) as many see God to be. You may ask if it can be true that the laughter of a baby, the soaring flight of an Osprey, a roadside ditch bursting with Ox-eyed daisies, and the simple tune of a gospel song reveal a bit of our heavenly Father to us. I say so. When I relax and open my mind as well as my eyes, I see wonder and purpose in most everything around me, even in the pains and hurts. When I allow my thoughts to drift into the words of Jesus or allow my feelings to be tethered to beauty in song, or marvel at the uniqueness of those around me and the very privilege I have in knowing them and spending time and energy with them, I sense a hand on my shoulder, a gentle tug at my heart, and an awareness of being connected to more than the eye can see or the ear can hear. Sound strange? Perhaps, but God's people have always been called a little strange (or maybe a lot strange!) because we dare to say with Ms. Browning, "earth is crammed with heaven, and every common bush afire with God."

During this coronavirus with all of its changes and strangeness where our routines are transformed and the possibilities of each day are narrowed, perhaps our sight can be heightened, and our awareness deepened as we sense God's revelation in the common things. And from time to time, when the insight touches within, we can "take off our shoes," for we find that we are truly treading on holy ground. I assure you that such times render time and effort holy, far more life- giving than the simple tasks (like picking blackberries) with which we often fill our time. Look around you, then. Our God, as Jesus told us, is with us.

God-shaped Vacuum

Blaise Pascal was a French mathematician, physicist, inventor, writer and Roman Catholic theologian, living in the 1600's. He was a child prodigy who was educated by his father, a tax collector in Rouen. Living in the Age of Reason when the most widely known philosophers were subjecting all assertions of truth to reason alone(*that is, it must be demonstrable and logical*), he nevertheless asserted and demonstrated that truth may also be known by the heart (*by what we would call insight and intuition*). He wrote once, "*If we submit everything to reason our religion will be left with nothing mysterious or supernatural. If we offend the principles of reason our religion will be absurd and ridiculous . . . There are two equally dangerous extremes: to exclude reason, to admit nothing but reason.*"

There are those who reject Christian faith because one cannot prove the existence of God and the stories of the Bible are too fantastic to believe by rational people. Equally, there are those who reject religion of any kind as based up wishful thinking rather than anything tangible and validated by objective standards of proof. On the other hand, there are those who believe just about anything that strikes their fancy, no matter how far from the real world it might be. Pascal is one of many theologians who tried to bridge this dichotomy.

One of his insightful statements has stirred my thinking and grabbed my heart as well. Said he, "*There is a God-shaped vacuum in the heart of each man which cannot be satisfied by any created thing but only by God the Creator, made known through Jesus Christ.*"

This insight, of course, is at the very heart of Christian faith. While our knowledge can point us very well to the possibility of a Supreme Being (reason), that which assures us of the reality of God comes through that which is provided us by God to attest to himself – namely, his revelation through the people of Israel and specifically in the life and death and resurrection of Jesus Christ as well as the movement of the Holy Spirit in our hearts and minds.. The human heart is seldom satisfied by the results of reason alone. That which anchors us in faith is our being touched within our hearts by the One who seeks to live there with us.

Each of us is born with both physical and spiritual dimensions. On the physical side of our lives, there are requirements for growth and the continuation of living: food, shelter, warmth, relationships, and understanding of environment. On the spiritual side of our lives, there are requirements as well: a relationship with the Other (God) that fills the places in our hearts that motivate us, provide values, and connects us with the Holy. Unless that "God-shaped vacuum" in our hearts is filled well, we shall wander spiritually through life, finding little to motivate us beyond the self.

Each believer has then to tend to this God-shaped vacuum in order for us to know that which is beyond reason, that which is at the very heart of the universe. That's why Christians pray. It's also why we gather for worship and seek to more deeply understand the revelation recorded in the Bible. It's why we seek to understand more. It's why we serve and share. It's why we find community with others. We are tending to that God-shaped vacuum within until that vacuum is filled by that which God himself provides.

Being at home as much as we are during the coronavirus can give us much more time and perhaps the desire to allow God to fill that God-shaped vacuum. Daily prayer, the study of the Bible, reflecting on life's ponderables, reading devotional materials, talking with fellow believers about things of the heart, and finding one's place in the great story of Jesus all are opportunities for the heart to hear more, grow more, and be more.

On Grace and Gratitude

Karl Barth was a Swiss theologian and Biblical scholar who lived through the twentieth century. His Biblical approach to theology has had an enormous effect upon both Roman Catholic and Protestant theology. In a word, he saved the modern church from drowning in Biblical literalism and theological trivia. He forever moved the goal posts in theology away from any kind of *quid pro quo* where what humans do affects what God does, and, like the Reformers who went before him (Calvin, Luther, *et al.*), underscored the profound effect that God's grace in Jesus Christ has on who we are and what we are to do as those who belong to him.

One of Barth's noteworthy statements is seared into my brain and into my heart. Some of you will remember that I have quoted it in several sermons over the years. It is worthy of quoting many times over the years. In thinking about the role of thanksgiving or giving thanks in our Christian lives, Barth offers us this descriptive picture of the depth and purpose of a grateful heart. Here's the quote:

Grace and gratitude belong together like heaven and earth. Grace evokes gratitude like the voice of an echo. Gratitude follows grace like thunder and lightning.

In my mind, just as heaven and earth describe a single unity – the universe in its entirety, so the awareness of grace filling our world and gratitude as the receptive way to respond to the grace that is there are a single unity as well. Where Christian people know this unity as a style in their living, they are both grounded within life and connected with what is above. This is a unity as well, to be grounded and connected.

Grace, of course, means "gift." It adheres to the giver as something set aside for the recipient. The recipient has no claim on it except to receive it. Upon reception of grace, the recipient is receiving something of the giver as part of the gift. In Jesus Christ God was giving the world a gift – a gift of himself in human form. Where grasped in faith, the gift of Jesus in our hearts and minds reverberates in our thinking, in our acting, in our behavior, and in our plans. In other words, that grace, received with gratitude, acts as a kind of <u>echo</u> in our lives – one can see it manifesting itself over and over. It affects one's style of living, this echoing grateful style does. Others know there is something special and real in the life of one who is grateful to God.

Gratitude, of course, means an "attitude of appreciation and thanks." It's something that is very hard to conjure up without grace evoking it. Of course, that's what God's grace in Jesus Christ evokes where one is open to God's

Spirit. God's grace grasps one's heart and mind and directs it toward love and appreciation, toward the things God has shown us, and to that which God has called us to be. And where gratitude becomes a deeper element in one's being, it acts out far beyond simple appreciation. It acts out in bold acts of kindness, justice, and service. That's why Barth says Gratitude "follows grace like thunder and lightning." Thunder and lightning are bold, direct, energetic, and have a real effect on the landscape it shows up in. So, too, gratitude. It strikes like lightning bearing with it the marks of the grace it has received and gratefully transmits it into a landscape being renewed by its effect.

Far too many Christians receive God's grace with thanks alone. To grow as God's people, however, is to allow that grace to produce a kind of gratitude which strikes here and there, everywhere, producing grace-filled and loving actions like thunder and lightning.

It's something to pray about each day.

Murmuring

I think I am getting better at it after all these weeks – murmuring, that is. Maybe you are getting better at is as well. Murmuring is defined as *"a soft, indistinct sound made by a person or group of people speaking quietly or at a distance."* And while it is looked at as more of a sound we can make at certain times of discomfort or worry, it is usually also made up of words. I wonder what are some of our favorite words for times of murmuring?

"Oh, my, will it ever be over?"
"If those in charge would only do their job."
"There's got to be a better way than this."
"I'm not sure how much longer I can hold out."
"I pray to God for this nightmare to end."

In Exodus 15 we find an interesting little vignette regarding Moses and Aaron on the one hand and the children of Israel on the other:

"Then Moses ordered Israel to set out from the Red Sea, and they went into the wilderness of Shur. They went three days in the wilderness and found no water. When they came to Marah, they could not drink the water of Marah because it was bitter. And the people murmured ("also translated 'complained") against Moses, saying, 'What shall we drink'" He cried out to the Lord; and the Lord showed him a piece of wood; he threw it into the water, and the water became sweet.

"There the Lord made for them a statue and an ordinance and there he put them to the test. He said, 'If you will listen carefully to the voice of the Lord your God, and do what is right in his sight, and give heed to his commandments and keep all his statues, I will not bring upon you any of the diseases that I brought upon the Egyptians; for I am the Lord who heals you.

"Then they came to Elim, were there were twelve springs of water and seventy palm trees; and they camped there by the water."

How like many folks they were. They had just been delivered from Pharaoh's army at the Sea of Reeds, and here they are murmuring over daily water. They had just been renewed from a slave people but let a little set-back come along and right off they murmur. I find myself murmuring every time I go to the grocery because there's no paper towels. I haven't seen a roll of paper towels in either of our two groceries in Beaufort in two months. So, I murmur. Doesn't do any good, I suppose, but I do it. I'll bet you a nickel some of you do as well.

There are bigger things to murmur over than paper towels, to be sure. It doesn't appear that this coronavirus is winding down at all and we fear how much longer we must practice our social distancing and masks and limited movement. Sounds like a pretty good time to murmur. Add to this that the nation as a whole seems to be coming to grips, however messily, with a time of reckoning about nascent racism which has been just under the surface in many areas of our common lives. That's a good thing. But when we see some of the excesses of this time of reckoning, it rattles us and we murmur.

Like smiling and laughter, murmuring and complaint mark us as human, though sometimes either can be excessive. We find murmuring all over the Biblical story, usually the excessive kind. The scribes and Pharisees murmured because Jesus hung out with and welcomed those they deemed as unclean and sinners. One time Jesus chastised them for murmuring, telling them not to complain among themselves over what he was doing. And in those early days of the church, some of the Jewish converts from among the Gentiles murmured against what Paul was preaching and doing among the very poor, leaving their families as among the last to be served.

Are there hints within our Christian faith that can help us in this time of murmuring? Of course, there is. The whole Biblical story is geared to draw us into a life with our God as we deal with the ordinary and extraordinary circumstances of life. And buried throughout the Biblical story are little nutshells of influence and meaning to snag our attention and reorient us along the way.

In the Exodus passage quoted above, we find such a nugget: *"If you will listen carefully to the voice of the Lord your God. . . .",* coupled with *"do what is right. . . ."* Listening and doing – of a specialized nature, tied to the God story, wrapped in the desire to live with our God, given to remind us even in those murmuring times of who we are and how to proceed.

We are learning how to live with this pandemic and to live with it carefully (social distancing, wearing masks, limited exposure to others, practicing wisdom) until the day comes when there is a vaccine. And we are learning anew that the task of fully integrating our society as one people is still an ongoing part of our journey where we are called to go beyond murmuring and into building at better society. Murmuring may come naturally in such a time, but it must be a prelude to faithful response for us believers, or it is wasted effort.

Choosing the Best Road

Many folks are familiar with the famous line in one of Robert Frost's poem – *"Two roads diverged in a wood, and I – I took the one less traveled by, And that made all the difference."*

Some commentators have said that Frost intended the poem as a kind of gentle mocking of indecision and that it was spurred by the many walks with his friend Edward Thomas. Evidently, Thomas had a hard time making up his mind which path to take on their walks. Later Frost was somewhat chagrined that most audiences took the poem more seriously than he had ever intended. For most readers over the years, the lines quoted above have come to reflect the challenge of living life.

In the two passages I list below, we find both Jesus and St. Paul being confronted by two roads, two paths for them to choose from. For Jesus it is to heal or not to heal on the Jewish Sabbath, something the Pharisees and their Scribes criticized him for as it appeared to them not in keeping with Sabbath law forbidding work. For St. Paul the two roads to consider were whether to live by the flesh (the self, and the things which gratified the self) or by the Spirit (living in light of God's presence and ways). In both cases, the men chose the road less traveled. Indeed, both men preached a road less traveled theme in their ministries. Not only did they preach such, they both traveled roads less traveled which is why we know of them and are continually instructed by them even to this day. And it has made all the difference to our lives with our God.

In the Romans 8:1-8 passage Paul challenges us to look at the decisions we make in living our life of faith and how often the choice of the road, the path that is less traveled can make all the difference. Like our world today, St. Paul encountered the road of materialism, power, influence, disharmony among peoples, and a great stress on "life is about me." This was the world of the flesh in St. Paul's mind. Paul, in his ministry over the Mediterranean world asked his congregations and through the Scripture asks us to consider another road, the road of the Spirit. It is a road where awareness of journeying with God, living in the light of God's care and God's ways, is the inner influence on our way. This less-traveled road assures that our journeys are toward that which lasts and in the light of a relationship with God.

In the Luke13:10-17 passage, Jesus is confronted with a woman who has been crippled by a spirit for many years. Jesus, rather than shunning her as obviously unclean, chooses the road less traveled by those of his day – the road of mercy and compassion which resulted in his healing her. The problem for Jesus in choosing this road was that it was the Sabbath day and the common view was that nothing of this sort was to be done during the Sabbath observance. Jesus takes the less-traveled road despite rebukes from some, and it makes all the difference in the world to the woman as well as those watching.

What's here for us? Namely this: In going through each day, particularly since we have to choose carefully during this time of pandemic, a conscious awareness of the road or roads we are on becomes a prime opportunity for choosing to live as God's people, valuing the journey from within God's perspective shown to us in Jesus, and choosing the Jesus Way which most probably will be the road less traveled. Just as St. Paul and Jesus had to choose the path they took consciously, so, too, is that our privilege and our responsibility as God's people. It will make all the difference for us and for others.

Rocks

I was watching <u>Schindler's List</u> the other evening for about the 20th time. It never fails to remind me that ordinary people can do extraordinary acts of goodness and kindness even in terrible and unsettling times. A greedy and selfish man, Oscar Schindler, was gradually moved to take extraordinary steps in protect the Jewish workers in his munitions plant in Nazi Germany, so much so that he kept some 1200 Jews from being exterminated in the Nazi camps throughout the war. At the end of the movie, Steven Spielberg, the Director of the movie, brought together hundreds of those that Schindler enabled to survive the Nazi horror. The final scene in the movie shows these survivors, now old, walking slowly past Schindler's grave in Jerusalem. As they walked by, each one placed a rock on the tomb as a token of gratitude and the recognition of how like a rock, he had helped each of them stand firm and alive throughout the war.

Rocks can do that, you know – stand for something quite important and vital in our lives. Moses struck the rock in the desert and water came forth to assuage the thirst of the Children of Israel (Numbers 20:11). This points to the reality that that which is firm and lasting produces the stuff of real life. Rocks have often been looked at as something like a fortress, a place of safety, a refuge. The Psalmist alludes to this in several places calling God the "rock of his salvation," and a place of "refuge for me" (Psalm 18:2; 31:2; 62:2). Isaiah says forthrightly that God's people are hewn out of this very rock, the strength and permanence of God himself (Isaiah 51:1). The prophet Jeremiah sees the rock as a place to hide – either for withering away if not faithful or for preservation until a better time (Jeremiah 13:4). And, of course, Jesus himself used the metaphor of a rock in several ways: suggesting that building one's house on a rock foundation lasts better than building one's house on sand, thus pointing to our life with God as a better foundation for life than anything else (Matthew 7:24); and, telling us in a parable that soil filled with rocks would interfere with growing a Christian life in that rocks do not allow for roots to go deeply into the soil (Luke 8:6). Paul calls Jesus the "spiritual rock" that seeks one out in life (1 Corinthians 10:4).

But perhaps the best use of the metaphor "rock" is found in Matthew 16:13-20, the account of Peter's confession as to Jesus being the Christ of God. After asking his disciples who people said he was and hearing the varied answers they gave, he asked Simon Peter (Simon was his Jewish name; Peter became his Christian name). And Simon said, "You are the Christ (the Messiah – the Anointed One of God), the Son of the living God." And Jesus looked at him and said, "Blessed are you, Simon son of Jonah! For flesh and blood has not revealed this to you, but my Father in heaven." And then he said this: "And I tell you, you are Peter (Greek = *petros*), and on this rock (Greek = *petra*) I will build my church, and the gates of Hades (death) will not prevail against it."

So, Simon gets a new name, his Christian name, Peter, the rock. And indeed, Peter stood like a mighty rock in those early days of the Christian church, preaching and serving fearlessly, like a rock, until the day that the Emperor Nero had him crucified in ca. 64 AD.

But Jesus said something more in his prophecy for the future in this encounter. He said he would build his church ("called out ones") on this *petra* (rock). What rock was he talking about? If he were talking about Peter, he would have used the proper gender for his noun (*petros* = Peter the rock, a man, thus the masculine form of the word). But he uses the feminine form, *petra* = rock. So, what rock is he referring to? There is only one possibility, and that is the confession of Peter itself. The rock upon which Jesus will build his church is the confession that "you are the Christ, the Son of the Living God." It is upon this confession by those called by God that Christ will build his church. That is the rock we are to build our houses upon. That is the rock out of which we are "hewn." That is the rock of refuge, the rock of salvation, the mighty fortress which God has provided, the rock into the cleft of which we are preserved and kept.

Kind of neat how all those different uses of "rock" join together into one: the rock of our salvation found in knowing that Jesus is Lord and that we live more boldly and fully as we join our lives to him. Then the old hymns begin to make sense: "Rock of ages, cleft for me; let me hide myself in thee. . . ," "he hideth my soul in the cleft of the rock that shadows a dry, thirty land; he hideth my life in the depths of his love, and covers me there with his hand, and covers me there with his hand."

During the continuation of the coronavirus pandemic, I can think of no better place to put our thoughts, our hopes, and our prayers, than in the "rock, from which we are hewn," the Lord Jesus Christ who leads us, teaches us, accompanies us, and renews us. Rock on, brothers and sisters.

Clouds

Susan fell and hurt her wrists and we drove to New Bern to the doctor (bad sprains, bruising, and wrist braces to be worn). Of course, as it must be, the safety protocols were to be observed (masks, distancing, sanitizing), and for that reason I was to wait outside while she saw the doctor. It was 96 degrees outside with a bright sun. Finding a place under the shade of a River Birch planted near the parking lot, I stood for almost an hour and a half taking in the very good breeze that conditioned my spot in the shade. Being a person who often is multi-tasking it was an unusual moment where there was literally nothing to do but to observe what was around me. I noted the various patients arriving and departing the doctor's office. I noted the myriad of auto types in the parking lot. There were several birds calling. But what caught my eye and my focus for a long while were the clouds - bright, deep blue sky accented continually by a parade of cumulus clouds slowly drifting by, shape-shifting on their way. It was one of those days where the clouds were billowy, strikingly dressed in the boldest white, and there for all of New Bern to see. I watched them come and go. In them I found faces galore, some that reminded me of church members. I saw animals, mountains, relatives, and fantastic creatures up there in the clouds. I was reminded that I ought to stop and watch the clouds more often. The time passed quickly watching those clouds.

I was reminded of other things while I watched as well. I started remembering the many, many ways that "cloud" is used in the Bible to express something intangible and ethereal about God and God's ways. And as I did so, my cloud-watching took on more of a cloak of insight and surprise. In remembering the use of clouds in the Bible, what was simply a way of passing time became a way of revelation and an occasion for sensing the holy, for sensing the ways of God. I had never thought of cloud-watching in such a way, but there it was — moments where I drew near to God. Can't beat that as a way of waiting for one's wife to finish with an appointment!

Not everyone enjoys a cloudy day, of course. Some researchers have developed a medical classification for the negative effects of cloudy days on the human psyche. Conversely, most folks tend to speak of the beauty of any given day in terms of how much sun and sky is there. However, Scripture encourages us to view the clouds in such a way as to think of the glory and presence of God. All over the Bible the imagery of clouds signal the immediate presence of God in time and space.

The first place where clouds play a prominent role in the redemptive history found in the Bible is in the flood narrative. When Noah and family came out of being shut in the Ark for so long, they saw a bow (rainbow) in the clouds — a reminder of the covenant of mercy that God was promising.

When the Lord brought his people out of Egypt in the Exodus, he led them out and through the wilderness for 40 years by means of the pillar of cloud – a theophany of promise that God would not forsake them.

There are numerous places where the coming of the Lord is promised and often it is discussed in terms of coming in a pillar of cloud. The Psalmist in 104:3 speaks of God "Making the clouds his chariot" as he comes to them. Here the metaphor is speaking of God making himself known.

The drama of Moses going up on the mountain to receive the Ten Commandments and the Covenant of God with his people is surrounded both in coming and going with clouds. We are told that "the glory of the Lord rested on Mount Sinai, and the cloud covered it six days. And on the seventh day he called to Moses out of the midst of the cloud " (Exodus 24:15-16).

On and on throughout the Old Testament, the Lord's presence is signaled by clouds – on the mountain, in the wilderness, and in the Tabernacle.

In the New Testament, Jesus is seen as the glory of the Lord in the midst of the people. As the one who enfleshes God, we read of him descending and ascending in a cloud in order to lead us and guide us to our eternal habitation with God (Ephesians 4:8-10). At the Transfiguration of Jesus (Luke 9:28-36), Jesus is revealed in a cloud as the fulfillment of both the law and the prophets (the Old Testament). As such, he brings to humanity God's new covenant sealed in Christ's blood. In the Transfiguration scene we read, "A cloud came and overshadowed them; and they were fearful as they entered the cloud. And a voice came out of the cloud, saying, "This is my beloved Son. Listen to him!"

After his resurrection, Jesus took his disciples up to a high mountain where "he was taken up and a cloud received him out of their sight" (Acts 1:9). And believers are promised that when he returns, "we who are alive and remain shall be caught up together with". . . those who have gone on ahead of us.

All in all, the Scripture utilizes the language and imagery of clouds to symbolize the presence of God. Cloudy days, then, are good days for us, and on those days when we gaze upon the clouds for a time, we, too, are invited into the presence of God Most High.

Standing near a parking lot on a hot day has its blessings . . . at least for me it did.

Birds

I belong to several Facebook groups that are devoted to birds and bird watching. It's fun to see what others are seeing and some of the very interesting observations and photographs that are posted most every day. On some occasions questions are raised about various aspects of watching and identifying birds. One question this past week caught my eye: "Should we take down our feeders during the hurricane?" Evidently, there was concern about the destruction of the feeders themselves or, perhaps, some concern over the safety of the birds if lured out into the open to the feeders during high winds.

Susan and I answered that question for ourselves many years ago. We never take our feeders down due to storms. Indeed, we have found that the birds flock to them during and after the storms in good number. The feeders are a dependable source of nutrition at a time when seeking the food amid wind and rain is more difficult. Birds have to eat each day, and the feeders are filled with birds particularly during the storms.

We have eight or nine feeders up and filled with food most of the time. During the storms, the Cardinals take the lower rungs on the feeders, the House Sparrows and House Finches take the middle rungs, the Titmice and Chickadees take the upper rungs, sometimes all at the same time. And, every once in a while, the Painted Buntings fly in and make a place for themselves. Insect and berry eaters like the Thrashers, Mockingbirds, and Catbirds fly in and out, and the Blue Jays scatter all of them for a time at the feeders. The Red-bellied and Downy Woodpeckers come and go, both to the seed feeders and to the suet. It matters not that some of the feeders a swinging rather wildly in the harsh wind, the birds are on them, riding the wind. That's persistence!

I have discovered that birds in one way or another are mentioned in 203 Old Testament passages and in 23 New Testament passages in the Bible. They are mentioned as metaphors for the presence of God (doves), symbols of ritual uncleanness (vultures), as sources of food among other uses as well as instruments of God's judgment on evildoers. In the Old Testament, birds are divided between those which are clean (may be eaten or used as a sacrifice) and those which are unclean (generally birds of prey which may not be eaten and often used as a symbol of evil or sin). The mention of birds stretches in the Bible all the way from the beginning in Genesis 1:20-22 (*And God said, "Let the waters bring forth swarms of living creatures, and let birds fly above the earth across the dome of the sky." And God created the great sea monsters and every living creature that moves, of every kind with which the waters swarm, and every winged bird of every kind. And God saw that it was good.*) to the great victory over evil empire found in the Book of Revelation where the birds of prey are instruments of God's judgment (Revelation 19:17-18: *Then I saw an angel standing in the sun, and with a loud voice he called to all the birds that fly in midheaven, "Come, gather for the great supper of God, to eat the flesh of kings, the flesh of captains, the flesh of the mighty, the flesh of horses and their riders – flesh of all, both free and slave, both small and great."*).

All this is well and good, but for my money (and my faith), one of the best mention of birds in the Bible comes from the mouth of Jesus himself. And it is certainly germane for us during this worrisome time of pandemic, protest, hurricane, and uncertainty. As believers we are bid by the Lord himself to **"Look at the birds of the air; they neither sow nor reap nor gather into barns, and yet your heavenly Father feeds them. Are you not of more value than they?** (Matthew 6:26). In other words, "Let not your hearts be troubled, neither let them be afraid" for life is about more than the worry which is at hand, and God continues to support us through life, through the storms, and even now. Just look at the birds clinging to their feeders in the midst of a hurricane. Just look at us, a congregation of God's people, hanging on in faith and hope, through the strength given to us through our Lord, Jesus Christ.

Brooding

I caught myself brooding last week. You know, that sense of getting lost in one's thoughts. Not just any thoughts, but particularly painful thoughts, painful or sad – or both. I'm generally quite up about things each day for there is always much to be up about. But sometimes, rather than being up, or down for that matter, I was brooding, allowing my mind to hover over what seems to be the effects of this interminable virus. Our Session, rightly so, has decided to put off any decision about in-person worshipping in our sanctuary until we revisit the issue again on Nov. 1. Bonny and I have been enjoying very much our Facebook Live service each Sunday, but it is nothing like a living, breathing, singing, laughing, fellowship-loving, meal-sharing, old-and-young gathering of our folks together each week for worship and a meal. When there are no voices lifted in song, no seeing the look of devotion in the eyes of each as we take Communion, no hearing the words of support and the requests for prayer and the announcements of what is coming and the sharing of gifts including food and clothing and the rhythms of the Christian year shared together each week in a communal setting for God's Spirit to come and to dwell among us takes quite a chunk out of what binds us together. And it takes quite a chunk out of me, too. So, I brood, I hover over what is not there, I nestle thoughts of what the immediate future might look like. I hope the congregation and its life won't slip away from us. So, I brood, and I pray. Maybe you do, too.

The terms "brood" and "brooding" are used in several ways in the Bible. When darkness and water covered what was to be the created order in the Genesis metaphor, we read that God's Spirit hovered over ("swept over" in some translations) the deep and provided the necessary order and purpose for the creation to come into being. In other words, through God's brooding he brought forth life, and because of that you and I are here.

The term "brood" is usually associated with chickens (and sometimes snakes). Mother hens who are "brood hens" lay their eggs and stay on them to incubate them until hatched. They even gather the little chicks in under their wings to protect them when they are very small. Most birds do this as well. This, of course, is an apt metaphor for our God who through his Son and his Spirit journeys with us through life, taking us under protective wings in ways we can see and in ways we can only discover from time to time. The Psalmist says it well: *"How precious is your steadfast love, O God! All people may take refuge in the shadow of your wings"* (Psalm 36:7). I find that if my brooding over the future is not placed into the context of God's continuing presence with us that God's wings cannot cover me, and my brooding can drift off to despair.

In addition to this, we find that the term, "brood" is used in another way in the Bible. Who can forget the several times that Jesus refers to the rigidity and lack of understanding of the Scribes and Pharisees as well as the lack of openness to God's refreshing word found in the Temple worship in Jerusalem which was under the leadership of the Sadducees with disdain by calling all of them a "brood of vipers." There's the snake analogy. Many snakes brood their babies just like birds do. But in the ancient world vipers (venomous snakes) were feared, disdained, and seen as unclean and evil. To call the Temple leadership and the religious leaders of the land a "brood of vipers" could get one killed. Indeed, it among other things did get Jesus killed. A "brood of vipers" was synonymous with a nest of corruption and evil.

There is little doubt that this coronavirus and its rippling effects on our land, on our churches, on our schools, and on our society, is something to brood about. But what kind of brooding shall we do? Brooding without end can lead to despair. Brooding only on the evil of the present can rob one of perspective. But, like those Old Testament guys who saw our life with God with all of its pain and promise as the location for God's purpose and love to "hover" over us and nestle us under his wings, we can brood in a way that allows for hope and for building up for the future. Creative brooding – allowing God's message of purpose, justice, hope and love to fill our minds as we brood, can lead us to better tomorrows and can certainly add blessings to our days.

Nevertheless

One of the first "big" words I learned as a small boy was one I heard my mother say often: *"nevertheless."* If I hadn't finished my tasks and though it was a beautiful day outside, *"nevertheless"* I had to stay in and do my jobs. If I had done something that normally would result in punishment, *"nevertheless"* sometimes I was spared the rod. It's a wonderful word, sometimes rendered as *"nonetheless"* as well as its shorter version *"and yet."* The dictionary reports that it is an adverb meaning "not the less; notwithstanding; that is, in opposition to any thing, or without regarding it." Example: "it rained, nevertheless, we proceeded on our journey; we did not the less proceed on our journey; we proceeded in opposition to the rain, without regarding it, or without being prevented."

Some version of the term "nevertheless" is found 237 times in our Bible. It is used in simple, ordinary ways like those mentioned above, and it is used to point to the profound mystery of our life with our God:

- In Psalm 73 we find the Psalmist lamenting that life appeared to him so unfair, that the wicked seemed to get away with their wickedness (*"For they have no pain; their bodies are sound and sleek. They are not in trouble as others are; they are not plagued like other people. . . ."*). Sounds right familiar, doesn't it? Of course, there is much unfairness in life, and many find it a stumbling block to faith. And the Psalmist here speaks for many of God's people when he complains that it should be this way with those who seek to serve God.
- Later in this same Psalm we hear the Psalmist trying to come to grips with this issue by humbling himself before God. Listen to him: *"When my soul was embittered, when I was pricked in heart, I was stupid and ignorant; I was like a brute beast toward you. Nevertheless, I am continually with you; you hold my right hand. You guide me with your counsel, and afterward you will receive me with honor. . . But for me it is good to be near God; I have made the Lord my refuge, to tell of all your works."*
- Did you hear the "nevertheless?" Life is not fair, especially to me, says he. "My complaints do no good. I could be embittered. *Nevertheless*, I will continue my journey with God; I will point myself upward. I will trust in the dark the nearness of God."

Not only is "nevertheless" used by believers as the turning point from despair to faith, it is used of God to denote his willingness to stand with his people even when they do not deserve it. In Psalm 89 we hear the psalmist speak God's promise: *"If [Israel's people] forsake my law and do not walk according to my ordinances . . . nevertheless I will not remove from him my steadfast love."* This promise of God's nevertheless is echoed throughout the Bible. We hear the prophet

Isaiah declare it forthrightly (Isaiah 30:18): *"Nevertheless the Lord will wait so he can be gracious to you; and thus he will rise up to show you mercy. For the Lord is a God of justice. How blessed are all those who wait for him."*

Jesus used the term to point to the necessity of recognizing God's will as primary to one's own will. He shows the picture of submission to the will of God as the underlying purpose of our lives. When he took Peter, James and John with him into the Garden of Gethsemane to pray shortly before he was arrested and taken before Pilate, his deep prayer underscored that in the face of evil, submission to God's will was his calling and ours. He wished the impending cup of death could pass him by, but he prayed that great prayer of faith and submission when he used the "nevertheless" word: *"Nevertheless, not my will but yours be done."*

The entire Biblical story is one of God's great "nevertheless" to his people. Though life is unfair, nevertheless God's ways will sustain us and God himself will be near. Though we stray and sometimes deserve rebuke and punishment, nevertheless God's mercy is everlasting for all. Though there is a blanket of darkness and evil alive in our world and all around, nevertheless God joins his people in their lives and holds them in the embrace of his love. The history of God's people down through the ages has borne fruit and given life because no final word is given to this world or to the evil of this life. In whatever darkness is around us or in us, God's word to us begins with "nevertheless."

On Standing

"Where do you stand?" It's a question sometimes whispered to us in our deepest thoughts, asked of us in gentle conversation, and even hurled at us in a demanding tone seeking to draw out of us some indication of where in the midst of a myriad of options we might locate our own thoughts, beliefs, life style or judgment. Indeed, we live in a time of political and social hype, often divided among several "stands" that can be taken on the issues at hand and on the political landscape as a whole. So, some folks wear their hats or fly their banners, or wear their buttons to show the stand they are taking. Others join in groups, put statements and memes on Facebook, and send messages to their friends indicating a particular stand and a desire for the recipient to stand there as well. Hopefully, it is with good spirit. Alas, sometimes it is not.

I thought about that funny little word, "stand," and thought about the many ways it is used. Someone is "left standing,' or "stands before," or stands beside." or stands fast," or stands firm," or stands in awe," or stands nearby," or stands still," or "stands up," or "stands down," or "stands with." It appears that "standing" is one of the major actions we take in life. Thus, it is important to think about where one stands and what one stands for. For it marks out a style, a location, and a position on things. One's moral "stance" marks one's values. One's thought-out political position indicates where one is with reference to others and the society. And one's direction taken in life shows how one's stance influences relationships and behavior.

For believers, knowing where one stands on the important areas of life is essential for faithful discipleship, for both believing in God and following Jesus Christ. Sometimes for believers we can get the believing and following part mixed up with some of the other "stands" we wish to take in life. Sometimes we separate our religious stands from other stands we take. Lest it be said that there is only one way to believe or be a Christian, let me point out that where we stand as believers is to become the groundwork for building our other stands. Where that happens, our stands on the outside are in sync with our stands on the inside, those of our hearts and minds. Where that happens, we find ample assistance in finding our way among the many choices for what to stand for on the outside. At least, I hope we do.

Biblically, there is much talk about *stand* and *standing*. It's used in all the regular ways including most of those I've mentioned above. The term "stand" in one form or another appears over 5,000 time in the Bible. But none, in my mind, is more important than the form that it takes in the New Testament that specifically points to the place where Christians stand as chief among all the other stands one can take. The word for *stand* in Greek is *stasis*. Literally it means "stand." It is joined sometimes with prefixes to make deeper words out of one's place of standing. For example, "ecstasy" comes from "*ek*" ("besides"), and when combined with "*stasis*" means "standing beside oneself" of "standing outside oneself." Neat, huh? But, most importantly, when "*ana* " in Greek is combined with "*stasis*" we get "*anastasis*" which literally means "to stand again." We translate it as "resurrection."

In Romans 6:1-5, we hear St. Paul at his best when he adjures the Romans Christians with these words: *"What then are we to say? Should we continue to sin in order that grace may about? By no means! How can we who died to sin go on living it? Do you not know that all of us who have been baptized into Christ Jesus were baptized into his death? Therefore we have been buried with him by baptism into death, so that, just as Christ was raised from the dead by the glory of the Father, so we too might walk in newness of life. For if we have been united with him in a death like his, we will certainly be united with him in a resurrection like his.*

For Christians, that is our "stand." God has claimed us in Jesus Christ, marked by Christ's resurrection. We are *"anastasis"* people before all things. All other "stands" show honor to our Lord as we each one stand on resurrection faith and follow a resurrected Lord as we begin to think of those other stands we might take. A good way to begin thinking about which hat we shall wear this election season.

Hold Your Horses

Twenty-five weeks is a long time. It's a long time to put off many of the good things about normal living – like mixing with friends, going to church, singing, visiting loved ones in the hospital, having folks over to eat, flying off somewhere for a vacation, going to school, and on and on and ON! For a people who have developed a finely-tuned sense of how long the normal activities of life take, the sense of never being able to get to those normal activities and actions creates static in our inner airways and can create some impatience or even anxiety in us and among us. So, from time to time we get beside ourselves and grow in the gardens of our thoughts and feelings a crop of impatience.

One can observe that impatience in countless ways around us (and within us as well). Outbursts of anger over whether one is wearing a mask or not. Bouts of incivility in action, word, or thought over even trivial things. Anger over the political views of someone you know and normally care about. Shouting at the news in frustration. A veil of tension over what used to be normal routine and interaction. Terrible things being said to one another on social media. I could go on, but you know what I'm talking about – the lack of patient understanding and patient life with others as we seek to endure and live as God's people during this pandemic. Of course, the political climate aggravates this situation. As many fall prey to polarization over the upcoming election, one often wonders how long we as a people and as we as individuals can endure.

One of my earliest memories of special words my mother said was her favored expression, "hold your horses!" In her country way she was helping us develop a sense of slowing down, learning to say "whoa" for a while, and "not getting ahead of ourselves." Maybe that earnest wisdom from my mother is good wisdom for us during this pandemic. Maybe taking things in stride, not imposing time limits on that which is ongoing, and thinking through what is appropriate is just the thing for dealing with a world off-center. Sure beats the stress and wasted energy one can put into impatience and frustration.

The Bible speaks of patience often. It is presented to us throughout the Bible as either forbearance (tolerance) or endurance (living with). God's patience with humans is one of the most frequently stressed ways of talking about God in the Old Testament. As it is put in Exodus 34:6 we hear what is an overriding word of confidence in the Bible: *"The Lord, the Lord, a God merciful and gracious, slow to anger, and abounding in steadfast love and faithfulness. . . ."* In other words, God is tolerant of his people. I'm sure glad for that. Imagine how it would be if God had no patience with us in this world. His forbearance is the ground upon which we can walk with our own struggle with patience, allowing his constancy with us to calm our spirits and soothe our souls to persevere in unsettled times. His patience with us is there to allow us to grow in our faith in him. Of course, his patience with us can also become a tool for us to become indifferent to his will as well.

In the New Testament, patience on the part of believers is what purifies one's faith. 1 Peter 1:6 describes this very well for us: *"In this you rejoice, even if now for a little while you have had to suffer various trials, so that the genuineness of your faith — being more precious than gold that, though perishable, is tested by fire — may be found to result in praise and glory and honor when Jesus Christ is revealed."* In other words, through our patient life with God, our trust in him grows, and our lives are more whole even in the time of testing. So, patience is not just good for wise living, it is the kind of forbearance that allows our trust in God to grow.

The result of such patience is endurance, which is the very problem outlined above as the result of this pandemic. So, what are we as believers to do with the vast amount of impatience found in these times? As an action borne out of our trust in God and God's ways, we can "hold our horses," and take some deep breaths from time to time and plunge on holding our own as God's people of forbearance and love. In Christ we can do this.

Goodbye

"We gathered there at the gravesite to say our 'goodbyes.'" So, I overheard at one of the two funerals I recently conducted. I've heard it many times. It's often said that this is the primary purpose of funerals, to say goodbye. Over the years I've wondered just what is meant by this, by saying our "goodbyes." For some, I am sure, it is a simple expression for putting a last word on one's relationship with the deceased, a way of saying it is now over, completed, the end. However, this hardly does justice to the word itself. "Goodbye" is a contraction from old English for "God be with you" ("Go b'wy"). As such, it is actually not a word of finality, closing the door, or ending the chapter. It is truly a blessing given to the deceased – "God be with you," "Go with God." While using the former definition of finality and conclusion is sometimes something one might want to avoid because of its sadness, nevertheless seen in this latter sense it can truly be a good thing to stand at the grave of a deceased loved one and say, "goodbye" ("God be with you."). It has with it a sense that it is not over, that there's more to come. "God be with you" for the journey. "God be with you" as you go to the Lord. "God be with you" for eternity.

While it is tempting for us to seek to know just what the journey is for the deceased or what is there when we give our blessing for one going to the Lord or just what we believe when we talk about God's blessing for one in eternity, the truth is that everything we can say about this mystery is dependent upon one reality: the life, death, and resurrection of Jesus. Without the reality of Jesus, everything we might wish to say about eternity is wishful thinking, a creation of our minds and our desire. What is it that St. Paul said: *"If Christ has not been raised, your faith is futile and you are still in your sins. Then those also who have died in Christ have perished. If for this life only we have hoped in Christ, we are of all people most to be pitied"* (1 Corinthians 15:17-19).

But Paul doesn't stop there. He goes on: *"But in fact Christ has been raised from the dead, the first fruits of those who have died.* (1 Corinthians 15:20). That fact is the basis for the hope we have for life beyond the grave. That fact gives us a basis for saying to our deceased loved ones, "God be with you" or, using its modern contraction, "Goodbye."

In my lifetime, I have said "goodbye" to my parents, to four of my siblings, to 272 church members, and to numerous friends. In each case, through faith in what God has shown us in Jesus, I have been comforted and strengthened by being able to say "goodbye," or better said, "God be with you."

Ubiquity

I wonder how many words each of us could come up with that begin with the letter "u." While "u" is one of the five vowels and therefore must be seen as important, in my estimation it is less to be admired than, say, "a" or "o." And so many of the words which begin with "u" are a bit more unusual than words like "artist" or "original" or any of the other thousands of words which begin with an "a" or an "o."

So, for this devotional I thought I would express the good Christian attitude of inclusion and focus a moment or two on the less well-recognized or celebrated letter "u." I guess we can't have a working vocabulary or a complete ability to write unless all the letters are valued and included, even a one utilized on a lesser scale like the letter "u."

Umbrella, umbrage, utility, umpire, upper, usual, utilitarian, unless, uncle, umbilical, ugly, ultimate, underdog, use, urgent, uranium, utmost, utopian - that's most of the words beginning with "u" that I can think of right off the top of my head, except for the jillion or so that have "un" or "up" in front of them. My "u" vocabulary appears to be rather limited. How about yours?

In the Miriam-Webster's Dictionary, the third word entry in the "U" section is an unusual word, the word "ubiquitous" followed next by "ubiquity." Strangely enough, I have found through the years that this unusual word is widely used – its use is ubiquitous ("ubiquitous ubiquity," if you'll excuse the pun). It means "present everywhere." Weather is "ubiquitous," at least on the earth. With five named storms whirling around in the Atlantic or Gulf of Mexico, we can get a flavor of what "present everywhere" might be. More to the point, there is no place in the world where the Covid-19 pandemic is not present and must be dealt with. The pandemic is ubiquitous. So are a whole host of other things that come to mind.

But for our purposes, let's focus on a form of "ubiquity" that can touch our hearts, fill our thoughts, and provide a place to stand and live each day in our lives. Let's allow the Psalmist to tell us of it (Psalm 139:1-12):

O Lord, you have searched me and known me.
You know when I sit down and when I rise up; you discern my thoughts from far away.
You search out my path and my lying down, and are acquainted with all my ways.
Even before a word is on my tongue, O Lord, you know it completely.
You hem me in, behind and before, and lay your hand upon me.
Such knowledge is too wonderful for me; it is so high that I cannot attain it.
Where can I go from your spirit? Or where can I flee from your presence?
If I ascend to heaven, you are there; if I make my bed in Sheol, you are there.

If I take the wings of the morning and settle at the farthest limits of the sea,
Even there your hand shall lead me, and your right hand shall hold me fast.
If I say, "Surely the darkness shall cover me, and the light around me become night,"
Even the darkness is not dark to you; the night is as bright as the day,
For darkness is as light to you. . . .
How weighty to me are your thoughts, O God! How vast is the sum of them!
I try to count them — they are more than the sand;
I come to the end — I am still with you.

More than the weather or the Coronavirus pandemic, as ubiquitous as they might be on the ordinary scale of things, the ubiquity of God, the ever-present reality of God who is with us, around us, in us, over us, out in front of us, trailing along behind us, and always near us is at the heart of the Christian faith. And for those who trust this reality through their own hopes and experiences, this is a pervasive (another word for ubiquitous) awareness. It's like always being aware of the weather. God is nigh, always. God whispers his presence into our special moments, always. God hear our cries of pain; they do not languish in the void. God is effervescent, breaking into our daily lives with comfort, hope, forgiveness, and love. Because of God's ubiquity, one can join with countless others and sing with voice and heart that great hymn of **the** ubiquity of God: "This Is My Father's World."

This is my Father's world, And to my listening ears
All nature sings, and round me rings the music of the spheres.
This is my Father's world, I rest me in the thought
Of rocks and trees, of skies and seas — his hand the wonders wrought.

This is my Father's world, the birds their carols raise,
The morning light, the lily white declare their Maker's praise.
This is my Father's world, He shines in all that's fair;
In the rustling grass I hear Him pass, He speaks to me everywhere.

This is my Father's world, O let me ne'er forget
That though the wrong seems oft so strong, God is the ruler yet.
This is my Father's world, the battle is not done;
Jesus, who died, shall be satisfied, And earth and heaven be one.

Shadow

When we were children playing outside on a summer day until just as nightfall came upon us and we could hear our mother calling for us to come in, we paid attention to shadows. Indeed, when the streetlight came on we would stand under it to see if we could make our shadows disappear. Then we would move away from the light and watch our shadows grow longer and longer until we were giants. Shadows were something to behold. One couldn't pin them down; ever they moved with us.

It should not surprise us that this illusive and transitory nature of shadows has intrigued humanity since ancient times. Indeed, the concept of a shadow has been used in many ways in common speech as well as in both literature and in religion. It has become one of those words that, while metaphorical in use, nevertheless conveys some pretty concrete ideas and meanings to us.

A shadow can point to that which is superficial. One might seek to get ahead of her shadow. Spies shadow their subjects. Some folks are afraid of their own shadows. Maturity might mean growing into one's shadow. The Shadow Knows radio mystery used to scare me. A conceited person thinks he is larger than his shadow. Some events plainly foreshadow what is coming. Shadows in pictures often help set the mood. Shadows in pictures bring out the three dimensional aspects of the picture. One's face takes on a different aspect when the eyes are shadowed. To grow up in someone's shadow is to be influenced by that one. Shadows can obscure. Shadows can be creepy. Shadows can give relief. Shadows can provide protection. Shadows are so important that the story of Peter Pan underscores the notion that one cannot grow into full life without one. On a summer day in these latter days of my life, rather than seeing how tall I can make my shadow, I am content to sit with Susan on our porch deeply enshadowed away from the sun and cooled by the breeze. *Viva la shadow*!

It should not come as a surprise that the Bible make great use of the term *shadow* as metaphor for some important things. Just as shade (shadows of rocks, landscape, trees, etc.,) offers protection from the desert sun, so, too, does God's care for us provide shelter in life or even protective power. In other uses, the term signifies the transient nature of life, fleeting like a shadow. The primary use in the Bible, however is that life under the shadow of God's wings or the shadow of his hand provides both the opportunity and the needed assurances for living as God's people in a world that is often, like a sun-baked desert, under stress.

In Isaiah 51:16, we find *"I have put my words in your mouth, and hidden you in the shadow of my hand, stretching out the heavens and laying the foundations of the earth, and saying to Zion, "You are my people."* As God's people we live under his protective and instructive shadow. This notion is echoed all over the Bible, sometimes using the picture of being shadowed by God's wings (Psalm 17:8).

Psalm 91:1 speaks of living in God's shelter (that's a picture of faithful living) and says that we are abiding "in the shadow of the Almighty." That shadow, of course, provides protection, direction, and instruction.

When the prophet Hosea spoke of Israel being returned to live as God's people, he used this vivid picture: *"They shall return and dwell beneath my shadow; they shall flourish like the grain; they shall blossom like the vine. . . "*

In the New Testament, Paul looks upon the perversions of life pictured as excessive use of food and drink and taking part in the pagan festivals that abounded in the Roman Empire as "shadows of what is to come." But in contrast to these shadows, the "substance belongs to Christ" (Colossians 2:16-17). Shadows are hollow and don't last. That which lasts is what God is providing.

In Luke 1:35 the angel told Mary that the Most High would overshadow her, and she would become pregnant and bear a child. Here shadow is used as the shadow of God. In Acts 5:15, they carried the sick out into the street hoping that Peter's shadow would fall on them when he passed by that they might be made well.

All this might lead one to ask and seek to answer several questions:

- What kind of shadow are you casting in your living?
- Under what or whose shadow are you living?
- Is your life in Christ foreshadowing how you live and hope in these days?

> *In the shadow of the cross, blessed place!*
> *Living only for the Lord, by his grace;*
> *What he says I'll gladly do,*
> *Ever standing firm and true,*
> *In the shadow of the cross, blessed place*
> *In the shadow of the cross I will rest,*
> *For with everlasting peace I am blest;*
> *Here I dwell in love unknown,*
> *Streaming down from heaven's throne,*
> *In the shadow of the cross I will rest.*
> *--old gospel hymn*

Mind

I've been thinking a lot about the various terms and expressions we use in ordinary speech that have great use in thinking about our responses to God in daily life. It's been fun and helpful in my own devotionals to explore certain terms and to seek to understand their place in the language of our faith. One term that readily comes to mind (no pun intended) is the word *mind*. Oh, how we use that word in some very important areas of our lives.

Is he out of his mind? I hope he changes his mind! Will you make up your mind? Who's going to mind the children? Do you mind if I go? He mindlessly argued the point. Please remind me of the next meeting. Mind your own business.

I wonder as well how the mind functions to produce the decisions and conclusions we arrive at. There are some things I don't understand fully about the workings of the mind. Last Monday Susan and I hopped into our truck and sped to Falls Dam (near Raleigh) to find a reported Kirtland's Warbler there. Our mind was on getting this new life bird. So much so was our mind on the goal that we failed at being "mindful" of the instructions for where the bird was to be found. We both read the emails several times. We kept at the forefront of our minds the destination as "Falls Lake Dam." We researched it on the map, planned our time with the destination in mind, and took off. However, the email information plainly said in several places, and we had read them several times, that the location of the bird was at "Jordan Lake Dam." How we couldn't see that when it was right in front of our faces shows the mystery of the workings of the mind. The mind can be influenced to work as we see fit. The mind can ignore what is real and go on its own. The mind can be influenced to see or think in a way that is contrary to fact and truth. Perhaps that should be kept in mind when we are thinking about the events of our present day. Maybe that's a factor for thinking about minding our votes come election day.

I wonder what comes to your mind (again, no pun intended) in our being mindful of this term, *mind?* At its root, the basic meaning of the term is both <u>what we think</u> (that's what's on our mind) and <u>how we think</u> (that's the process of minding). It involves giving attention in a complete and responsible way to something or someone. It means matching what we think with what is there or what is possible or what is true. Which leads me to the Scriptures where it is revealed that to be a Christian believer in truth has a great deal to do with what's on our minds, in our minds, and the product of our minds. Try these words of St. Paul as you are mindful of your faith journey. They describe a mind filled with God's movement toward creating abundant life. The words are found in Philippians 2:1-11:

If then there is any encouragement in Christ, any consolation from love, any sharing in the Spirit, any compassion and sympathy, make my joy complete; be of the same mind, having the same love, being in full accord and one mind. Do nothing from selfish ambition or conceit, but in humility regard others as better than yourselves. Let each of you look not to your own interests, but to the interests of others. Let the same mind be in you that was in Christ Jesus, who, though he was in the form of God, did not regard equality with God as something to be exploited, but emptied himself, taking the form of a servant, being born in human likeness. And being found in human form, he humbled himself and became obedient to the point of death — even death on a cross. Therefore God also highly exalted him and gave him the name that is above every name, so that at the name of Jesus every knee should bend, in heaven and on earth and under the earth, and every tongue should confess that Jesus Christ is Lord, to the glory of God the Father.

Paul is encouraging believers to share life in one accord, being of the same mind. But, more importantly, he describes that "same mind" as being filled with Jesus Christ, that is, allowing who Jesus was/is and what Jesus preached, and the emphases of Jesus' preaching and the way of thinking about life and others that Jesus displayed, to fill our minds as we live each day. I don't believe that doing such is so hard. I do believe we will do it only if we make up our minds to do so. So, in this week's prayers and thoughts, we might bring these things to mind.

Single-minded

"Hear, O Israel: The Lord is our God, the Lord alone. You shall love the Lord your God with all your heart, and with all your soul, and with all your might. Keep these words that I am commanding you today in your heart. (Deuteronomy 6:4-5).

With this keen insight that God is the only God, ancient Israel separated herself from the rest of the world, a world filled with belief systems of gods, demons, and multiple explanations for understanding the world. Israel, through her experience of deliverance and provision in the wilderness, came to know that all beliefs in what humans think might be or wish to be a god or gods were forms of wishful thinking. Out of her experience and insight, no other explanation or experience could provide what centering life around the one God of creation and of the universe provided. That oneness centered Israel's life and hope.

Centuries later as it became apparent that Judaism had limited even this understanding, God underscored the centrality of his lordship by showing the people what the one God was like and was about. That's what the coming of Jesus revealed. The one God wasn't limited to following the rules, important as they may be. The one God was about taking the one God as Jesus was revealing him, into one's heart as the source for living, or as Paul Tillich put it once, as "the ground of our being." This, of course, moves God out of the place of distant honor and allows God a place at the core of our hearts and minds.

St. Paul, the great missionary and teacher of the first century AD offered us a definition of what taking this one God revealed in Jesus Christ into our hearts looks like: *"I therefore, the prisoner in the Lord, beg you to lead a life worthy of the calling to which you have been called, with all humility and gentleness, with patience, bearing with one another in love, making every effort to maintain the unity of the Spirit in the bond of peace. There is one body and one Spirit, just as you were called to the one hope of your calling, one Lord, one faith, one baptism, one God and Father of all, who is above all and through all and in all"* (Ephesians 4:1-6).

I suppose there are a number of ways one can be single-minded. Stubbornness centered on one's likes and desires rather than reflection on what is true might be one form. Refusal to accept any authority other than oneself might be another. Make-believe and fantasy as a form of making one's desires the authority for what is true can become another as well. But there is little doubt that at the center of Christian faith there is a single-minded adherence to the one God revealed through the teachings and the life, death and resurrection of Jesus Christ. As our hearts and minds are centered in him, the one God becomes the focus of who we are and what we think. Our unity as people comes from such singlemindedness. Our life together as a church community thrives on such singlemindedness. And our hopes for each day in this life and for the new days coming in the life to come find their truth in this singlemindedness as well. Thanks be to the Lord God, the Lord alone. That singlemindedness is ours to live by.

Pass

In this devotional I hope to "pass on" to you a little thought about the frequently used word *pass*. It's such a little word. But its use is quite large. The basic meaning of *pass*, of course, is *to move* or *proceed*. We "pass" the football (move it from here to there); we get "a pass" to transfer from one place to another; we "pass away" or "pass on" as we move from life to death; we "pass" our school course as we move on to another; we "pass through" the river (cross it); and we travel through the "pass" in the mountains (allows us to go from here to there). This, of course, doesn't begin to exhaust the various ways we use this remarkable word denoting "movement," but it gives us the flavor of it.

Interestingly, the word is an important word in the Holy Bible. It is used in its variety of ways 1,244 times throughout the Scriptures. One of the most important usages of it is found in the story of the Exodus from Egypt. You no doubt remember the plagues that were heaped on Egypt at the time Moses was demanding the release of the Hebrew people from bondage so they could go to their homeland. Remember the last plague – the one where death came to each household of the Egyptians but "passed over" the households of the Hebrews. The central celebration of Judaism to this day is "Passover," memorializing that event. Look it up in Exodus 12. Isaiah uses the imagery of the Hebrews going through the waters of the Sea of Reeds (Red Sea) during the Exodus as a picture of God's promise to deliver his people always (Isaiah 43:2 – "When you pass through the waters . . . "). Jesus mentions that though heaven and earth will "pass away," his words will last (Matthew 24:35). Jesus went on to ask God to allow "this hour (impending death on the cross) to pass from him (Matthew 14:35).

Perhaps the most pivotal use of this little word is found in John 5:24 ("Very truly, I tell you, anyone who hears my word and believes him who sent me has eternal life, and does not come under judgment, *but has passed from death to life.*") But there's more: The Seer in the Book of Revelation sees into the future and reflects on how the "first things" (the creation and life on earth) won't last. Listen to him in Revelation 21:3-4: "And I heard a loud voice from the throne saying: *See, the home of God is among mortals. He will dwell with them; they will be his peoples, and God himself will be with them. He will wipe every tear from their eyes. Death will be no more: mourning and crying and pain will be no more, for the first things have PASSED away.*"

To my thinking, what the multiple uses of this term in the Bible and in our common life connotes is a basic truth which we can hardly ignore: **life is ever on the move and no matter what happens "This, too, shall pass."** While that phrase is not found directly in the Bible, it is implied throughout. "Don't be anxious about tomorrow," "God walks through every valley with you," "Death is no longer victorious," "Sing a new song." On and on, the direct implication that "this, too, shall pass."

Someone told me recently of watching an Indian standup comic who was having some fun with this phrase, "this, too, shall pass." During his routine he commented on the fact that this sentiment is meant to remind us that not only the bad things will pass (as many tend to use this phrase, especially now during the COVID-19 pandemic), but that we also have to realize that the good things are temporary as well, and thus we should not get too attached to them either. Point made.

I have been hearing from many of our church family about how they are faring during this unusual time. The partial isolation, the major change in routines and habits, the vast difference the shut-down has made on schools and education, the fact that some we know or know of have contracted the virus and have actually died – together with a political campaign of enormous import – all these have the potential of numbing us, worrying us, demoralizing us, and in some cases even making us sick. It becomes all the more essential for our well-being to remember that in God's scheme of things, nothing is permanent ("This, too, shall pass!") except for God himself and the grace he pours out upon us in good times and in bad, in darkness and in light.

Drawing Upon What is Known to be True.

One of my favorite family stories (that some of you have heard me tell before) involved my younger sister, Anne. When we were young children (she being about 3 and I about 5), we shared "the children's room" for our sleeping and toys. It was adjacent to our parents' bedroom in our large two-storied Florida frame house. The children's room was a corner room with windows facing two directions and the roof over our house's porch just outside. Since this was Florida and in the days before air conditioning, the windows were open except for screens to keep out the mosquitoes. Our house sat on an acre of property with grass and trees galore – a wonderful place in which to grow up. And, we had cats! There were always one or more cats who had made a home with us. We learned about babies and parenting and fun with others from watching our cats.

One warm night Mother had put us to bed. And after our prayers and her singing to us, we were sternly warned not to allow the yellow cat into the house. You see, all of our cats learned to climb up the avocado tree and get on the porch roof and meow outside our screened windows to be let in. We often let them in and played with them on the bed. But this night, no yellow cat was allowed. She was expecting a litter of kittens at any time. Of course, this meant little to my sister at her age and around midnight the old yellow cat started telling us to let her in from outside Anne's window. The streetlight outside gave off enough light to give a dim view of things. So, Anne, ever the cat lover, let her in and put her under her covers. Ignorance is such sweet bliss! Not long after that Anne felt movement under the covers and little mew sounds. When she pulled the covers back she saw very dimly in that faint light little squiggly things moving around. Not aware of what that might be she drew the only conclusion she could and jumped out of her bed, fleeing into our parents' room, and with excited voice exclaimed, "Mother, come quick! The cat fell apart in the bed!"

I think that was pretty smart of her. That is, at the tender and unexperienced age of 3 Anne came to the only conclusion that made sense to her. Not understanding about having kittens, she saw the little things moving about and concluded that where there had once been something larger (the mother cat) there were now several squirmy things – and the only conclusion is that the larger had come apart to make several smallers. Good thinking.

This can be a parable for us, for it is so true that we can draw conclusions based on limited understanding and match those conclusions with what we know whether it is correct or not.

Perhaps this explains why folks have drawn so many unworthy conclusions about the world we live in. If we have little understanding of science, it makes more sense to deny climate change. If we don't see or experience racial bigotry, all the hoopla about it seems far-fetched. If we don't have much exposure to a faithful understanding of life, it doesn't appear necessary to spend much time on God or the Christian story. And, if our understanding of God is limited to childhood versions of the wise old gentleman who makes things better, it becomes confusing when we see so much in the world that isn't better. You get the drift.

Once long ago, a believer much like ourselves, one who had been exposed to the insights of his forebears about the nature of God and his role as creator and sustainer of the universe, and one to whom life was to be lived, stood outside on the hillside and looked up. He was struck within at what he saw – a vast panoply of stars, glistening in the darkness. And it pointed him to the creator.

Anne tried to make sense without much to work with. That Hebrew psalmist drew on his learning and his own journey to know what was truly there. Listen to him:

> *O Lord, our Sovereign, how majestic is your name in all the earth!*
> *You have set your glory above the heavens.*
> *Out of the mouths of babes and infants you have founded a bulwark because or your foes,*
> *to silence the enemy and the avenger.*
> *When I look at your heavens, the work of your fingers,*
> *the moon and the stars that you have*
> *established; what are human beings that you are mindful of them,*
> *mortals that you care for them?*
> *Yet you have made them a little lower than God,*
> *and crowned them with glory and honor.*
> *You have given them dominion over the works of your hands;*
> *you have put all things under their feet,*
> *all sheep and oxen, and also the beasts of the field, the birds of the air,*
> *and the fish of the seas.*
> *O Lord, our sovereign, how majestic is your name in all the earth.* (Psalm 8)

As we continue our way through this pandemic and this election and the economic problems facing so many, we are encouraged to draw upon what we know to be true as we seek understanding and form our conclusions. And what we in the Christian community know is that God is present always to carry us through the darkness and into the light, to whisper his words of encouragement and hope into every time of fear, to provide for us a groundwork upon which to stand as we seek to do what is right, to maintain our stance toward love, and to live humbly with our God and each other.

Strength Alongside

Her father had just died after a years-long battle with a debilitating disease. She was fourteen years old, the oldest of three children in a very close family. She had watched him slip deeper and deeper into dependency until the day came when he was unable to breathe on his own. His death was a bitter end to a bitter battle at a most critical time in her life. She suffered with his death. As she told me about her inner struggles with this great loss, she was able to verbalize a precious feeling so essential to each of us. After talking about the pain of watching him suffer and die, she tearfully said, ***"Now, I don't have anyone to cry to."*** That was one of the many roles her father had played in her life. When she needed to cry, she had someone to cry to, someone who provided that element of strength alongside of that we call "comfort." Indeed, that is what the term "comfort" literally means – Latin word *fortus* meaning strength (we get our word "fort" from this, a place of strength) and Latin word *com* meaning "with" or "alongside of."

There is little doubt that one essential thing about being human is our capacity for and need of comfort. We are well-equipped to give it and well-disposed to receive it from others. Indeed, one of the important aspects of our belonging together in families, communities, churches, and to our God is the glue that comfort provides for our times of need. Strength alongside. Yes, there are times when we get by with a little help from others. When someone is there sharing the moment, his or her presence draws us beyond ourselves and into a fellowship that can provide some relief from any burden. That's why children run to a parent when hurt or afraid. That's why we turn to others when we suffer or fear. That's why we pray most in times of suffering and hurt. It is one of God's greatest provisions that we are made to both need and give comfort.

Is it any surprise that this is one of the primary roles of God identified by countless witnesses throughout history and in the Biblical story itself? I checked on some of the best passages in the Bible, describing God's role in our lives. I've quoted several of them here. I invite you to read through them and let the import of the declarations and hope expressed in them draw you into a sense of God's comfort for you even now, and perhaps equip you for days ahead when God's "strength alongside" will be most needed and welcomed by you.

2 Corinthians 1:3-4 ESV / Blessed be the God and Father of our Lord Jesus Christ, the Father of mercies and God of all comfort, who comforts us in all our affliction, so that we may be able to comfort those who are in any affliction, with the comfort with which we ourselves are comforted by God.

Psalm 23:4 ESV /Even though I walk through the valley of the shadow of death, I will fear no evil, for you are with me; your rod and your staff, they comfort me.

Matthew 11:28-30 ESV /Come to me, all who labor and are heavy laden, and I will give you rest. Take my yoke upon you, and learn from me, for I am gentle and lowly in heart, and you will find rest for your souls. For my yoke is easy, and my burden is light."

Psalm 119:76 ESV /Let your steadfast love comfort me according to your promise to your servant.

Psalm 119:50 ESV /This is my comfort in my affliction, that your promise gives me life.

Matthew 5:4 ESV / "Blessed are those who mourn, for they shall be comforted.

Psalm 91:1-16 ESV / He who dwells in the shelter of the Most High will abide in the shadow of the Almighty. I will say to the LORD, "My refuge and my fortress, my God, in whom I trust." For he will deliver you from the snare of the fowler and from the deadly pestilence. He will cover you with his pinions, and under his wings you will find refuge; his faithfulness is a shield and buckler. You will not fear the terror of the night, nor the arrow that flies by day, ...

Matthew 5:1-48 ESV / Seeing the crowds, he went up on the mountain, and when he sat down, his disciples came to him. And he opened his mouth and taught them, saying: "Blessed are the poor in spirit, for theirs is the kingdom of heaven. "Blessed are those who mourn, for they shall be comforted. "Blessed are the meek, for they shall inherit the earth. ...

Romans 8:26-28 ESV / Likewise the Spirit helps us in our weakness. For we do not know what to pray for as we ought, but the Spirit himself intercedes for us with groanings too deep for words. And he who searches hearts knows what is the mind of the Spirit, because the Spirit intercedes for the saints according to the will of God. And we know that for those who love God all things work together for good, for those who are called according to his purpose.

Isaiah 49:13 ESV / Sing for joy, O heavens, and exult, O earth; break forth, O mountains, into singing! For the LORD has comforted his people and will have compassion on his afflicted.

John 16:22 ESV / So also you have sorrow now, but I will see you again, and your hearts will rejoice, and no one will take your joy from you.

Isaiah 51:12 ESV / "I, I am he who comforts you; who are you that you are afraid of man who dies, of the son of man who is made like grass,

Psalm 86:17 ESV / Show me a sign of your favor, that those who hate me may see and be put to shame because you, LORD, have helped me and comforted me.

As we draw God's Spirit into our hearts and minds, there we find the comfort God has spread over his creation and into the lives of his people. As we continue the journey through the anxieties of the pandemic and the divisiveness of our time and the economic and social uncertainties of our time, I hope we can remember how well-positioned we are because we have someone "to cry to."

"Rent Space" in Our Minds

Why the tendency to absolutize the major events and circumstances of our lives I wonder? I really do wonder at it. Maybe you do as well. We break an arm and suddenly it becomes the consuming issue of our lives. No day goes by without complaint, explanation, or comment about the broken arm. Daylight Savings Time comes to an end and we can't get our sleep and wake cycles back in whack for a time and it becomes our focus all day long even to the point of complaining about it. Somebody doesn't wear a mask when standing next to you in a public place. It makes you uncomfortable and you complain inwardly for a time — maybe even outwardly as well. You have a "discussion" with someone who believes strongly in the other candidate and political party than yours and the words of that person echo in your mind all day long and you spend time and energy thinking of what you should have said in order to straighten out their thinking. Sometimes recently, such division in thought and belief has caused friendships to end and words to be exchanged that will be very hard to take back adequately. You see what I mean about the tendency to absolutize? One man I know has called it the tendency to allow an issue or a person or an event or a belief to "take up rent space in our minds." That's absolutizing.

As I write today, Americans across the country and its territories are at the polls rendering final judgment on who will be elected as leaders both local and national. While such a decision time has always brought out absolutism to some degree in the past, this year the danger of it is paramount. Each of us probably has one or more friends, acquaintances, or family members that we cannot talk with about the election because of the rancor, anger, and distain that such an attempt would bring. On the streets and in the communities, some have fallen out with others over their political beliefs. There has even been some violence and chicanery including conspiracy theories about how badly the other side is behaving and what must be done about it. Absolutizing, I would say., climbing into hardened mental positions that take up enormous "rent space" in the minds of those who have absolutized. I'm afraid that it is leading some into depression, resentment, unresolved anger, and mental disdain.

Need I point out that in the realm of Christian faith, such absolutizing of these things can rob us of our Christian trust in God, our understanding of life with our God, and our daily journey with the Lord. I know some today who fear all is lost if their candidate does not win — that the nation and our communities and our life in a decent America will be lost if the election does not go the way they absolutely believe it should. And, I say, how faithful to the Lord of all life is that? Such absolutizing may even become a form of unfaithfulness, for it places limited beliefs into a supreme position. And that's dangerous to the heart. It's dangerous to one's faith. It's dangerous for it substitutes frail absolutes for those that last, substitutes which inevitably divide folks from each other and render judgments that do not hold up.

Our brother Paul the Apostle continually encouraged Christians living in those hard times as the church was just beginning. They faced the excesses of the Roman Empire, the real possibility of torture and death under certain of the Roman rulers, the criticism of many in the pagan religions, and the ongoing temptation to believe God had abandoned them (that's absolutizing) when they encountered hardships. Listen to Paul's words drawing them back to the real Absolute and how life with their Lord offered them the sure way in the midst of their fears and faults. Philippians 4: 4-9:

Rejoice in the Lord always [here is found that which one truly can absolutize about]; *again I will say, Rejoice. Let your gentleness be known to everyone. The Lord is near. Do not worry about anything* [nothing is absolute but God himself] *but in everything by prayer and supplication with thanksgiving let your requests be made known to God* [talk your fears and uncertainties over with him]. *And the peace of God, which surpasses all understanding, will guard your hearts and your minds in Christ Jesus* [It will certainly change your focus].

Finally, beloved, whatever is true, whatever is honorable, whatever is just, whatever is pure, whatever is pleasing, whatever is commendable, if there is any excellence and if there is anything worthy of praise, think about these things [absolutize on those things which are God-given and will last]. *Keep on doing the things that you have learned and received and heard and seen in me, and the God of peace will be with you.*

The sun will come up tomorrow and the next day and the next. We can depend on that so long as the universe survives. Political movements will come and go. Leaders will shine and grow dim. A decision to move to red or to blue will be a rather small thing when compared to the gift of life and the love of God. I pray that we will let that have "rent space" in our minds for the days ahead.

On Being Shaped

The word that came to Jeremiah from the Lord. "Come, go down to the potter's house, and there I will let you hear my words." So I went down to the potter's house, and there he was working at his wheel. The vessel he was making of clay was spoiled in the potter's hand, and he reworked it into another vessel, as seemed good to him.

Then the word of the Lord came to me: Can I not do with you, O house of Israel, just as this potter has done? Says the Lord. Just like the clay in the potter's hand, so are you in my hand, O house of Israel. At one moment I may declare concerning a nation or a kingdom, that I will pluck up and break down and destroy it, but if that nation, concerning which I have spoken, turns from its evil, I will change my mind about the disaster that I intended to bring on it. And at another moment I may declare concerning a nation or a kingdom that I will build and plant it, but if it does evil in my sight, not listening to my voice, then I will change my mind about the good that I had intended to do to it. Now, therefore, say to the people of Judah and the inhabitants of Jerusalem: Thus says the Lord: Look, I am a potter shaping evil against you and devising a plan against you. Turn now, all of you from your evil way, and amend your ways and your doings. (Jeremiah 18:1-11)

What we have here is a vivid metaphor of the reality and revelation that God is continually shaping his people. Sometimes it is quite apparent how he is shaping us. Sometimes we have to wait until God is finished with the shaping. But here and in numerous places in the Bible, God is seen as shaping – not manufacturing, but shaping; not mechanically assembling, but moving through events toward God's purposes. As we look at the events through which we are traveling today (or any day for that matter), Christian faith rests on the awareness that this is our Father's world and God continues to shape his people through the events and processes of their day. The pity is there for those unable to see, as Jeremiah is hinting at through this metaphor concerning the people of Judah in the face of the Babylonian insurgence.

The episode described in this passage may have unfolded like this: It began with a call to the prophet: "Come, let us go down to the potter's house." Jeremiah is one of the Bible's vivid characters. He was eccentric, did things his own way, and had some laughable moments – including being thrown into a pit, buying a junk piece of land that everyone knew would only be ransacked by the Babylonians, and wearing a yoke around town. But his actions invariably discomfited people, because in some strange way they revealed what was true about their world. So, here, he goes into a potter's place of work and watches him go through the process of making a clay jar (which could sometimes be six feet deep).

Perhaps you can picture the scene: the potter, while kicking the wheel with one foot, grabbing a lump of clay, dropping it nearly on center in the middle of the wheel, and then working it up and down with both hands. Maybe there is a flaw of some sort and he tears it up and remakes the lump and begins again. It was a marvel to watch the lump slowly take shape until it was finished and could be taken off of the wheel and placed outside to dry.

On that day, the process of the potter's art struck the prophet as a profound metaphor for the activity of God in the world. He surmised that God's creative relationship with humanity was something like (not exactly like – after all, this is God we are talking about!) the potter's creative relationship to the clay. God worked ceaselessly through people and events for the well-being of humanity, but some people fell short of God's best intentions. Jeremiah saw in the beautiful forms of freshly thrown clay jars an image akin to the beauty of people who act righteously. The potter who critiqued the aesthetic value of his own pots was quick to cherish some or rework others. Likewise, God was critiquing the moral value of divinely created humanity and was quick to act dramatically in judgment where people failed to act justly.

When we read the Jeremiah story and focus too narrowly on our assumptions about how God is like a potter, we can easily miss an important lesson., "Come, go down to the potter's house, and there I will let you hear my words." God does not send him to the temple, the desert or even the royal palace. Instead of a religious institutional setting, the prophet finds insight and meaning by venturing into the workspace of a craftsman. Further, he does not find his insight by gazing at finished masterpieces but by observing the creative process used by the potter. In fact, his insight relies on watching the potter at work. The story invites us to appreciate the possibility of discovering God's word to us not only in obvious or prescribed venues but in myriad creative and even unlikely situations. Here, the prophet comes to an awareness that God was shaping his people through the current threat and unrest in the world in which they lived. The shaping was to be seen in how well God's people saw God at work for righteousness and then responded in faith and righteousness in the midst of the shaping experience.

Perhaps, we might look more closely at how we are being shaped as God's people through the threats and events of our own time. For, most surely, God has not abandoned us, but is ever reworking that lump of clay toward righteousness.

Living With Fear

I happily belong to a group of Presbyterian ministers who began their friendships when we were together as students at Union Theological Seminary in Virginia. We began our friendships by hiking together once a month or so while we were students. Since 1978, we have met annually in the mountains of West Virginia and now in Virginia for three days of sharing, laughter, theologizing, joking, and what all. In the early days we hiked, canoed, and explored flora and fauna. These days (before being shut down this year) we sit more and tell stories and reflect on the church, the world, and our lives. Two of our number have died. Since we have not been able to meet this year, we have been meeting each Monday morning for an hour on ZOOM. It has been most entertaining and refreshing to gather with these guys through the years and now on Zoom. While we have made no "last-man-standing" agreements, we shall continue to meet until there are none of us left.

I share this with you in this devotional because one of the most frightening experiences of my life took place with this group while we were in seminary. One of our number is an expert spelunker (cave explorer), well known in the spelunking world for his expertise in this endeavor. Through his tales about the caves he had explored he invited us to join him in a cave in West Virginia that would not be too rigorous for all of us novices. So, one Saturday we drove two carloads of us into West Virginia, equipped with helmets, lights, ropes, and rough clothes for a day of caving. We entered the cave at the base of a mountain. It was a walk-in entrance, with the trail winding through passages we could manage while standing upright. Soon we entered a huge dome – a room over 200 feet wide and long right in the center of the mountain. This was my first experience with total darkness. When the lights were off, one lost orientation to some degree because it was the thickest of blackness. But we had plenty of lights, so it was an experience rather than a threat.

Then our spelunking friend told us that at the top of the mountain we were within there was another large room like the present one and this one had crystal formations and other interesting rock formations. How do we get there? Our guy told us that there was a small opening in the wall of the present room and after going on our bellies for about twenty yards we would come out into another room about 200 feet wide. So, one after the other, we belly-crawled through the narrow passage and we, indeed, did come into the other 200 foot wide room. What he didn't tell us was that this room was only three feet high. Then for the next four hours we worked our way sometimes crawling, sometimes on our bellies, occasionally walking stooped over, as we made our ways through this room and on up the interior of the mountain. We finally emerged into the large room with the crystals and rock formations. And after exploring for a while, we used our ropes and made our way out of an opening at the top of the mountain. It was exhilarating. It was also, for me, very frightening, especially those four hours crawling through the narrow passageways. At one point two of us got separated from the rest. I was close to panic during that time. I could imagine all sorts of scenarios that ended in the dark. Our leader realized the two of us were not with the group and came back and guided us.

Three things helped me with the fear in that caving experience: confidence in our leader; my companion with whom I got separated and with whom I could share the experience at the time; and very real prayer seeking the confidence that comes with knowing that I was not alone and that God carried my heart and mind while I was focusing on getting my body to a more secure place.

I would suggest today that these three things can help each of us during this unsettling time. I say unsettling, because we are dealing with at least three very threatening circumstances that is breeding much fear in our society and among us as well. They are: (1) this Coronavirus which is very much on the increase at present – a very dangerous time; (2) the political scene with all of its anger, distrust, and accusations as well as the divisiveness it has deeply infused into our society; and (3) economic stress particularly for small businesses, essential day workers, and the self-employed. I have no need to enumerate much about the stress and fear that these three realities have foisted onto our people. It has led to irrational outbursts, refusal to deal with facts, estrangements among friends and family, quantities of anger, and a general uncertainty about the future. Fear and uncertainty have increased around us and among us.

I would suggest in such a time that the three things that aided me in my cave-fear can be of utmost help to each of us during the uncertainties and fears of our time: (1) confidence in our leader – as new leadership comes into power, it is hoped that that leadership will bring in more certainty and hope in dealing with our national ills; (2) companionship that offers trusting relationships to fend off a sense of isolation. While different than in normal times, keeping up with friends and family via social media and other means is vital to take the emphasis off of our fears; (3) A very real focus on our inner lives – seeking to journey through the dark times with conscious awareness of ourselves as God's people and opening our hearts and minds to prayer, clarity in thought, and awareness that we are never alone.

As we continue to worship together via Facebook Live and continue to share thought and prayer as we use these weekly devotionals, together with contacts made with fellow church members and friends, and hopes for our new leaders in the days ahead, my hope and prayer is that we can keep fear from dominating our lives and becalm those times when we are most afraid.

Thanksgiving

The young man had just turned eighteen. He could vote now. He could serve in the armed services now. In the eyes of society, he was a man now. But as he waited to board the Amtrak train which had just pulled into the station, those things were far from his mind. He was off to college. His foster parents had gotten up early to bring him to the station where he would go off to another state to begin the next phase of his life.

The earlier stage had been a non-conventional one. His birth parents had died in a fiery crash that killed them immediately. He was not in the car with them but had been playing with a neighbor child at home. He was eight. He was eight and the only one left in his family. No siblings, no grandparents, only an older cousin out West somewhere. The County Department of Social Services and his church family had stepped in to care for him in those first dreary days of confusion and uncertainty. But what was his future? Where would he live? With whom would he live? These questions frightened him more deeply than he could have told you at the time. But the answer to them came rather soon and in a profound way. The answer was Bob and Rita.

Bob and Rita were members of the lad's church. He had known them through the years as kindly old folks who never failed to speak to him and his parents at church. They were in their early sixties when the accident had occurred. And they took him in to live with them. They had no children of their own, so this was a new venture for them, but one they readily and lovingly embraced. They took the boy in and raised him with love, wisdom, and kindly attention to his journey through childhood and adolescence. Now he was a man. Now, his life was before him to choose. They had nurtured him to this point. Now it was time to leave home.

At the station, they said their goodbyes, tearfully, quietly. The young man, never one for many words, embraced Bob and Rita and stepped back, looking into their eyes. He said to them, "How can I ever repay you for all you have done for me?" Bob put his hand on his shoulder and said, "Son, love can never to be paid back, but it can be passed on. It's your turn now."

With that, the young man boarded the train.

(I've told that story several times over the years. It's true. And it points me to the essence of thanksgiving. Thanksgiving is not about settling debts. It's about showing appreciation in response to grace. It's about gratitude. And while it is essential to develop such an attitude throughout life, Thanksgiving in our society is a reminder that the train we board for our journeys in life are provided by others along the way. I'm glad God has made life that way. Happy Thanksgiving!)

Advent

For some years, now, I have been collecting material and evidence, looking things up, visiting special sites, reading local histories, talking with newly-discovered cousins (most of them third cousins once removed!), and exchanging information on my family history and genealogy. It's fun. It's also consuming. I find myself thinking about it in odd moments, going over new information as I lie in my bed, staying up later to add just one more thing to my research. As I place myself into the line of antecedents and descendants of our family, I have begun to be aware of my age. Soon to turn 77, noting the ages of those who have gone before me, keenly aware during this pandemic of the early deaths of forebears who had no defenses against measles, the Spanish flu, polio, smallpox, and other such scourges, my fortune to live this long as well as my awareness that I *have* lived this long, all have underscored that I am OLD! Not too old, but old. Might as well admit it. While I haven't needed a walking cane yet, I did feel that I should mark this awareness in some tangible manner, so while I work at my desk and care for the odds and ends of my restricted life (by the pandemic), I decided to mark my status by wearing red suspenders! If I'm going be old, I'm going to look the part! What with shaggy hair and beard from lack of going to the barber together with my red suspenders, by golly, I look the part!

The segue from that thinking into something to draw us upward is not a hard one to make. There are a number of parts. First, we all come from somewhere and from some people. And if there had not been love back then and care given along the way, we wouldn't be here. That's what providence looks like. So, thank you, forebears who came across the ocean for good purpose and who helped establish this land where, in time, I could be born. Second, having come from this long line of forebears and watching the growth of my children and their children, I gain a sense of connectedness that transcends the biology of it all. I belong to some folks and they belong to me. Something vital transmits in that belonging. Third, when I'm gone, my place in the story will not be eliminated, but remembered, hopefully with honor and love. And lastly, having witnessed the role of Christian faith through the past generations and being a part of the community of God's people in the present and knowing that my children and their children are carrying on the faith, I rest in the confidence that my identity will be more than an item on a genealogical chart. It will be inscribed with countless others in the Book of Life, by God's own claim on us all.

We are entering the season of Advent this week. Like my genealogical study, Advent involves a looking back, a present involvement, and a vision of the future. Christ, God's way of reaching out to humanity, was looked for quite a long time. In the looking forward to his coming (that's what Advent is), expectations are born. Folks lived out of those expectations even before he arrived. Then he was born among us and his ministry, culminating in his death and resurrection, changed forever the ways of the world. Like us he had a special place on the genealogical chart. And we have ever followed after him down through the ages, noting how he continues, through his Spirit, to affect the present and draw us toward the future. Someday, the story will be completed and the Book of Life will be filled to running over with the names of his people. As we embrace his coming once again during this preparatory time, be assured that the timeline we are on is God's own and that the awareness of such is what we celebrate in these weeks leading up to Christmastide. A good thing for each of us to do is to remember the timeline of our lives and see how it joins with the timeline of God's people from the beginning all the way to eternity. Man, now I do need to wear those red suspenders! May these days of Advent expectation be a time of heart growth and faith growth and confidence growth for us all.

Waiting

Waiting can become mighty tiresome. At least some kinds of waiting can. We're all burdened by the long wait until we've each been vaccinated and can return to normal activities – especially getting back into our time together in worship and fellowship as a community of faith. How long, O Lord? - the words of the ancients echo in our minds and seem peculiarly relevant to us today.

It seems relevant in ways other than hoping for an end to the pandemic, too. For there are, of course, the normal kinds of "waiting" that are a part of human life – waiting to grow up, waiting for the baby to be born, waiting to get well, waiting for the election to finally end, waiting . . . and waiting - certainly a frequent part of our lives. And here we are in the midst of the Advent season for Christians, and what does that season mean but more waiting – waiting through the month until the Christmas celebration comes, waiting in our hearts for Christ to come to us in renewal once again, waiting, at least in our thinking, for the return of Christ when God fulfills and completes the story. It would seem accurate to say, then, that one of the descriptions of the Christian life is that of waiting.

In the Bible, there is a lot of waiting. Indeed, the term is often used throughout the Bible, and it is used in two primary ways: (1) A term denoting duration of time as one waits for something expected to finally happen or arrive; and (2) A term denoting confidence and hope as one describes the stance one is taking as one goes through life towards its goal. Noah represents the duration meaning when he waits for the flood to abate. But the primary use of the term, "wait" in the Bible has to do with expectant confidence as the stance one will take until the anticipated conclusion finally arrives. It has to do with hope and confidence "in the meantime."

This second meaning of the term is for growing Christians. Beyond simply complaining that the Lord hasn't come yet or done what one wants yet so that waiting is a more like a "downer," the deeper waiting of God's people is an expression of confidence and hope for "the meantime." Listen to Isaiah (40:31): ***But they who wait for the Lord shall renew their strength; they shall mount up with wings like eagles; they shall run and not be weary; they shall walk and not faint."*** Waiting, then, is a form of hopeful living in the midst of the present. It is the confidence that our inner lives, touched by God through our trust, will be encouraged, strengthened, readied, and prepared for what is coming. Waiting becomes the path we trod, the avenue for our hope, and the form our vision takes in the present. And when we wait faithfully, God is there with us, all the way. This is a life-stance for making our way through the long periods of the other kind of waiting, like the one we're in with this pandemic. We are to be reassured that in the midst of waiting our

Lord is walking with us, just as he will be at the end of it all, coming toward us in love and victory.

Let our thoughts during this time of waiting echo the words of the Psalmist when he proclaims: *"Wait for the Lord; be strong, and let your heart take courage; wait for the Lord"* (Psalm 27:14).

Stars

"O star of wonder, star of night; Star with royal beauty bright; Westward leading, still proceeding, Guide us to thy perfect Light." So we sing the celestial words of John H. Hopkins in his traditional Christmas Carol, "We Three Kings of Orient Are." *". . . Field and fountain, moor and mountain, Following yonder star."*

While we know that the universe operates in dependable ways that we understand through the observations and discipline of science and, thus, have accumulated great knowledge concerning the solar system, galaxies, and the far-flung stars which ever shine upon us, the stars and planets upon which we can gaze have an enduring history in inspiring poetry, metaphor, and myth. Religious people have long associated the stars with the revelation of the gods or, in our case, God. So, in your mind's eye, come with me for a few moments up to a rocky outcropping upon the top of a mountain in Shenandoah National Park in Virginia, on a clear summer night in June:

It's midnight and a group of us, without flashlights, travel by starlight (Yes, in the utter darkness of that moonless night with the stars literally blazing away like a blanket of mini-lights stretching from horizon to horizon, we could see our way.) up the narrow trail to the outcropping filled with large boulders. We spread out, each choosing a boulder upon which to lie back upon and to take in the twinkling drama that practically absorbed us. No sound. No light from the world. Hardly breathing. Mesmerized by the sheer grandeur. Humbled into prayers filled with both words and sighs of exhilaration. A holy moment, whereby God moved in through the sheer magnificence of his created universe spread out before us. One could almost hear voices coming from the points of light. One could see the constellations given names by the Ancients most clearly. And the reverence was punctuated by the meteors, silently on their way toward destinations beyond our scope. No wonder the Ancients studied the stars as portents for what lay ahead. Surely, such magnificence pointed to something grand and worthwhile.

We spent three hours utterly transfixed up there on those boulders. The memory of that night is so solidly engraved into my brain, that when someone speaks of the stars, images of that night under God's own blanket comes to my mind.

In the year that Jesus was born, there was violence, chaos, political and social unrest. It was a dark time. Our tradition (cf. Matthew, chapter 2) tells of the Magi who found the infant and his parents by way of a star. Whether it was a supernova, a comet, or the conjunction of two or three planets together, the tradition is that this sign led them to the Christ child, surely a sign that something wonderful and great was happening. They followed the star to Bethlehem where his family was living temporarily, and, bringing gifts, worshiped. In a time that was dark, light was brought in to our world. As we believe, Jesus stepped into the chaos and brought peace.

Now, fast forward to the year 2020. It, too, is a time of violence, chaos, political and social unrest. It, too, is a dark time, especially with the pandemic savagely upon us. It is dark. Winter Solstice, December 21, is the time where the day is the shortest and night is the longest. It's literally the "darkest day," and is the beginning of what most would say is the cold, dark winter season.

How marvelous for those with a poet's heart to know that on the darkest day of this year, Jupiter and Saturn meet (at least to our eyes), giving us the Christmas Star once again! How fitting, that in the moment of time during the Christmas season that we get to see this beautiful reminder that even in the darkest of times, Light will, and has, and does step in. In our chaos God continues to remind us that He is here with us. He continues, always, to bring light . . . and hope.

Stories

"What's your story?" So the question goes when people talk with each other. Oh, they might not ask it outright, but our conversations often echo the story or stories which are playing in our lives and influencing what we think and what we do.

For example, in talking with veterans of war, these survivors of often unimaginable fear and horror may look at their world interpreting things through the lenses of fierce loyalty and sometimes disdain for those who do not fit their story's picture of what they were fighting for.

Another example would be the story of the way things are and are supposed to be which shapes the life of someone who was raised in a loving home that taught a clear morality and offered much encouragement for life. Folks raised like that often have a most positive outlook on life and seek to contribute as a primary desire far more than they seek to take. They live out the story they received in growing up.

You see the point? We are living our stories in some very real ways. And we do so either consciously or unconsciously, perhaps both.

In this time of political and social unrest, aggravated by the tensions which are influenced heavily by the pandemic, the people of our country seem divided by the stories citizens hold to as the frame of reference for decisions, opinions, voting, conversations, and attitudes. That division holds true throughout our society and is reflected even among church folk like us. And, sometimes, the stories found in a divided society are so majorly different, that conversations are hard, disdain abounds, and there can be a tendency of dismissing those who do not reflect the same story one himself or herself might hold dear. We can see this division in the fact that some folks trust only certain media and leaders, that on some very bad occasions fighting has broken out in the streets, and, in some churches, members have quarreled, ministers have resigned or been fired, and the tendency to think that if one isn't telling the same story as one's own, then that person is wrong and should not be heard or included. Stories are important.

It seems to me that in such a setting and with the importance of the stories which influence us, that here at Christmastide, we have a wonderful chance to re-evaluate the basic story or stories which shape us and guide us in our lives.

John the Baptist lived with a basic story guiding him. It wasn't one he invented. He was called to be the Messenger, to point the Way for God's Messiah. He lived most simply because his story demanded his attention to other things. He challenged the authorities who talked one way and lived another. He dared to challenge King Herod, denouncing him for his adulterous life with his brother's wife. John's story pointed folks to the coming of Jesus. His baptism of folks was to help them retool the stories which were guiding their lives. And it cost him his life.

What story do you think those shepherds were sensing and following when the very stars out there in the fields sang angelic songs to them and made them aware God was up to something? Surely their stories included the possibility that God can and would reveal himself to folks.

The same can be said for the Wise Men and their visit to the manger-side. Their stories included reading the heavens for patterns they found reflected on earth. And when the unusual star appeared, their story allowed them to believe God was up to something and they went to find out.

As we come to the Christmas celebration once again this year, maybe we can find this a time to evaluate the stories that are guiding us and our behavior. Could it be possible that we should allow the story of God's Son come among us to outrank any or even all of the stories that shape our thoughts and actions? I say so. Maybe this will be the essential step we must take to put away the stories conjured up by hateful conspiracy theories (which are actually stories that have begun to shape lives), by partisans of hate and distrust, and by misplaced loyalties. Maybe the story of God so loving his people that he has come among us in the most basic way – in the birth of a child who was destined to lead us to a more essential story for our lives, just maybe (I'll bet on it!) that story can lead one away from anger, fear, and hate Maybe the story of Jesus can once more become the guiding light to shape and influence all the stories we tell ourselves and act out of. It seems to me that is the way to receive this gift from God, allowing his love in his Son and through his Son to shape us, shape our stories, and shape the stories we believe.

So, what's the story we each one are living? What is the essential story we each one believe? My prayer for us all is that we continue to be shaped by the Greatest Story Ever Told.

Gifts

I can't help thinking about gifts and giving as I write. Christmas time certainly brings that subject up for most of us in that we've spent time both giving gifts and receiving gifts during this last week. Of course, the age-old questions of why in the world we go through such endeavors each year have been asked and probably answered in some way that allows us to feel good about the custom. We've probably been reminded of the Wise Men who brought their gifts to worship the newborn King and been gently urged to think of our giving at Christmas time as one way we can honor our King as well. And that's all well and good. Such a thing as God sending his Son to us is more than a worthy encouragement for us to be *gifters*, to make *gifting* a way of honoring our God.

I shall wear my new clothes and eat the delicious goodies and reread my Christmas cards with a great sense of having been *given to*, of having been *gifted*.

Is not all this awareness of the *giftedness* of the Christmas celebration but an illustration of one of the fundamentals of the life that God seeks for us? In studying the Bible as a source of revelation into the mind and will of God, one can be amazed at the hundreds of references to *gift* and *giving* found there. Indeed, it is apparent that the very substance of the nature of our God is profound *giving* and *gifting*. And if one reads further on the subject in the Bible one finds that it is equally apparent that the very substance of the nature of life for God's people is to be profound *giving* and *gifting* as well. Evidence of this is found all over the Bible.

The Scriptures point to three primary contexts in which *gifts* are given. First, there are the numerous passages which describe God as the *giver* of *gifts* to humanity. Among them are sustenance and the ability to be sustained by the creation itself; work and the possibilities of being able to build one's livelihood; wise leadership from those God calls to serve him; the Holy Spirit as the inward testimony of the love and purposes of God in one's heart; and grace as the profound claim God has upon his people out of his nature as a loving God. If we were to stop with the knowledge of just these *gifts* it would be enough. But, there's more.

Secondly, the Scriptures describe the hope of humanity *giving gifts* to God as symbols of appreciation of and thankfulness for God's *gifts*. The animal sacrificial system in the Old Testament was an example. However, both Testaments look at the ways the faithful serve God by serving others and living by God's ways as their *gifts* to God.

Third, the Scriptures over and over point to the possibility and the necessity of people giving *gifts* to each other. Indeed, it is a mark of the covenant of *giving* illustrated by God's *giving* Christ to us and Christ *giving* to us his ministry, teachings, and life, that an essential aspect of Christian living is profound, continued, appreciative, and helpful *giving* to others.

The whole of the Christian story and the endeavor of living as Christian people is underlain by numerous strata of *giving, gifting, and gifts*. Such is the heart of life in Christ and life in the Christian church.

What this brings to mind for me is the fact that God sees us as *gifted* people. We are endowed with the necessary ingredients for *giving*, we are equipped with certain qualities and abilities that fit us for *giving*, and we are given special *gifts* by God himself that allows our *giving* to enhance the quality and success of life together as we *give* them.

As people *gifted* by God himself, we are enabled through our faithfulness to live out our *giftedness* by living in response to God. St. Paul describes what the *gifted life* looks like in Romans 12:9-21:

[9] Let love be genuine; hate what is evil, hold fast to what is good; [10] love one another with mutual affection; outdo one another in showing honor. [11] Do not lag in zeal, be ardent in spirit, serve the Lord.[a] [12] Rejoice in hope, be patient in suffering, persevere in prayer. [13] Contribute to the needs of the saints; extend hospitality to strangers.[14] Bless those who persecute you; bless and do not curse them. [15] Rejoice with those who rejoice, weep with those who weep. [16] Live in harmony with one another; do not be haughty, but associate with the lowly;[a] do not claim to be wiser than you are. [17] Do not repay anyone evil for evil, but take thought for what is noble in the sight of all. [18] If it is possible, so far as it depends on you, live peaceably with all. [19] Beloved, never avenge yourselves, but leave room for the wrath of God;[a] for it is written, "Vengeance is mine, I will repay, says the Lord." [20] No, "if your enemies are hungry, feed them; if they are thirsty, give them something to drink; for by doing this you will heap burning coals on their heads." [21] Do not be overcome by evil, but overcome evil with good.

Through *gifting* the world with these *gifts*, our lives, our families, our homes, and our communities will be blessed. I pray we go into the new year bearing our gifts to share with others.

On Feeding

Like many of us as we age, I have idealized my hometown of Dunedin, Florida. Living there in the forties, fifties, and sixties, I experienced its movement from a small, Southern town somewhat akin to Mayberry into a thriving and much-desired small city on the edge of the huge metropolitan areas around Tampa Bay. Our home was just across the railroad tracks from the depot where my father was the ACL Railroad agent and station master. We lived in a large, two-storied frame Florida house built to catch the breeze in those days before air conditioning. The house sat on an acre lot loaded with trees, many of them fruit trees of various kinds. While our house faced a warm and friendly neighborhood on Scotland Street and Douglas Avenue, just immediately behind our house and just across from the depot there was something unique as far as we children were concerned. There, propped up on cement pillars, sat an old, weather-beatened feed store owned by our neighbor Mr. Brandenburg. For we children, the feed store was a wonderful place. I can smell the feed piled up in sacks in the back part of the store even now. But the wonder of it all was the access we had to the back warehouse where we could hide and play among the stacks of fertilizer and feed. Of course, we weren't supposed to play there, but, hey, this was Mayberry, remember, so we got away with it. On occasion, the store featured baby chickens and baby ducklings for us to watch. There were feral cats always hanging around the store hunting the rats and mice that inevitably found food and safe haven there. It was just the kind of place for cowboys and Indians, or Hide and Seek, or secret meetings of our "gang." I ran across a picture of that Feed Store in my collection the other day and it reminded me of the role the Feed Store played in my childhood. And that got me to thinking about the term "feed store" and some of its possible uses as metaphor for an important part of our Christian faith.

There is much about "feed" and "feeding" in the Bible. While it often refers to actual food with which to be fed, it also is used frequently as a metaphor for taking care of and providing for others, offering others spiritual food and support, and a picture of what God provides for us when he feeds our spirits and fills our hearts with love. A quick trip through the Bible finds "feed" as an important ingredient in our faith journeys with God.

- Elijah, fleeing from the wrath of Queen Jezebel, is guided by God to the Wadi Cherith where he is told that the ravens will feed him there. (God will provide for him.) I Kings 17:4.
- In Psalm 81, God adjures the people to listen to him and walk in his ways, saying: "I would feed you with the finest wheat, and with honey from the rock I would satisfy you." (God is providing better days as the people listen to him.) Psalm 81:16.

- In Proverbs 10:21, it is claimed that righteousness feeds many, but fools (not righteous) die for lack of sense (unfed).
- Isaiah 40 is one of the great passages in the Bible where we are promised that God is our shepherd who is faithful in feeding his flock. Who can forget the tenor solo at the beginning of Handel's Messiah quoting Isaiah: "He will feed his flock like a shepherd. . . ."
- God's love and purposes are seen as bringing harmony pictured in Isaiah 65 as the wolf and the lamb "feeding" together.
- In the Sermon on the Mount (Matthew 6:25) Jesus tells us not to worry about our lives, to look at the birds of the air - "they neither sow nor reap nor gather into barns, and yet your heavenly Father feeds them." Feeding is the metaphor for care and purpose.
- When Peter and others are with Jesus as he is about to depart from them in the Ascension, he tells Peter three times that it is his role (and the church's) to "feed my sheep." (John 21:17)

What this all brings to my mind is the idea that the church, in all of its manifestations, is truly to be a kind of "feed store" in our life in our communities. While it is tempting to take the metaphor too far and indulge ourselves in thinking about all the birds, lions, lambs, ravens, and other such creatures we might represent in using the metaphor, the main thing is the role of "feeding" that God's people represent. At our "feed store" – the church family:

- we are fed God's Word,
- we listen for God speaking (feeding us),
- we do God's bidding (feeding others),
- we seek to care for our neighbors (feeding others),
- we forgive as God forgive (a special kind of feeding),
- we allow Jesus' words to become our words (thus feeding our minds and others),
- we pay attention to the "still, small voice" which is feeding us,
- we recognize when we are unfed or underfed and seek to be better fed,
- we support the work of the Feed Store as it seeks to provide for the many,
- and we gather around the Table where we "feast" with our Lord.

Feed Stores are quite important for any number of reasons, but the church as our "feed store" is part of the feeding provision of our God for us. And we can feed together there and feed one another.

Brandenburg's Feed Store Opposite Dunedin ACLRR Station. Facing East, March 3, 1989

Cold Water

As many of our church folk know, Montreat, NC, is a village near Black Mountain, nestled in a hollow formed by Graybeard Mountain and the Black Mountains. It is the home of many Presbyterians, seat of one of the offices of the Presbyterian Historical Society, site of many Presbyterian conferences, home of Montreat University, and a place most-favored in the summer by long-time Presbyterians. I have been there many times, enjoying both leisure and conferences. The first time I was there, I was a Junior in High School, attending the World Mission Conference along with about 300 other youths. It was a great experience.

One thing that will forever remain in my store of memories of Montreat is my encounter with Lake Susan while at that conference. Lake Susan is a six or seven acre lake formed by damming the main creek that runs through the hollow where Montreat sits. In those days, one could swim in it and there was a floating platform out in the middle of the lake where one could play. Coming from my home in Florida, I was used to the lukewarm waters of the Gulf of Mexico and the occasional cool waters of some of the fabulous Florida springs. I was not prepared for Lake Susan.

A friend and I donned bathing suits and walked to the lake intent on some water fun. Great was the anticipation therein. Great also was the surprise awaiting us therein. We both dove in eager to swim to the floating platform. Egad! I certainly was not prepared for the shock that the cold mountain water of Lake Susan had in store for me! It was electric! It literally took my breath away! I started swimming with all my might, determined to escape the electricity surging through my body. I couldn't get a breath. I swam on autopilot. The cold hurt! And in record time, I made it to the floating platform, there to stay for an hour trying to get the courage to swim back. It surely did take courage, because swimming back was even worse because I knew what was coming. It took the rest of the day for me to warm up.

This episode as long been in my memory. It has given me a vivid picture of what putting "cold water" on something is like. Of course, putting cold water on something means to demean it, put it down, discourage someone about it, etc. It sure discouraged my swimming back or ever swimming in Lake Susan again.

The Bible speaks of "cold" in several ways. It is a measure of the weather and is one aspect of life (Genesis 8:22 – *"As long as the earth endures, seedtime and harvest, cold and heat, summer and winter, day and night, shall not cease."*).

It is a metaphor for what is refreshing and restorative (Proverbs 25:25 – *"Like cold water to a thirsty soul, so is good news from a far country."* Matthew 10:42 – *". . . and whoever gives even a cup of cold water to one of these little ones in the name of a disciple – truly, I tell you, none of these will lose their reward.").*

Paired with "warm" it is also a metaphor for being committed or showing a diminishing of commitment: (Revelation 3:15 – *"I know your works; you are neither cold nor hot. I wish that you were either cold or hot.").*

To "throw cold water" on something means to temper excitement or enthusiasm or to discourage or try to prevent a plan from being carried out. It is to be unenthusiastic about something or to express misgivings about or disapproval of something. All of us have those moments when someone threw cold water on a plan or belief or idea.

We are living in a time when it feels like "cold water" has been thrown on our lives and on our life together here in our land. Can't worship together; must keep our distance; must protect others from ourselves with our masks, travel is hard, deeply worried over the civil strife and political divisiveness that is sucking the energy out of our lives much like that cold water of Lake Susan sucked the will to go back in the water out of me. Indeed, to many the pictures in our minds of what our society is like and is to be have had cold water thrown on them by the beliefs and deeds of others. Will we get back to normal again, many ask?

The answer is that we shall get back to normal, a changing normal as always. But in the meantime, it often feels like we're sitting on the floating platform waiting to plunge back in. It is here that our life in Christ becomes essential.

This is our Father's world. Nothing can separate us from him or his work in our hearts and minds ultimately. This is the floating platform in which we await. The words of the prayer Jesus taught us are for all times and especially for these times:

"Thy kingdom come, thy will be done, on earth as it is in heaven.
Give us this day our daily bread,
and lead us not into temptation, but deliver us from evil. . . ."

Jesus warned his disciples about what cold water can do: Matthew 24:12 –

"And because of the increase of lawlessness, the love of many will grow cold. . . ."

But we can swim through the cold water; yes, we can. And we must if we are to continue on. And we do so in the confidence that our Father is on the shore beckoning us toward him as we swim. That's God's promise.

*****

Cold, cold water surrounds me,
And all I've got is Your hand, Lord;
Can you hear me now?
Don't you know I love you, and I always have.
Hallelujah! Will you come with me?
Cold, cold water surrounds me now;
And all I've got is Your hand.

-Song by Damien Rice

Gladness

"I am so glad to see you," I told him. After months of relative isolation due to the pandemic, seeing a dear friend lightened the load I was carrying in my heart and refocused my attitude and thoughts for a while. Gathering with the Men's group even under social distancing and masking circumstances, did the same. It made me glad. Glad to see faces I knew and cared about. Glad to share time and space once again. Life together does that, you know – make us glad. I hear that the helplines are especially busy right now in this pandemic because isolation deflates – it lessens the lightness of one's heart, it stifles gladness. I take part in a Zoom meeting each Monday with old seminary friends. We each look forward eagerly to it and the result of sharing even electronic space with each other brings on hearts of gladness. Perhaps not being able to worship together on Sundays in person adds to a dampening. But I see the notes church members put on our Facebook Live service each week greeting each other. Even that gladdens the heart.

There is much in the Bible about *gladness*. The term *glad* is often paired with *rejoice*. I note that to "re-joice" is to be joyful "again." The Psalmists invite us to be glad over and over. Listen:

- *"Let the heavens be glad, and let the earth rejoice, let them say among the nations: The Lord is King!"* (I Chronicles 16:1)
- *"Be glad in the Lord and rejoice, O righteous, and shout for joy, all you upright in heart."* (Psalm 32:11)
- *"My soul makes its boast in the Lord; let the humble hear and be glad."* (Psalm 34:2)
- *"I was glad when they said to me, 'Let us go to the house of the Lord.'"* (Psalm 122:1)
- *"Worship the Lord with gladness; come into his presence with singing."* (Psalm 100:2)
- *"Therefore, God, your God, has anointed you with the oil of gladness. . . ."* (Psalm 45:7)

Some Biblical writers connect gladness with anointing ("oil of gladness"). One may remember that the Jews had anointing ceremonies for various acts in their lives – for birth, for marriage, for death, for worship, for repentance and cleansing. They believed that such anointing "covered" them (literally and figuratively) with God's redemption and grace. Through such actions, they changed the trajectory of their lives for those moments and the subsequent relief and renewal sparked "gladness." Where one's heart was in it, that gladness was real, that joy was uplifting as the renewal took hold.

Thus, it is not surprising to hear Isaiah exult about the relief that comes with God's delivering the people from captivity. It is through God's redemption which "covered" (anointed) them once again as his people. Thus, the prophet says: *"So the ransomed of the Lord shall return, and come to Zion with singing; everlasting joy shall be upon their heads; they shall obtain joy with gladness, and sorrow and sighing shall flee away."*

There is no magic to all this. One doesn't say a word or do an action and then suddenly find joy in the heart and gladness once again. What one does is to begin to live out of a different story in the mind than the story one was living out of before.

As we go through our days, we have an inner voice/ picture/narrative going on. In fact, sometimes there's more than one going on at the same time. We go to work and while the story at the front of our minds is about the task at hand, the back story is one of worry about a loved one or about a fear or some guilt or some plan for another day, etc. We humans are capable of multiple stories going on all at the same time. There's the right-now story, the family story, the relationships story, the work story, the to-do story, the wishful thinking story, the regret story, God's story, and so forth.

However, we generally bring one of those stories to the forefront of our minds in each moment. And here is where gladness as a result of being "covered" by our faithful walk with God comes in.

We are "anointed/covered" by our Lord as we allow our story of faith and trust in him to come to the forefront of our minds. As we do that throughout the day, consciously remembering God's promise never to leave us, God's promise to renew our lives through his love, God's promise to walk with us down every path even one in the shadow of death, God's delight in his creation and God's delight in us, and can hear the words of Jesus as we move, showing us the more sure way to live, and can sense his presence in the pictures that come to mind, we are "covered" from above. And, there is gladness.

Brother James, an old Roman Catholic monk, called this "the practice of the presence of God." It has to do with what story we are telling and listening to in our minds. Gladness comes as we live out of God's story as we live out those many others that are a part of our lives.

Try this picture for the next few moments:

Make a joyful noise to the Lord, all the earth.
Worship the Lord with gladness; come into his presence with singing.
Know that the Lord is God. It is he that made us, and we are his;
We are his people, and the sheep of his pasture.

Enter his gates with thanksgiving and his courts with praise.
Give thanks to him, bless his name.
For the Lord is good;
His steadfast love endures forever,
And his faithfulness to all generations.

--Psalm 100

Doesn't that make you glad!?

Awake

Hey, Rich! Wake up! The President has been killed!" Those words will forever be etched into my memory store. It was November 22, 1963, and it was the rudest of awakenings for me. President John F. Kennedy has just been assassinated by Lee Harvey Oswald, a gruesome act captured on live TV. I had been taking a nap right after lunch. It was as if I had been awakened into another world, so forceful was this event in my consciousness as well as in the life of the nation and world. I looked out of the window of my dorm to see the flag over Anderson Hall, the centerpiece of our campus, flying at half-mast. As we limped through the following days of sorrow and uncertainty, it was as if our lives were at half-mast as well. Each person who was alive on that day can tell you details about their own awakening to this new and unsettling reality. That's what awakenings can do, you know, open us up to new and sometimes unsettling realities.

The term *awake* is found all over the Bible. It is one of those words used to draw the reader into the story or situation being presented. It is used in at least three ways in the Bible.

First, it is a general term used in the familiar way of rallying one's attention like my friend did for me in drawing my attention to the President's death. For example, the psalmist and prophet ask God to *awake* and take action on the people's behalf (Psalm 7:6; 44:23, et al.). To *awake* in this general sense can refer to emotional states as in the soul being *awakened* in joy and praise (Psalm 57:8); love being *awakened* as passion kindled between lovers (Song of Solomon 2:7).

But there's more. Secondly, *awake* can mean to restore someone to a conscious state, whether from sleep (1 Samuel 26:12; Psalm 102:7) or death, as when one "sleeps with one's ancestors" (1 Kings 17:17-24; Matthew 9:18, 23-24). Brother Paul says that those who "sleep" will be the first fruits of the resurrection (1 Corinthians 15:20) as they *awaken* to new life.

On a deeper level, *awake* often describes a state of spiritual readiness and preparation. Jesus asks his disciples to stay *awake* with him in the Garden of Gethsemane as he agonizes before his arrest. The disciples fall asleep literally and figuratively; they do not keep vigil with him and then disown him when he is arrested (Matthew 26:40-41; Mark 14:34-38). Parables of the kingdom of heaven exhort listeners to "stay awake," to be prepared at any moment for the coming of Jesus because they do not know the day or the hour of his return (Matthew 24:42-51; 25:1-30; Mark 13:35-37).

As we continue our journey together as a congregation as well as friends who read this in other locations, I find that all three ways of using this little word can well apply to our lives. What we're about in the Christian community is seeking to gain each person's attention to the things of and ways of God including the sense of who God is and how God has reached out to us in Jesus Christ and continues to nurture us through his Spirit. I know many persons who have never been awakened to this reality. They are conscious that there is a God, they believe in God, but have not been awakened in the sense of getting their real attention in the midst of life. Worship, prayer, Scripture, celebration, sermon, singing, the story – all are to get one's attention .

Likewise, our life together has a restorative aspect to it – it is to restore one to a conscious awareness of who one is as belonging each day to the God who calls us awake. Not only does the congregation's life offer this opportunity, but one's own journey can do the same as the process of daily living continually draws one into questions about meaning and change. Just as President Kennedy's death set off a chain of events that motivated multitudes to re-examine what they believed and how God was moving in the events of the day, so too can the circumstances of our time and lives do the same. They can restore our conscious awareness of the deeper things, of the reality of God and God's purposes, and the sense that God is among us along the way. The recent turmoil of the insurrection attempt on our nation's Capitol has done this for many, reawakening the deeper questions of who we are and what we believe as citizens, as well as to re-examine issues of truth versus falsehood and questions of the future. I do hope many have been awakened to ask the important questions and seek for ways to continue to enact our life together in accordance with our deeper beliefs.

All of life in general and our faith journeys in particular offer us the third way of *awakening,* for they offer us opportunities for sensing God's Spirit among us, awakening our inner selves to the sense of God's presence and truth, preparing us for daily journeys with him. If each new day doesn't invite our readiness to continue our spiritual journeys with our God, then we will have missed out on one of the ways God provides for us. God has set things up so as to continually *awaken* us for loving our neighbors, serving our God, giving praise to him, sensing him in the "still small voice," acting for justice and righteousness in our world, and hearing him speak to our hearts and minds. My prayer is that as we continue our journey together, even if remote for a time, that this will be a time of *awakening* for each of us.

Seeing Clearly

The Scripture for this week is to be found in John 9:1-12 (see below), one of the stories of Jesus healing a blind man. This is the one where he puts mud on the man's eyes and tells him to wash it off at the Pool of Siloam and assuring the crowd that the man's blindness was not punishment for sin, neither the man's nor his parents'. The theme is "seeing clearly," something most pertinent in the unclarity so prevalent among the peoples of today.

While this event was a sure enough miracle of Jesus, there is a lot more going on here that just the description of a miracle. This is a story of faith, a faith that sees clearly. It is set in the setting of several other characters, each of whom suffers from blindness of one kind or another.

First, there were the disciples. They suffered from the blindness of limited theological understanding. They believed, as did the folks of that time (and some today), that blindness (and other afflictions) was because of sins, either the man's own sins or that of his parents. They believed God punished sin in some tangible way, illness and affliction being among the ways. While God does not afflict folks in this way, there is a connection, not from God but from reality, between a person's setting and influences and how clearly or less clearly one sees what is real and true. Those who are under the sway of prejudiced or hateful thinking and behavior are often limited in how clearly they can see reality and truth. There is much of this going on in the present climate of our society, I'm afraid.

Second, there were the neighbors. They were blinded by denial. "Wasn't this guy the beggar?" No, can't be him, he was a blind man." He told them he was indeed the beggar, but they did not believe him. Denial. There is great evidence in our time that this is the affliction of those who want reality to match their preconceived beliefs. Some are even willing to accuse every other voice, even those based on solid evidence, of being untrue. "Don't confound me with the facts," is a saying rampant today. Or, rather, let me have my own facts instead than what is demonstrably true. It was the beggar who demonstrably was able to see, but it was easier to deny it because it didn't fit their "alternative facts." Oh, how comfortable it is to deny what we don't like even when it is true. It enables us to resist change or realities we dislike.

Then, there were the Pharisees. They suffered from the blindness of righteous indignation. How dare Jesus break the rules and heal someone on the Sabbath! And worse, "How can a man (meaning Jesus) who is a sinner perform such signs?" It is true that one's belief system can often stifle an acceptance of reality. "Don't tell me Magellan sailed around the world; you know the world is flat!" "None of the main news companies tell the truth, so I will find my own truth somewhere else." It's an old story, not seeing clearly.

Fourth, there were the blind man's parents. They suffered from the blindness of selfishness. They didn't want to lose their seats in the synagogue. "They were afraid of the Jews; for the Jews had agreed that anyone who confessed Jesus to be the Messiah would be put out of the synagogue." Rather than believe their own son, they chose to distance themselves from him (and the truth) in order to save themselves. Not seeing clearly truly can cause harm to others.

Finally, there was the crowd. They suffered from the blindness of rejection. It is unclear just who was challenging the man on his new sight, but the implication is that all of society wanted him to reject what Jesus had done for him. Yet the evidence was to the contrary and all the man knew was that he was blind but now he could see. But, not wanting to hear that testimony, they drove him out of town. How many times has a version of this taken place throughout the world! I don't like what the evidence shows, so shut it down, drive it away,

The blind man was surrounded by a community who all suffered from some form of spiritual blindness; they could not see clearly. Sadly, no one acknowledged that a miracle had taken place. No one rejoiced or praised God for the man's ability to see. No one asked him what it felt like to be able to see his family for the first time. Instead of being excited that God had intervened and helped a man to see, they all rejected him because of his faith in what Jesus did. Rejecting the evidence, they could not see clearly. Point made; lesson learned; reflection is in order.

One thing is clear to me: The charge to the community of faith is to learn every way possible to see more clearly. See what God is doing among us. See how God's ways continue to move throughout the world. Hear God's word so that we have substance to work with more than opinion or desire. Free the truth from the blindness which can beset any society or group. Live toward what God is revealing. *We must no longer be children, tossed to and fro and blown about by every wind of doctrine, by people's trickery, by their craftiness in deceitful scheming. But speaking the truth in love, we must grow up in every way into him who is the head, into Christ, from whom the whole body, joined and knit together by every ligament with which it is equipped, as each part is working properly, promotes the body's growth in building itself up in love.* (Ephesians 4:14-15)

Coming Clean

As I write I note that today is Ash Wednesday, the beginning of the forty-day Lenten period of preparation for the celebration of Christ's resurrection at Easter. Historically Ash Wednesday is a day of prayer and fasting and in some churches is marked by the placing of the sign of the cross on the foreheads of believers after their prayers of repentance. The sign of the cross is done with ashes made from the burning of the palm branches of the previous year's Palm Sunday celebration. Thus, this shows the meaning of discipleship as it moves incessantly between repentance and celebration.

In thinking about the holy drama that the Jesus story presents for us, I found myself pausing once again to reflect on that which is at the very heart of the Lenten season - which is penitence. In my experience in a lifetime in the church, I have found that often the whole notion of penitence, confessing sins, spending time in reflection on my failures, and coming clean with myself and with God about my deeper self is something I often avoid. It's not comforting in itself. It hurts one's self-image, and sometimes leads one to resent acknowledging that this area of one's life is precisely where God's grace and truth is perhaps needed the most.

The old-time preachers spent 90 percent of their sermons on arousing a sense of one's sinfulness so that one would be motivated to repent and get life on the right paths (and frightened many with Hell if they didn't repent!). Indeed, so ingrained is the notion that preachers and preaching is best avoided because it inevitably brings up one's sinfulness, that a person once told me that whenever he saw me (as a minister) he felt guilty. That, to wit, is topped by the experience I have had a number of times in meeting someone on an airplane or in some other setting who, when it was discovered I was a minister, immediately began to tell me why he or she doesn't go to church or why they avoid the things of God. In other words, because of the emphases in the past and present of some forms of Christian preaching on our sinfulness and our need to repent or one will burn in Hell, some folks just avoid the subject and the church that goes with it altogether.

Lest we throw the baby out with the bath, however, one can claim a more active faith when one addresses this whole confession and repentance business than when one avoids it or rebels against it. Indeed, the central drama of God seeking out his people, coming among them in the person of Jesus of Nazareth, signaling to them in cosmic words and actions his forgiveness of all that stands in the way of their life with him and with a loving life with others, is provided to claim our hearts and minds, cleansing them of thoughts and deeds that transgress his will and his ways. If our faith in God's great word to us in Christ's suffering and death does not enable us to grapple with our own shortcomings and misdeeds and hateful thoughts in ways that move us toward love and harmonious living, then we have missed the point of God's work in Jesus Christ.

The period of time prior to both the birth celebration of Christmas (Advent) and the crucifixion and resurrection of Jesus (Lent) is one way to encourage believers to tend to their hearts, to take part in some spiritual housecleaning, and to clear the way toward unencumbered celebration and continuation of the Christian journey.

God's purpose has never been to burden us with our sinfulness, but to draw us forward into new life. Listen to Jeremiah as he speaks words of God's intentions and, therefore, the people's hope as they were in captivity in Babylon. These are words for all times, even for this Ash Wednesday:

For surely I know the plans I have for you, says the Lord, plans for your welfare and not for harm, to give you a future with hope. Then when you call upon me and come and pray to me, I will hear you. When you search for me, you will find me; if you seek me with all your heart, I will let you find me, says the Lord. . .

During the season of Lent, I hope we shall come before our Lord in honesty about those areas where we have fallen short or not gone far enough. In a spiritual sense, let us carry the sign of the cross on our heads and on our hearts.

A Room Called Remember

The writer Rumer Godden in her book, <u>A House With Four Rooms</u>, builds her reflection around an old Indian proverb. The proverb speaks of each person being a house with four rooms: a physical, a mental, an emotional, and a spiritual room. She goes on to say that "most of us tend to live in one room most of the time, but, unless we go into every room every day, even if only to keep it aired, we are not a complete person." I find this thought an apt analogy for thinking about where we are in our minds throughout the day. It's hard not to go into the physical room what with the need for food and drink as well as care for our person throughout the day. I guess some people spend inordinate amounts of time in this room and others would like to have more of the needs of that room met. The mental room is where we go to think, to comprehend, to plan, and to communicate. For some, this room is more habitual than thoughtful. For others there is great pleasure in where one can go and what one can learn in using one's mind. The third room is the room for emotions. This room often takes little thought and is more reactive to circumstances, real or imagined. It is the seat of emotion, of love and hate, anger and friendship. It is often where we find motivation for caring for others. Unfortunately, it also can be where we store up anger and hatred, locked in places we can visit to soothe our hurt and released sometimes in hurtful actions. The fourth room is the spiritual room, the room where our thoughts are lifted and our values formed and enhanced. A purpose or purposes for life can come from this room as well as decisions about truth and hope. We meet God in this room, at least we can. Perhaps it would be a good exercise to reflect on how we spend time in each of these rooms in our ongoing lives. Maybe we will discover that we tend to live in one room more than the others with decidedly marked results.

While our awareness of the four rooms is a mental exercise, one should not limit the self to these rooms alone, for I can think of at least one other room that I have found important in my life – a room that is built off of all four of the other rooms. Let's call it what one writer has named "A Room Called Remember."

In that room is the great storehouse of memories we either treasure, learn from, or are haunted by. Some folks actually live in that room most of their days, especially folks who are haunted by failures of the past. Spiritual health would dictate that they should not live in that room alone if they want to grow beyond its entrapments. But it is an important room, for our treasures are there as well. Our room called remember can motivate us toward change, it can bog us down in the darkness of unresolved grief or pain, it can pretend to be the only thing in our lives, and it can enliven us with the memories of successes and victories. I am comforted and motivated by much in my room called remember. I hope you are as well.

However, for the purposes of this devotional, there is an additional matter to consider. To what degree, if any, have we allowed the God who loves us, the Father of our Lord Jesus Christ, as well as his Son Jesus himself, and the awareness of God's Holy Spirit to inhabit the rooms of our minds with us? It is very possible, you know. Inviting God into our physical surroundings is like asking a blessing for our physical lives. Inviting God into our mental room is like a walk through our thoughts with an important friend. Allowing God into our emotional room can give balance to our emotions which can sometimes vary so widely. And, of course, inviting God into our spiritual rooms is like inviting the host to come into our midst to oversee the party and to renew our lives. I often ask God about what I have learned and what I have seen in my room called remember. Perhaps the reason some find God so distant and the awareness of his presence in one's lives so fleeting is related to how actively and willfully one allows him to enter the physical room, the mental room, the emotional room, the spiritual room, as well as the room called remember in one's life. Allowing God into those rooms is an activity over which we exert control. This is why Christians gather to worship, study, share, and serve together in Christ's name. That's why Christians pray for one another. Such actions allow us and encourage us to invite our God into our lives. And, altogether, this makes living in the house of our minds and hearts a home.

Seeking the Welfare of Others

"Years ago, anthropologist Margaret Mead was asked by a student what she considered to be the first sign of civilization in a culture. The student expected Mead to talk about fishhooks or clay pots or grinding stones.

But no. Mead said that the first sign of civilization in an ancient culture was a femur (thighbone) that had been broken and then healed. Mead explained that in the animal kingdom, if you break your leg, you die. You cannot run from danger, get to the river for a drink or hunt for food. You are meat for prowling beasts. No animal survives a broken leg long enough for the bone to heal.

A broken femur that has healed is evidence that someone has taken time to stay with the one who fell, has bound up the wound, has carried the person to safety, and has tended the person through recovery. **Helping someone else through difficulty is where civilization starts**, Mead said." – Ira Byock

As interesting as this is in terms of civilization, it is also at the very base of what being a Christian in the world is all about. While there is little doubt that one's inner person is deeply involved in being a Christian – our relationship with Jesus Christ and through his revelation with God Almighty, nevertheless, being a Christian does not stop at nourishing the inner person. Indeed, for one's faith to activate, to be real, to become vital, to be authentic, it becomes so by placing attention on others. Especially those in difficulty. It can be said that **seeking the welfare of those in difficulty is where Christianity starts**. Christianity is a religion of focus on God and neighbor. As we watch and listen to Jesus as revealed in the Bible, we can both hear and see this. Loving one's neighbor as self, loving one's enemy, welcoming the stranger, making a place for children, seeking the welfare of those on the outside (in his day, lepers, women, slaves, Gentiles, mentally ill, prisoners, tax collectors, Romans), reaching out to those who were ill, those who were lost and confused, and sinners of all stripes and shapes; all of these actions, and those similar, is where Christianity starts, is where Christianity is alive.

In my own Christian journey, over and again I have had to rethink what I believe I am about as a Christian believer. When I hear the harsh words some have for immigrants, for minorities, for the poor among us, for the elderly, for the mentally ill, and for anyone who is "not like us," I have to rekindle just what my inner self truly believes. When I hear fear and resentment about others who, it is supposed, will "take what I've worked so hard for," I have to have a talk with God and with myself about what belonging to Jesus Christ is all about. The words Margaret Mead had about where civilization starts point me over and again to the many words of Jesus about where Christianity starts – seeking the welfare of those in difficulty. Does this mean wearing a mask for the sake of vulnerable others? Does it mean getting vaccinated for the sake of vulnerable others? Does it mean fighting the urges to harden my heart toward others, especially those who are not like me or don't believe the things I believe? Does this mean seeking to make peace in my inner life about God's care for those who frighten me? Each believer must come to one's best response to questions like these in relation to his or her own walk with the Lord. But as I do so, I have to begin my thoughts with this notion: seeking the welfare of those in difficulty is the beginning of Christianity. It also continues civilization at its best.

With Wings Like Eagles

I am a birder. So is my wife. And so are numerous friends. We spend time and energy seeking birds, learning their habits and songs, drawing deep satisfaction from knowing about them and finding them. Interestingly, once someone knows one is a birder, the questions begin to flow. "There's this bird that comes to my feeder that . . . . What is it?" People like birds and generally are interested in naming what they are seeing. It is a genuine and frequent connection to the natural world available to all.

There are two species of eagles that live in the Lower Forty-eight United States. One is the Golden Eagle, found more readily in the West, mostly in the Rockies and other mountain areas (we even get a few here in North Carolina in the winter). The other is the better known American Bald Eagle (our national bird; often in the ancient world as well as in scientific nomenclature white on the head is called "bald."). When I was in college in the early 1960's, the Bald Eagle was scarce and in trouble. DDT, used as a pesticide, rendered Bald Eagles and many other bird species sterile or their eggs so unformed that they got crushed in the nest. It was so bad that in 1962, the total number of Adult Bald Eagles in the Lower forty-eight numbered fewer that 5,000 and half of them were sterile. If DDT hadn't been outlawed, the fate of our national bird would have been extinction. However, with the establishment of the Environmental Protection Act, DDT was taken out of use and species like the Bald Eagle began to recover. Today, there are over 150,000 Adult Bald Eagles in the Lower Forty-eight. Hooray! This bird has been used in our culture as a symbol of strength, courage, and power.

Eagles are used symbolically in the Bible as well. There are four species of eagles that can be found in the Biblical lands. But the one most often referred to in the Bible is the Golden Eagle (the same species as the Golden Eagle we have here). Several Biblical writers use this eagle as a symbol for the ways of God. When the collector of the Book of Proverbs named the four things most impossible to understand (30:18-19), "the way of the eagle in the air" came first. When the voice of God hurled at Job his challenge of power, one question was: Does the eagle mount up at your command? Isaiah 40:31 promises the strength of eagles to those who serve the Lord. Renewed youth like the eagle's is the pledge of Psalm 103, for people of olden times saw magic in the way an eagle's beak stays scimitar sharp and strong, even in old age – never guessing that it was daily stropping and cleaning that kept youthful strength renewed.

Eagle swiftness is praised in nearly a dozen passages, and both Golden and Bald Eagles have actually been clocked in power-dives at around 120 miles per hour. Their usual cruising speed is much slower, however. These kingly birds have tenderness to match their power, usually mating for life and guarding their young with patient care. Deuteronomy 32:11-12 gives one eagle watcher's report of their home life, describing how the female arranges and rearranges the nesting material and how the mother spreads fluttering wings over the downy young, shielding them from rain or hot sun or biting wind. And, the Biblical writer notes how she coaxes the full-feathered young to follow her in gliding flight, letting them find their wing power in triumph – or buoying them with updraft current from her own wings.

Many ornithologists have thought that the Bible picture of an eagle carrying her young was merely figurative, but in recent years certain observers have actually seen a parent bird let its young rest for a moment or two on the feathered back – especially when there was no other roosting place in sight. When an eagle nests on the ledge of a sheer-walled canyon, many feet above the earth, with no jutting tree root or protruding rock to break the fall, the quick movement of a mother bird to offer her own back to a frightened fledgling may be the only way to let it live to try its wings again. Just so did the power of God reach out to Jacob (the people of Israel) as we see in Deuteronomy 12:

> He sustained him in a desert land, in a howling wilderness waste;
> He shielded him, cared for him, guarded him as the apple of his eye.
> As an eagle stirs up its nest, and hovers over its young;
> As it spreads its wings, takes them up, and bears them aloft on it pinions,
> The Lord alone guided him; no foreign god was with him.
> He set him atop the heights of the land, and fed him with produce of the field;
> He nursed him with the honey from the crags, with oil from flinty rock. . . .

Watch an eagle in flight yourself, the lines seem to suggest, and know how great the strength of the Lord must be.

One of the assurances given to Christians as we look both above and within is the sense that no matter the struggle, God is there holding us, buoying us like the parent eagle. That is the gift God has offered his people from the beginning. It is an act of faith to trust this. And when we do, we see life's circumstances differently, think of them differently. When we remember and read or say the special words of Scripture, we can find ourselves buoyed as well. When we place ourselves into his presence and word, we are often instructed or led. Truly, life with our Lord bears us up "with wings like eagles."

Gethsemane

A Meditation for Easter Preparation

Go to Gethsemane; it's necessary, you see. For in the figure of Jesus kneeling there under the hungering shadow of death, struggling with all his might to find the will of God, we see a picture of us in our Christian lives.

"In the days of his flesh," we read, *"Jesus offered up prayers and supplications with loud cries and tears, to him who was able to save him from death, and he was heard for his godly fear."* (Hebrews 5:7) He was heard yet the struggle at Gethsemane did not change God's mind about what it means for Jesus to be obedient: he was to die. God did not change his mind, but the struggles in Gethsemane put Jesus' ideas in the right place - for out of the struggle he knew obedience to death was the only way the will of God could be carried out in him.

Go to Gethsemane; it's necessary for us, you see. For three things happen in the Gethsemanes of real life:

1. There we struggle for the will of God.

2. There our wills are enlarged to include God's will and way.

3. There we leave the childhood of faith behind and enter Christian maturity.

Of course, what this scene of Jesus in the garden praying his heart out points us to is the startling reality that if our Christian faith is to be truly an on-going journey with our God, it depends upon our prayers – our gathering our inner selves in the presence of God as the basis for who we are and what we are to do.

"Go to Gethsemane and learn to pray." So we're told. And so it happens. Gethsemane - no land of Oz with wishful thinking, but the place within us and around us which speaks of stark realities and real struggles - of matters of life and death, of the things of joy and love.

Yet such prayer doesn't come easy to us, at first at least. And we tend to be like the disciple of Jesus who one day said, *"Lord, teach us to pray."* One often wants some kind of a manual of instruction, a formula, a short cut around the honest struggle with God and God's will which deep prayer really is.

As we move toward the Gethsemanes of our lives, we find that there are three types of experiences that always seem to summon prayer from within us. One is the experience when we are convicted of sin. It is not enough to ask forgiveness of the one whom we have wronged, not even enough to forgive ourselves, often a harder task When we are truly beset with an awareness of guilt, there is an anxiousness to get it purged and cleansed. There, we turn to God.

The second type of experience in which we instinctively turn to prayer is that of some shocking catastrophe when we are thrown off-balance by some event in life. We feel a sense of ultimate helplessness, and yet in the midst of that helplessness, there can come a hope that help might be there. Whenever something harmful or terrible happens among us here in our community, don't we instinctively join in prayer and ask others for prayer?

And the third experience when we turn instinctively to prayer is that which comes when we are lifted outside of ourselves into some joyous appreciation of life. Somehow we become aware that there is more to life and more to the world than we can encompass with our feelings and our own understanding.

Who among us has not found himself or herself reaching out to say thanks to someone - to ask help from someone - to say "Forgive me, someone?"

You see, the question, "Should we pray?" is academic. We DO pray - instinctively, intuitively, at some points in our lives. Queen Victoria's Prime Minister, Lord Melbourne, in conversation once with the Archbishop of Canterbury, said, *"I have only two questions: To whom should one pray, and about what should one pray?"*

Jesus answered them both in his New Testament teachings. He said to his disciples, when you pray, say, *"Father,"* for *"what father among you if his son asks for a fish, will instead of a fish give him a serpent?"* And what does it mean to reach out into the universe and cry, "Father," except to affirm a "Who" instead of a "What" who is in control of human destiny? The very use of the word "Father" colors our whole concept of prayer. More than anything else, what we get in deep prayer is the sense of God with us, bearing us up, moving us into the future with courage. And for many, that sense of being borne up leads one into a hopeful place.

And what should we pray for? All things, of course. But not in the sense of going to the supermarket and asking for one of everything we want or need. Not in the sense of rubbing Aladdin's lamp and wishing for everything. No, in the sense of Jesus at Gethsemane, wrestling with stark realities in conversation with God.

And, of course, that is the issue at the heart of both prayer and faith - obedience. Go to Gethsemane; wrestle with God about your values, about your decisions, about your politics, about your loves and your hates, about your hopes and fears. Be sure to include your commitment to God as the basis for prayer. Struggle aloud with the issues. Sort them out in the holy presence of God himself. And seek for obedience rather than self-indulgence, moving God's will genuinely rather than immediate happiness.

This is at the heart of Christian living. It is in putting our own desires alongside God's purpose that we find our way with God. It is in seeking consciously and deliberately day-by-day for life with him in all that we do, that the ups and downs of life take on their positive meaning, that we are released from those captivities of hopelessness and fear. It is in constant awareness of his significance and our dependence upon him that we gain proper perspective as to how life should be sorted out. It is in time spent on our knees that we are enabled to walk as adults in such a wind-tossed life. And it is in seeking God's will that we are prepared not only to live, but to die - in the very hands of God.

Go to Gethsemane, then. Go to Gethsemane during this Lenten time, this preparation for Easter time. Go to Gethsemane every day. For there in prayer and the inward struggle in our hearts and minds stands God who is for us. For there awaits our source for both living and dying as people of God.

Easter (1)

It's Easter time, the time of new beginnings and new hopes as we are reminded in graphic terms that the second of God's cosmic acts which have benefited humankind has taken place and is ours to dwell within just as is the first. His creation of the universe has provided us place and time. That's the first cosmic action. The resurrection of Jesus has given us authentic life and eternity. That's the second cosmic act. Both continue to shape our lives and that of this planet. For twenty-one centuries we have benefited by what God has provided in Jesus Christ. Perhaps, then, it's time for a story.

Peter and the Resurrection

Profound sadness coupled with terror wrapped Peter's stomach and clenched it into a tight, painful knot.

Yes, Jesus had told his disciples that he would be killed, even that he would be crucified. But Peter hadn't believed it. When you see daily miracles and hear incisive teaching from a confident public figure, you refuse to acknowledge that anything could ever change.

But overnight, Peter's world collapsed.

They had eaten Passover together on Thursday night. But only few hours later, Jesus was under arrest. A hasty trial lit by flickering lamps in the high priest's palace condemned Jesus. Then early-morning shuttles to Pilate, then Herod, then back again to Pilate sealed his fate. By 9 am soldiers were pounding nails into his wrists and feet, jerking him upright on a cross to let him hang in the sun -- until the sun itself hid its face and left the onlookers to watch the Master die in the eerie chill of this very black day.

Peter had fled. In fact, none of the Twelve remained to see him buried. Only Mary Magdalene and a couple of wealthy followers were left to take his body down, carry it outside the city, and entomb it.

If you've ever felt despair at the pit of your stomach, then you know what Peter felt. When he did go out, he would walk in a kind of daze, utterly disoriented, shattered, the center of his world now a black hole, an empty void.

How could the Messiah, the heir of David's throne, be executed? It went against all logic. It was impossible — yet it had happened, and oh so swiftly!

Peter slept fitfully Saturday night and when his eyes opened Sunday morning, the doom of death was heavy upon him. He pulled his cloak over his eyes, hoping he could fall back to sleep, but knowing he wouldn't.

All of a sudden someone was banging on the door. Soldiers! Peter got up with a start. How can I escape? Then he heard Mary Magdalene's voice, and his terror fell back into depression. Mary was breathless, troubled, her face stained with tears.

Peter grumbled, "Why did you have to wake me so early?"

Mary blurted out: "They have taken the Lord out of the tomb!"

Peter pulled his fellow-disciple John to his feet, slammed the door behind them, and began to run through the narrow streets, out the city gate, and then on to the tomb.

The great stone that had sealed the tomb stood open. As they entered, the sepulcher was empty, except for some folded graveclothes. The body was gone.

Folded? That was strange. Folded graveclothes but no body. Hardly what you'd expect from grave robbers.

John seemed convinced by the graveclothes that somehow Jesus had been resurrected or something, but Peter wasn't so sure. How could he believe that after so much had happened? He walked slowly back towards the city pondering, thinking, wanting to believe, but afraid to hope.

Suddenly, Jesus appeared. Peter, the so-called "rock," had publicly betrayed him. He had shouted, "I don't know the man!" He was so unworthy. And yet here was Jesus before him. Peter fell to his knees and wept for joy.

Peter never said much to the others about this meeting — what had been said, what had transpired. But after that you'd sometimes see Peter deep in thought, pensive. Then he would nod his head and traces of a smile would begin to transform his face into one written with thankfulness and joy and peace.

Peter had been whipsawed from his pit of despair and pulled by the Master into peace. Life had changed for the good. Peter began a new journey as emissary of the Lord. And since then many have found this same peace, this same smile of wonder at God's amazing grace through his Son. Human frailty is just the place where God in Christ seeks us out. Jesus had risen — and Peter never doubted him again.

That was twenty-one hundred years ago . . . and here we are.

Thought for the Day:

You probably do not remember the name Nikolai Ivanovich Bukharin, nor should you.

But during his day he was as powerful a man as there was on earth. As Russian Communist leader he took part in the Bolshevik Revolution 1917, was editor of the Soviet newspaper Pravda (which by the way means Truth), and was a full member of the Politburo. His works on economics and political science are still read today.

There is a story told about a journey he took from Moscow to Kiev, in 1930, to address a huge assembly on the subject of atheism. Addressing the crowd he aimed his heavy artillery at Christianity hurling insults, argument, and proof against it. An hour later he was finished. He looked out at what seemed to be the smoldering ashes of men's faith.

"Are there any questions?" Bukharin demanded.

Deafening silence filled the auditorium, but then one man approached the platform and mounted the lectern standing near the communist leader. He surveyed the crowd, first to the left then to the right. Finally he shouted the ancient greeting known well in the Russian Orthodox Church: "CHRIST IS RISEN!"

En masse the crowd arose as one man and the response came crashing like the sound of thunder… "HE IS RISEN INDEED!"

Have a Blessed Easter and Rejoice… for Christ is risen! Hallelujah!

Redemption

The two women were talking, as old friends do, about their thoughts on Easter which had just been observed. It was an earnest conversation, indicating both insight and wisdom. While they discussed some of their Easter memories, their conversation centered on the question: **What has the death and resurrection of Jesus achieved?** In other words, how is salvation connected with this strange and memorable event of so long ago? What was the connection of the "then" and the "now?"

Of course, that is the question that should be asked in every generation if the Christian faith is to be more than a treasured relic of a bygone time.

So, they went to talk with an old teacher of Bible and theology about it. And they both reviewed and learned a great deal. Here's some of what they learned:

> • That all ways of talking about what Christ's death offers us are pictures, stories, figures, metaphors, parables for the mystery of God's love and action on behalf of all humanity.
> • That to make these pictures too literal can lead to distortions in understanding what God was doing in Christ.
> • That the issue God has resolved in Christ's death and resurrection is the destructive nature of sin in our lives (individually and collectively) and the endless nature of death.

As they discussed this issue and how they saw the human problem illustrated in the many destructive

and harmful actions in ordinary life by people in general and in one's own life, as well as in the awful toll the reality of the death of loved ones and others has taken on so many people (especially during this pandemic), they began to relate more to the various pictures of what Christ's death and resurrection were about.

When they discussed the picture of Christ's death paying the penalty for our sin, they discovered that this wasn't a way of saying God is out to judge people and convict them for their sin, but, rather, a way of saying that Christ's death and resurrection is God's way of showing that he claims us nonetheless. Thus, they considered being **justified** ("made right") as the work of Christ in one's life as the meaning of the picture of Christ paying our penalty. They delighted in seeing that it is God who is paying the penalty.

Likewise, when they discussed the picture of Christ's death being a ransom to pay the debt incurred by our sin, thus **redeeming** us, they once again saw the picture as pointing to God's actions in Christ, signaling to humanity in the cross and resurrection that he claims us nonetheless. Redemption is a way of describing living with the action of God in Christ at the heart of faithful living.

And, again, when they discussed the picture of Christ's death being a sacrifice offered on our behalf by God himself, they saw this picture as pointing to God's actions in Christ, signaling to humanity that he claims us and that if sacrifice is needed to help us, then he is offering the sacrifice, thus **reconciling** us.

When they discussed these three pictures for a long while, they asked the teacher whether these pictures made God out to be somewhat cruel if it were true that those who aren't believers are not justified, redeemed, or reconciled. They were reminded that these are pictures, not automatic systems, that the heart of each is a picture of God in Christ seeking his people and providing for them even in darkness, sin and death.

They are not pictures to divide the sheep from the goats or in any other way. These depict what God is doing for humanity.

The discussion went on for hours. They looked at the **moral influence** of Jesus, especially in offering himself in love, as pivotal in what God was doing in Christ's death and resurrection. They considered a more philosophic picture which showed that behind the scenes of history and life there is a horrific struggle going on between evil and darkness on the one hand and righteousness and light on the other. That struggle has been depicted as warfare between Satan and Christ. In this picture it appears that Satan wins (indeed, many have concluded that Satan is winning). But the resurrection is God's seal that the ultimate darkness (death) cannot hold us, that God's light shines even there.

Interestingly, they considered how often believers have divided the world or their lives up into those who are "in "and those who are "out." Some, it appears, have drawn this from some the pictures they had discussed. Thus, some have picked "outcasts" of one sort or another (Jews, Commies, Gays, Liberals, Hispanics, Muslims, Women, Non-believers to name a few) and scorned them, thus adding grievously to the problems of our world. The old teacher pointed out that throughout the Bible, it is precisely the "outcasts" that God seeks to protect and include (one might think of Abel, slain by his brother, Cain; or Joseph, scorned and sold into slavery by his brothers; or Israel, scorned by just about everyone and trampled upon by whatever powerful nation that happened to be around; or Jesus, scorned unto death by the "greatest power" on earth – Rome). The pictures don't point to exclusion, but to inclusion.

All well and good. They had sought out more understanding of Christ's death and resurrection and wanted to ponder on it for a while. So, they concluded their discussion with a reminder from the writings of St. Irenaeus in the second century AD when he said, "Christ became what we are in order to enable us to become what he is." Christ lived, he loved, he shared, he suffered, he died, he was raised ("he became what we are") in order that "we might become what he is" (living a life in Christ). After discussing this for a while, the discussion ended with the reminder that St. Paul gave to the Corinthians: *"So if anyone is in Christ, there is a new creation; everything old has passed away; see, everything has become new"* (2 Corinthians 5:17)."

Weeds

I've been thinking about weeds of late. In getting our gardens in shape for the year as the plants, trees and shrubs are leaping forth in new growth, we're once again experiencing the annual emergence of a healthy crop of weeds as well. Weeds – of various types and shapes. Weeds – some of them not so bad in appearance, but so prolific they take over a whole region of the garden. Weeds – with the ability to override the more desired plants and even choke them out if not tended to. Weeds – seeming to spring up almost overnight sometimes. Weeds – rapidly growing again if simply mowed down. I've been thinking about weeds a lot of late.

Jesus used weeds in one of his more famous parables (The parable of the Weeds among the Wheat – Matthew 13:24 – 40). Weeds were so common in his day and so problematic that to use them as a picture of those who are indifferent or hostile to God would be readily understood. The proliferation of numerous species of weeds in cultivated fields was a continual problem for farmers in ancient Israel. Part of the problem was the inability of these farmers to plow furrows deep enough to turn up the bulbs to allow the sun to dry them out and thus destroy the next generation of useless weeds. As a result, these noxious plants intermingled with the grain, stealing its moisture and sometimes overwhelming the edible plants. At harvest time, it was often difficult to separate the stalks of wheat or barley from the weeds. As a result, their seeds, which often look quite similar to the wheat, were mixed together, and when the sowing occurred in the next growing season both good seeds and bad seeds were cast into the newly turned furrows. The prophet Hosea used this fact to compare lawsuits and "poisonous weeds in the furrows of the field" (Hosea 10:4)

What has caught my eye in thinking about weeds as well as this parable is that Jesus implies that there will always be weeds in life, that it is part of reality. And while it is incumbent upon us to deal with them in such a manner to allow our good plants to thrive, any thought of total domination or elimination of them is perhaps wishful thinking. Maybe that's why Jesus' attitude toward enemies and those lost in sin was not as condemnatory as the Pharisees wished. Maybe Jesus' attitude of condemning the sin but not the sinner was so startling to those who were so much more authoritarian. Maybe that's why some today, focusing on the weeds, are so ready to destroy the whole crop including the good plants in order to eliminate the weeds. Indeed, there are times when some tend to spend their time thinking about, worrying about, even fretting angrily about, the weeds found in life, so much so that nourishing the good plants gets left behind. It appears that Jesus is pointing us toward a focus on the good plants, taking care not to let the weeds overwhelm to be sure, but providing nurture for that which provides the good in life and serves our Lord as the primary emphasis.

There's no doubt that this pandemic has been one giant weed system in our lives. It needs to be dealt with and dealt with decisively. But there is so much more out there as well. Hopefully the Easter celebration just past is a reminder that while the weeds thrive for a while, God's ways are eternal. It is incumbent on us all to do our part in dealing with the threat of Covid-19, but spring is here, our church is slowly opening up, children are going to school, most of us have gotten or will get our shots, and the good possibilities of life and life together abound.

When I look out over the gardens here at home, I want to see the beauty and value of the garden more than the weeds so I can watch a visual picture of God's provision for us in a world where there are both "wheat and weeds."

Tending

Several of the men of our congregation gathered recently to cut down the bushes that surround the church as well as two Dogwood trees that had died. The bushes had been trimmed several times over the years, but never to the point where cutting them was easy. Indeed, it took a chainsaw this time to cut them down to about two feet high. It was easy for us to think while we were cutting away that this would have been easier if the bushes had been tended to regularly through the years. With little attention over the years, they became more difficult to cut and manage.

What a wonderful thought – "tended to." The root meaning in English is "to show a liking or proneness for something." As a verb it means "to take charge of especially on behalf of another." My family "tends" to be talkers. The woman feels "tender" to her baby. I have a "tendency," to notice birds wherever I am. The fire will go out if no one "tends" to it. We "attend" meetings and at them someone might take "attendance."

I remember a passage in Leviticus (6:8-13) where the instructions were given to Aaron and his sons (who were priests) to "tend" to the fire on the altar in the tabernacle of the Lord. The Hebrews believed that God was traveling with them during those days of the exodus from Egypt, and God's presence was marked by the flame on the altar in the tabernacle (traveling tent where the "Holy of Holies" was). The priests and their assistants were admonished to always tend to this fire so that it never went out. It was a desecration to God's presence with them to allow the flame to be extinguished. Thus, "tending the fire" was a major job of the priests and their company.

This, of course, can become a wonderful metaphor for our spiritual lives, "tending" the flame of our faith and discipleship. On the hearts and minds of Christians there can be an inner flame of God's presence and truth. We even use the language of fire to talk about a living faith: *"Did not our hearts burn within us as he spoke,"* some of his disciples said on that road to Emmaus after Jesus' resurrection. John Wesley described his conviction of God's call to him as *"I was strangely warmed."* And some folks in the church talk of *"a red-not faith"* and *"a burning desire"* to serve God. And, of course, similar to the times of old, the fire of faith and conviction that glows in the interior life of believers must not be allowed to go out. It can do that, you know.

There are many potential threats to the interior life of each believer, threats which, if they are left unchecked, can extinguish the fire of our devotion to God and the benefits we derive from a conscious life with our Heavenly Father. I can think of three right off:

1. Exhaustion. Truly. No fire can burn without adequate fuel. Yet many folks struggle through their lives in the throes of spiritual and emotional exhaustion. Whatever resources one had for spiritual growth get used up and the flame of faith is depleted. When the flame of faith is not tended to because of exhausting oneself on the tasks of living, that flame can burn low and even go out. One would think that this is a fine argument for taking time for spiritual reflection and prayer. Jesus told those who were sorely pressed by the needs of others to "come away by yourselves to a lonely place to rest awhile." Tending the fire.

2. Neglect. For a people who cannot exhaust all the opportunities a day provides what with job, family, social media, maintenance of hearth and home, and other interests and responsibilities, it is easy to neglect one's faith, treating it more as something on which to focus on rare occasions or for rare circumstances. Like those bushes that have often been neglected through the years and get out of control, a neglected spiritual life and faith slowly slips away until, for some, it becomes a dim memory. If one does not tend to his or her garden, it gets smothered with weeds or overgrown or dries up. How like the journey we are invited on with our God if not tended to.

3. Compromise – those times when deeply-held convictions get bartered away for other quests. When this happens, say in moral, legal, or social settings, they can dampen the flame of devotion and a heart purified by cleansing and active faith is smudged. When values are sullied in trade-offs for acclaim, power, security, or pleasure, more always is lost than is gained. Jesus asked once, *"What has a person profited if one shall gain the whole world and lose one's own soul?"* Tending the flame of faith is a call to fight with all our conscious powers to retain integrity and inner character regardless of cost. St. Augustine once said with piercing insight, *O greedy man, what will satisfy you if God will not?"* Compromise can quench the flame, yes it can. But character and courage, drawn from the shared strengths of friends in Christ, the Spirit of Christ, and the Word of God can kindle and enflame anew our relationship with him.

The altar of each person's heart is a place deep within that is a place for a fire, a fire of faith, kindled for the most part by the grace of our God. On this altar rests the deepest allegiance of life given to God, the flaming presence in our lives of the Risen Christ. Our opportunity as well as our task as God's people is to tend to those fires – to keep the flame burning. Whatever else may slide or be deferred, keep the fire burning. God, whose mercy through the cross first brought that flame to life, will not leave us alone in this. As was told to Aaron and his priest so long ago, *"The fire must not go out."*

Smile

He entered Jericho and was passing through it. A man was there named Zacchaeus; he was a chief tax collector and was rich. He was trying to see who Jesus was, but on account of the crowd he could not, because he was short in stature. So he ran ahead and climbed a sycamore tree to see him, because he was going to pass that way. When Jesus came to the place, he looked up and said to him. "Zacchaeus, hurry and come down; for I must stay at your house today." So he hurried down and was happy to welcome him. All who saw it began to grumble and said, "He has gone to be the guest of one who is a sinner." Zacchaeus stood there and said to the Lord, "Look, half of my possessions, Lord, I will give to the poor; and if I have defrauded anyone of anything I will pay back four times as much." Then Jesus said to him, "Today salvation has come to this house because he too is a son of Abraham. For the Son of Man came to seek out and to save the lost."

The question is always worth pondering: does the Gospel of Jesus Christ, God's way of reaching out to the world, the very picture of God's graceful nature, ever make one glad? Smiling glad? Heart-filled glad? Warmth from within, lip-smiling glad?

It should, you know. The writer of Ecclesiastes tells us that *"there's a time to weep and a time to laugh, a time to mourn and a time to dance."* While life sometimes gives us weeping times and mourning times, there are gladness times as well and the gospel of God's grace especially gives us times to be glad.

This familiar story of Zacchaeus is a story to smile at, particularly when one finds the self in it. It's the kind of story I love to read in the Bible, for it spells out in story form the miracle that God has wrought among us. It's the kind of smile-when-you-read-it story one finds when one reads of Noah or of Jonah.

It's the kind of story heard when one is told of ancient Sarah, Abraham's wife, giving birth to a son in her old age, and naming him Isaac (which, by the way, means *laughter*), because of how it all struck her.

It's David's kind of story; at least it expresses the kind of joy one feels when one sees that king of kings dancing before the altar of the Lord in sheer delight. And it's akin to that marvelous story of Elijah, hollering taunts and teases at those prophets of Baal who can't seem to get their fire started up there on Mount Carmel.

And it's Jesus' kind of story as it carries the same irony and delight in it one finds in his parable of the vineyard owner who hired men early in the morning to work in his vineyard. Then he hired others at mid-morning, others at noon, others in mid-afternoon, and still others at 5:00 PM. And then, gladness upon gladness, at the end of the day, he paid them all a full day's wage! It's a parable of God's generosity and pleasure at serving his people with his love and one will smile because the ending is so unlike us and yet so like God.

This story of Zacchaeus is written to make us smile as we take in its truth. It's a story filled with incongruity and surprise in a close encounter Jesus had with this unlikeliest of characters. Children remember the story well. It's about a small man who can't see over the crowds. But he was a rich small man, and that makes it all the more interesting for us because you know how Jesus felt that riches often interfered with a person's life with God. Indeed, the story of the rich young ruler whom Jesus told to sell everything and give to the poor is in the chapter just before this one.

And yet (that's one of the key statements in Christian belief -"and yet") salvation comes to this despised, crooked, rich, little man's house. Salvation comes and Zacchaeus gives one half of his goods to the poor and promises to pay back fourfold to anyone he had cheated. Gladness observed here! Gladness in action! This little man had done a remarkable reversal of his life when he encountered Jesus.

Let yourselves smile at him: a powerful man, undignified up there in that sycamore tree looking over the crowd at this man from Nazareth. Let yourself smile when you hear Jesus call him by name before all the people who clamored for his attention and see him go walking off arm in arm into his house.

And let yourself smile when the crowd acts so predictably selfish and jealous, standing around murmuring to themselves about how Jesus is spending time with such a notorious sinner.

Let yourself smile because this story is also a story about repentance, about new life, about getting one's mind right, and about Jesus involving himself with a person so that his whole life was directed. When Jesus encounters any of us at a point of real need and captures us with his acceptance and love of us, he stamps upon us the feeling, the knowledge, the renewal of what it means to be a person, to be fully human - and that's something worth smiling about. When we catch a glimpse of the Jesus way, it brings out the best in us and we smile.

There was Zacchaeus, an easy target for hatred because of his cheating heart. There was Zacchaeus, responding to the first adult acceptance and love ever given to him, the first touch he had with the large, God-dimension in life. There he was, turning around in his life (that's what repentance is: turning around). There he was changing his mind, seeing things more for real, and then giving one half of all he has to the poor and repaying all he had wronged four times over.

There can be no cheap grace, you see. It has not been experienced as true grace unless there is some outpouring of life on the part of the receiver of grace, some outpouring in moral action taken in real life.

And that's the message for Christians to hear time and again. How does one respond to the acceptance and love God has offered in Jesus Christ? How does one respond to the comfort he gives, the sense of his presence he provides, the hope one can find for life here and beyond only in him?

For the gospel is to lead us to joy in our lives. Joy because God comes to us, because God loves even the least of us, the Zacchaeus' of this world, even the Zacchaeus within each of us.

For behind Zacchaeus' story, and behind our own stories, in faith we can hear joyful laughter, divine laughter, warm, accepting laughter. Salvation has come to this house. Even to Zacchaeus, of all people. Salvation has come to this house. Even to you and me, of all people. And that's something worth smiling about.

Seasons

Seasons. They come and they go. Seasons of the year. Seasons of one's life. Seasons in relationships. Seasoning for taste. Baseball Season, Football Season, Soccer Season, Hunting Season. The atmosphere around the Croatan community changes when Deer Season begins. That's because seasons affect us.

I was in the North Carolina mountains last week visiting kin and doing some birding. My siblings and I are in the latter season of our lives and it is important to stay in touch in these days. And the season of the year affected the birds I was able to see as well. Indeed, a microcosm of the effect of seasons was well-illustrated to me as I birded the lofty peaks and valleys around the Blue Ridge Parkway in the Asheville, NC, area. Here it was the end of April and the beginning of May, certainly well into spring down here on the coast. And at the lower levels (up to 2,000 feet in altitude) of the mountains, it was certainly spring as well. Indeed, the dogwoods had all leafed out and every plant was well into its leaf. The birds of that elevation had already mated and were on nest. But hike into an elevation above 2,000 feet and up to, say, 4,000 feet and it was early spring – with new buds on the trees, flowers on the dogwoods and birds beginning to call for mates. It was another story altogether when I got to above 4,000 feet in elevation. It was still winter – at least in terms of plant growth and bird activity. Just the beginning hint of buds on the trees. Few birds could be heard singing. The stark stillness of a winter landscape spread over the mountaintops. Lower temperature and fewer birds. Seasons affect us and the whole wide world.

The Bible speaks of seasons in many places. In ancient Israel, the calendar revolved around four periods of about three months each with an emphasis on the agricultural cycle and defined by the position of the stars. More generally, *season* referred to the appropriate time or period for something to happen (In Ecclesiastes 3:1 ff., we read *"For everything there is a season, and a time for every matter under the earth . . ."*). This gets close to our lives as we often define our lives in terms of the season *we* are in.

Noting the seasons of one's life or the seasons of some period of our lives is to note that life is not static, fixed, or a repetitive cycle. There is a certain dynamic involved in moving through the seasons of our lives. The coming and going of the seasons give us more than the springtimes, summers, autumns, and winters of our lives. Martin Luther remarked that "Our Lord has written the promise of the resurrection, not in books alone, but in every leaf in springtime." In other words, the seasons of life reflect the deeper realities of living. Winter is the quiet time for slumber, dormancy, reflection, and renewal. A time leading to the agitation period of spring is the time of rebirth, rejuvenation, and growth. Summer is the season of joy and fun – a period that is full of life, yet we tire to slow down into autumn's annual wane. Then back to winter to reflect on what was and to prepare for what is to come. Just as this may well be an annual cycle for us, it may also reflect a day in one's life or one's whole life altogether. For everything there is a season.

For the entire world this past year and these next months have been a season of fear due to the pandemic and the continual dramas of political agitation, conspiracy, and unrest. Out of that fear has been born for some, seasons of discontent. For others, it has birthed hostility and dread. For still others, it has led to serious division, even rejection of things like science and truth. Yet despite these areas of discontent, many have persisted with courage, never forsaking basic decency, always seeking to help their neighbors, and living in each season with confidence in God. One could call it a season of discontent, but like all seasons, it is not permanent. Seasons of discontent are the best times for sowing seeds of renewal and growth. Seasons of fear can push one toward seasons of love. Indeed, as Mother Teresa said once, "Love is a fruit in season at all times, and within reach of every hand."

The same is true for believers when we join hands with our Lord in whatever season we may find ourselves. In a time of great discontent, St. Paul addressed the churches through his second letter to Timothy (4:1-5): *In the presence of God and of Christ Jesus, who is to judge the living and the dead, and in view of his appearing and his kingdom: I solemnly urge you: Proclaim the message; be persistent whether the time is favorable or unfavorable; convince, rebuke, and encourage with the utmost patience in teaching.*

In other words, every season is a time to trust and follow our Lord.

Propensity

Ever know someone whose propensities were observable and usually consistent? Such as:

- A propensity to over-indulge in something
- A propensity to procrastinate
- A propensity to exaggerate
- A propensity for hostility
- A propensity for kindness
- A propensity for enthusiasm
- A propensity for delusion
- A propensity for fear or anxiety
- A propensity for judgmentalism
- A propensity to believe fantasy
- A propensity for empathy

Perhaps we can observe or are aware of certain propensities that are a part of our makeup as well, because we all have them. Call them inclinations or tendencies or leanings, an observable part of the make-up of each of us includes our various inclinations. Some are actually quite helpful in daily living. Of course, some are harmful to one's self and/or to others. We might suggest that a good way to describe someone would be to note the various propensities that define the person.

One of the great joys of living is to live with those who have a propensity to care and share – certainly a propensity that has to be nurtured in order to continue to be one's inclination. On the other hand, one of the flaws in life together which can make life so painful is that it is peopled with folks with tendencies toward selfishness or hostility to others. A deeper reality is that in varying measures, most of us carry both of these propensities.

In the great drama presented to us in the Bible, there is a clear delineation of human tendencies. Left to ourselves, the propensity toward selfishness most often becomes dominant. That, of course, is a gentle way of describing sin – living on one's own without regard to our place as God's people including living in contradiction to the ways of God. That contradiction would include all manner of evil and anguish from the sublime to the blatant. It is the propensity to sin that the Bible is addressing throughout. Asking how one can live in the world with this as a basic propensity, the Bible offers two ways one can tame this propensity, one inferior to the other. The inferior way is through law. One does not have to go far in the Bible to find much about laws for living (many of them still quite timely and germane) – all the way from the Ten

Commandments to discussions about what is wise and helpful for life together (like in the Proverbs or in Paul's letters to the churches). The superior way is to call one into encounter and relationship with what God seeks to do in our hearts and minds through Jesus Christ. This is the way of salvation. The Bible portrays God has making covenants with his people to draw them to himself in order that they might "live." And the covenant of grace made in Jesus's death and resurrection is offered to claim our hearts and to retool our inclinations. To be "saved" is to be saved from our own tendencies that defy our God and God's rule in our lives. To be "saved" is to live in a loving relationship with Jesus. To be "saved" is to allow the propensity for love, sharing, kindness, justice, hope to become the heart of our living. Perhaps the next time someone asks if one has been saved, one might bring to mind the degree that one's life in Christ has influenced and claimed one's propensities.

Life in Christ is sometimes described as being easy. But it is easy in the same way that love is easy – it must be nourished continually in order to be active and alive. That it is not always as easy as one might think, we remind readers of Paul's struggle to keep his propensities in line with God's ways and love. Romans 7:14-25 is a good place to hear him as he works "out his salvation."

But in an outpouring of enthusiasm, listen also for Paul's description of the propensities of one who lives with Jesus (Romans 12:9-21): *Let love be genuine, hate what is evil, hold fast to what is good; love one another with mutual affection; outdo one another in showing honor. Do not lag in zeal, be ardent in spirit, serve the Lord. Rejoice in hope, be patient in suffering, persevere in prayer. Contribute to the needs of the saints; extend hospitality to strangers. . . .*

I'm inclined to take Paul seriously. I hope each of us is as well.

Precious

The word *precious* is a wonderful term. We use it very sparingly because it is so . . . well, precious. A little girl, all dressed up in a new dress and ribbon in her hair evokes the sentiment that *"She's just precious."* We treasure special moments spent with treasured loved one and call those moments "precious." The same is true with memories of great value and meaning – they are "precious memories." The dictionary tries to capture the specialness of this word with descriptions such as: *Of great value or high price; highly esteemed or cherished; excessively refined.* As such, we use the term to describe the worth of jewels, the rocks out of which precious stones are hewn, special moments and memories, and anything which can be seen as greatly refined. *Precious* can be something that is in the eye of the beholder (*"That was a precious moment for us."*), or it can be assigned as a component of an object *("precious jewels")*. It can even be used in a darkened manner to denote excessive value placed on something perverse (*The Lord of the Rings* fans will remember how Gollum, the distorted creature, focused all his attention and feeling on possessing *"The One Ring to Rule them All,"* calling it repeatedly *"My precious."*).

The Bible uses the term *precious* well over a hundred times as well as using its synonyms frequently (*valuable, treasured, esteemed, highly regarded*). For the purpose of this devotional, I invite the readers to consider just how precious we feel God's work in seeking out our devotion and trust is for our lives, for throughout the Scriptures *precious* is the term used to describe it.

Psalm 36:7 – "How precious is your steadfast love, O God."

Psalm 116:15 – "Precious in the sight of the Lord is the death of his faithful ones."

Proverbs 31:10 - "A capable wife who can find? She is far more precious than jewels."

Ecclesiastes 7:1 – A good name is better than precious ointment. . . "

Isaiah 28:16 (prophecy of the coming Lord) – "Therefore says the Lord God, 'See, I am laying in Zion a foundation stone, a tested stone, a precious cornerstone, a sure foundation. . . .'"

Luke 12:24 – "Consider the ravens: they neither sow nor reap, they have neither storehouse nor barn, and yet God feeds them. Of how much more value (precious) are you than the birds!"

1 Peter 1:7 – To you then who believe, he is precious. . . ."

1 Peter 1:18-19 – "You know that you were ransomed from the futile ways inherited from your ancestors, not with perishable things like silver or gold, but with the precious blood of Christ, like that of a lamb without defect or blemish."

2 Peter 1:4 – "Thus he has given us, through these things, his precious and very great promises, so that through them you may escape from the corruption that is in the world . . . . "

When God's love is for the world, God's way of coming among us is through promise and the person of Jesus Christ, and when God's continuing journey is with us into each new day, surely there is no other word to describe his actions other than "precious." Precious, indeed!

Journey

It's been a long journey through the pandemic, longer for some than for others. A year of interrupted patterns, limited possibilities, and a real slow-down in connections with others. But, happily, we are coming out of the limitations to resume our lives, at least to a large degree. The vaccinations are doing their job, offering a way forward with a far less chance of serious illness and death.

One resumption I am hoping for in the next few weeks is a resumption of our worship and fellowship life as a congregation during April and May. While there have been around twenty attendees at the in-person service each week and another 80 or so who tune in to our Facebook Live service, I look forward to the feel of life together again as we worship and fellowship in full as we move through the summer.

In thinking about the journey we've been on, I couldn't help but think of how the metaphor "journey" is often used, especially in our lives as God's people. The Bible is full of journeys, you may remember. One can recall the Abrahamic stories, the genuine journey of the Exodus, the Exile to Babylon of the people of Judah, Jesus' movements from Galilee down to Jerusalem, and the several missionary journeys of St. Paul. Add to that the journey of the early Christian disciples into "all the world." The metaphor is especially useful in describing our own experiences with God. We say things like, "on my faith journey." We talk about God "walking with us" in times good and bad. We might even say something like, "Since my father died, I've come a long way in my inner life with God." So, it is quite easy to envision the experience of faith as a journey.

There are several reasons why "journey" is a helpful metaphor for Christians. First of all, "journey" focuses on the process of getting somewhere, not on the destination. Christians grow into the image of Christ *"from one degree of glory to another"* (2 Corinthians 3:18). This is a process and for those who seek to follow Jesus (there's that journey idea again), it continues throughout our lives. We continue the journey until we draw our last breath, never fully gaining the destination until we are claimed by Christ in the resurrection. So, when we talk about faith as a journey, we are emphasizing progress, not perfection. Our worship and prayer life as a congregation are part of the equipment we use to guide us on our journey.

Secondly, a journey implies changes, transitions, challenges, and remakes. Indeed, our lives with our Lord teach us to be more open to meeting God in the unexpected and amid the places I might least likely expect him. On our Christian journey we never know what is just around the next bend in the road. However, we do know who will be there with us.

Another aspect of our Christian journeys involves travel companions. Sometimes our travel companions accompany us on the entire trip, and other times we meet with a short-term travel companion. What is life in a Christian community such as ours but the gift of travel companions who care about us as we journey along together. They also give us great opportunity in growing the art of caring for and about others.

One more dimension of our Christian lives as a journey can be seen in the way focusing on our faith journey enables us to lighten the loads we carry along the way. Jesus reminds us in Matthew 11:30 that journeying with the Lord is an unburdening experience *("Come to me, all you that are weary and are carrying heavy burdens, and I will give you rest.")*. Does not prayer help us vanquish anger? Does not forgiveness allow renewal and change? Does not life in Christ enable us to unburden and to lighten the load?

I wonder how strengthening it could be in our daily lives if we were able to view them as one more day on the journey with our Lord. Certainly such a view would dampen any anxiety we might have about the future. It would as well, enable us to view the scenery of each new day with the eyes of the traveler who knows where he or she has come from and where one is going as well as knowing first-hand who travels with us along the way. As we move on toward regaining our congregational life, know that it will be one more step on our journey together.

P

Pleasure

It was the summer of 1951 in a small town in Florida. He was 7 years old and had been allowed to walk the block from his home to the barber shop nearby. Feeling every bit grown up, he hadn't needed to sit on the board across the arms of the barber chair this time because he was tall for his age. After the cutting and trimming had ceased, he looked forward to the final touches of this tonsorial experience – the moment when the barber sprinkled some sweet-smelling hair tonic and rubbed it into his hair. After the final combing and the required inspection in the mirror, the lad was ready to walk back to his home. On the way, however, the final part of this ritual of independence was a stop at his father's office where he proudly and with great pleasure asked of all gathered there, "Want to smell my haircut?"

Life is filled with moments which allow us to give and receive pleasure. An unexpected surprise, a kind word, an act of love, a special moment, a time of victory, a recovery, a mystery solved, intimacy – the possibilities for giving and receiving pleasure are unlimited. One of the persistent secrets of being an active Christian is that serving our Lord also and especially brings and gives pleasure. Not the pleasure of the flesh, however. Nor is it the pleasure of the ego. No, it is a pleasure of the heart, a moment or time where the heart is touched from beyond the self and brings forth a sense of being cared for, affirmed, and accepted. Is this not a way of describing the experience of being loved?

The Bible offers many examples of that which can bring pleasure by bringing one close to God. In the Old Testament, it is affirmed over and over that the Law of God and the focus thereupon brings to believers that sense of being pleasing to God and being on a path that brings purpose and dignity to life. Psalm 1:1 states it very well: *Happy are those who do not follow the advice of the wicked, or take the path that sinners tread, or sit in the seat of scoffers; but their delight (pleasure) is in the law of the Lord, and on his law they meditate day and night.* The prophet Isaiah in seeking to draw Israel back to a focus that takes pleasure in their life with God says, *If you refrain from trampling the sabbath, from pursuing your own interests on my holy day; if you call the sabbath a delight and the holy day of the Lord honorable; if you honor it, not going your own ways, serving your own interests, or pursuing your own affairs; then you shall take delight (pleasure) in the Lord, and I will make you ride upon the heights of the earth; I will feed you with the heritage of your ancestor Jacob, for the mouth of the Lord has spoken.* (Isaiah 58:13-14).

Maintaining a sense of pleasure in the things of God is not always constant nor easy. There is much about our world and about our own makeup which draws one to distracting kinds of pleasure and other delights. St. Paul in his letter to the Romans speaks of how maintaining the sense of pleasure in the things of God is not always easy (Romans 7:21-23): *So I find it to be a law that when I want to do what is good, evil lies close at hand. For I delight (find pleasure) in the law of God in my inmost self, but I see in my members another law at war with the law of my mind, making me captive to the law of sin that dwells in my members.* However, to this conundrum, we have the assurance of God's constant presence, seeking to touch our inner selves with his good pleasure. Jesus even calls such pleasure as comes from life with God a "treasure." Listen to him addressing the crowds about worry and anxiety in Luke 12:32: *"Do not be afraid, little flock, for it is your Father's good pleasure to give you the kingdom. Sell your possessions, and give alms. Make purses for yourselves that do not wear out, an unfailing treasure in heaven, where no thief comes near and no moth destroys. For where your treasure is, there your heart will be also.*

What this collection of thoughts brings to mind for me is the question, "Do we find pleasure in being a Christian?" In its simplest form, do we sense something like the pleasure of the little boy whose haircut smells so delightfully good to him in our daily journey with God in Christ? As we reach out in acts of kindness, as we take part in the acceptance and affirmation of others, as we are able to forgive others, as we let go of any hardness of heart, and as we participate in the worship of God with others, is there the sense of being in God's good pleasure? I can think of little other than this sense for maintaining an active faith in our daily lives.

In the book and movie <u>Chariots of Fire</u>, the true story of Scottish runner Eric Liddell and his win at the 1929 Olympics, we can hear Eric affirm this sense of God's pleasure when he said, *I believe God made me for a purpose, but he also made me fast. And when I run I feel his pleasure."* As we live on in the awareness of God's care and purpose for us, we can feel God's pleasure as well. Want to smell my haircut?

Lagniappe

I learned a new word when I served as Pastor of Lakeview Presbyterian Church in New Orleans, LA, for six and a half years long ago. The word was *"lagniappe,"* pronounced "lan -yapp." Mark Twain learned the term in New Orleans as well. In his <u>Life on the Mississippi</u> (1883), he writes: *"We picked up one excellent word – a word travelling to New Orleans to get; a nice limber, expressive, handy word – "Lagniappe." When a child or a servant buys something in a shop – or even the mayor or governor for aught I know – he finishes the operation by saying, 'Give me something for lagniappe.' The shopman always responds; gives the child a bit of liquorice-root."* Based on an Incan word adopted by the Spanish and brought to the Spanish Empire in Central America and southern North America, it was part of the Creole language. When the French Acadians settled in southern Louisiana, the word took on its French pronunciation used today. It's basic meaning is "a little extra."

What a wonderful term, describing one of the better aspects of life – something "a little extra." As such it can well be understood as a deeply Christian term as well. Grace as provided by our God is always known as something extra, something provided by our Lord beyond expectation. Grace is always present but is seldom flashy and is actually seen through the eyes of the beholder. That's why some people never know the lagniappe of God's provisions. They haven't allowed themselves to trust what God is providing and, thus, they seldom see.

Add to this that God's grace as known through his revelation of it in Jesus Christ is the actuary in whatever sense of "abundant life"(that's a living sense of lagniappe) the believer experiences. So let's link these two terms for our thinking today: *lagniappe* (grace = something extra) and *abundant*.

There's no doubt about the fact that the experiences of believers in both the Old Testament and the New Testament show that they know quite well the lagniappe that God provides to human life. Indeed, one might say that we *abound* (the verbal form of *abundant*) because of it. To know God's provision for us by the marvelous way the human body is put together, ordered, and provided for is indeed an experience in abundance = lagniappe. The Creation itself is beyond description in its wonders and processes – all provided for us in abundance = lagniappe. When we are loved, we abound. When we share with others, we all abound. When we are sacrificed for, we abound. When we are healed, we abound. We abound all around all the time = lagniappe.

However, to participate in our journeys with what God provides as well as in company with God himself as we are claimed in our hearts by his love and forgiveness, and especially by his continued provisions for us in faith and spirit, is to know that the heart of God and the heart of our lives with God is truly lagniappe. Through our walk with him, we abound in whatever we are dealing with, whether it be life or death.

We might listen for our Lord as we visit six passages (of well over fifty) which speak of our abounding through him:

- Proverbs 28:20 – *The faithful will abound with blessings* . . . .
- Romans 6:1-4 – **What then are we to say? Should we continue to sin in order that grace may abound? By no means! How can we who died to sin go on living in it? Do you not know that all of us who have been baptized into Christ Jesus were baptized into his death? Therefore we have been buried with him by baptism into death, so that, just as Christ was raised from the dead by the glory of the Father, so we too might walk in newness of life.**
- Romans 15:13 – *May the God of hope fill you with all joy and peace in believing, so that you may abound in hope by the power of the Holy Spirit.*
- 1 Corinthians 15:58 – **Therefore, my beloved, be steadfast, immovable, always abounding in the work of the Lord, because you know that in the Lord your labor is not in vain.**
- Philippians 4:12 – *I know what it is to be abased, and I know what it is to abound. In any and all circumstances I have learned the secret of being well-fed and of going hungry, of having plenty and of being in need. I can do all things through him who strengthens me.*
- 1 Thessalonians 3:12 – **And may the Lord make you increase and abound in love for one another and for all, just as we abound in love for you.**

Jesus Christ, God's gift of himself to our world, is the testimony to God's grace. He is in every way God's "lagniappe" for us in all things. It is true that our lives bear that "something extra" as we live in him and through him.

Locusts

As the summer unfolds before us now that the solstice has been passed by, a number of things come to mind as to the landscape of our time: heat and rainfall, long hours of daylight, keeping an eye on the Tropics for possible hurricanes, the continuing march of the pandemic though now in the face ever-increasing vaccinations, folks moving out of house and home for activities left behind during the past year, fresh vegetables from farm and garden, flowers and birds in diverse appearances, outdoor activities for all, the upcoming 4th of July, the resumption of public worship, and hopes for better solutions to the proliferation of dark themes and irrational stances taken by many in public places, to mention a few. And in certain parts of our country the landscape includes noise – unusual noise, sometimes deafening noise, often times irritating noise – the noise of **Cicadas** singing their choruses throughout the long hours of the day, often in such volume, like loud static, as to interfere with both mind and heart.

Here in America there are twelve broods of 17-year Cicadas centered in lower New England and the heartland of America including the upper South. There are also three 13-year broods centered in parts of NC, SC, GA, AL, and Missouri and Illinois. This year is the year for Brood X to appear and appear they have by the jillions, though few of them have affected North Carolina. Our time comes in 2024 when Brood XIX hatches. These broods of thousands of Cicadas emerge after living underground for their allotted time only to live as adults for about six weeks where they mate, lay eggs in live plants and trees, and then die. The eggs hatch, the nymphs drop to the ground and burrow under the soil, to live in darkness until their appointed time to emerge.

While Cicadas are not specifically mentioned in the Bible, Locusts sure are, and Locusts and the reality of Locust swarms have plagued the Biblical lands as well as much of Africa for eons. Locusts swarm also appear in the United States, mostly in the West from time to time, triggered by lots of rainfall. Locusts and Cicadas are often confused. They are really quite different from each other. Locusts are a type of grasshopper while Cicadas are cousins of crickets. Locusts eat live plants. Cicadas suck the sap out of trees. Locusts are immensely destructive to crops, especially when they appear in swarms of millions. Both are edible and are used as food and fertilizer in many parts of the world.

I am bringing all this to mind because of the roles swarms of insects and plagues of Locusts have played in biblical thought as metaphorical indicators of evil forces and of the providence and judgment of God. There are over 30 mentions of Locusts in the Bible, in 17 Old and New Testament books. Bible passages with detailed images of Locusts and historical accounts of Locusts' devastation to crops are found in Exodus, Psalms, Jeremiah, Joel, and Revelation. Locusts are mentioned as food in Matthew and Mark.

In terms of being indicators of evil forces, one might think of the 8th plague Moses oversaw in Egypt when he was seeking the release of the people of Israel from bondage. Indeed, the plagues in Exodus were seen as the result of evil in a society which deemed itself irreproachable and secure in its own wisdom. Evil most often results where arrogance to justice and harmony are disregarded. Egypt as captor of the Israelites and cruel slave-owners, was vulnerable to larger forces, especially those in nature, that they could not see nor be prepared for until the plagues were upon them. Israel, on the other hand, was prepared for what was to come by the wisdom and leadership of Moses. Lesson: blindness to the way reality functions breeds vulnerability to the downside of that reality. In other words, dependence upon one's own power and sight alone, makes vulnerability to the forces of nature more acute – a lesson one might consider in thinking about vulnerability to the pandemic as a plague in our society or our own society seeking to live with little regard to the forces of the natural world.

In the long history of humans learning to live with the natural world provided to us by God, plagues of Cicadas and plagues of Locusts or any other natural phenomenon are apt indicators of our vulnerabilities to those phenomena if wisdom and knowledge are not utilized. The way many have responded or not responded to the plague of this pandemic is a good illustration of the same story of humanity that has been taking place since the beginning. Slowness in recognizing how devastating this plague is and resistance to the wisdom needed to combat it has cost 600,000 lives in our country alone. The Biblical story, with its emphasis on presenting to us God's way and will, seeks to lay the groundwork for humility and wisdom in the face of the natural world as well as the way to work together in seeking a better life when the plagues do come.

Hidden

Does God hide from us? Or to put it another way, how can one know God and the things of God? It is the question behind the query as to who God is, what God's will is, and what, if anything, might God reveal to me? And in a time when there are so many clamoring voices alleging that God's will is such-and-such, that God is saying this, that God wants that particular thing, that God has spoken to this particular person and not that one, and that the will of God is "as I see it," it is easy to understand why many people park the question on the roadside and move on to other things content in not knowing much about such a God, or worse, content in believing that God does not have much to reveal to us at all, that much about God is hidden.

There's a lot about God's hiddenness in the Bible, displaying a broad spectrum of ways to talk about it. Nothing is hidden from God (Psalm 139:15; Isaiah 40:27; Daniel 2:22), which is comforting for penitents (Psalm 19:12; 38:9) and devastating for the sinful (Jeremiah 16:17; Amos 9:3; Job 34:22). God by nature is essentially hidden from humans, as are God's plans (Deuteronomy 29:29; Psalm 10:1; Isaiah 45:15; Job 28:21). Therefore, God must reveal God's will if it is to be known. The hiddenness of God is presupposed in the New Testament: God's kingdom is compared with a hidden treasure (Matthew 13:44); true knowledge is hidden from the wise (Matthew 11:25; Luke 10:21), yet everything hidden will be disclosed (Mark 4:22). In Jesus, God has revealed his hidden wisdom (1 Corinthians 2:7); God's hidden mystery must now be proclaimed (Ephesians 3:9).

Facing the real possibility that we can make up our own versions of God, that we can say that God is this or that, and that God's will is this or that, one is moved to find some true ways of considering the hiddenness of God and how clarity in who God is and what God wants becomes paramount if the Christian journey we are invited onto is to be more than a reflection of ourselves.

First, consider objective thinking as a means of realizing the possibility of God as Creator and Lord. It makes sense to think of One from whom the created order has sprung, much more sense than thinking that the universe sprang up on its own. It makes sense also to consider that just as there are laws of nature which we can perceive and understand by which the natural order operates, that there are also ways built into reality for life to function more agreeably with some ways of behaving far better than others. These we can figure out by objective experience and thought. However, if objective thinking allows for the reality of God as plausible, it also leaves much that is hidden about him. This is certainly part of the widespread experience of humans the world over – believing in a higher power makes objective sense.

Second, consider the subjective nature of being human – that ability of people to intuit some aspects of reality as valuable and true or not. No one has to explain a mother's love for her child to convince that child that its mother's love is real. The same is true in many areas of life. We can perceive much about what is good or not so good by intuition and by reflection upon both experiences and their effects upon us. Being a part of a loving congregation provides a setting whereby one might intuit through experience something of the nature of the God we worship.

Third, we might consider the impact of collective experiences and the story they tell as basic in learning the lessons of the past. Thus, the witness of others as to their insights and conclusions can go a long way in introducing and nurturing one's own understanding of one's journey. The hiddenness of God becomes less hidden and the purposes of God become more clear. And when the insights and lessons of the past are collected and shared as part of a people's collective memory, that shared story becomes a point of growth in insight and revelation for one's own journey. Certainly, this is the role of the Bible for Christians.

However, the crucial aspect for Christians is the inward testimony of God himself in our hearts and minds as we deal with life. In measuring what we have learned objectively with what is witnessed to both outwardly by others and inwardly through insight and reflection, one has the opportunity to "hear" God speaking to one's own life. It is this inward revelation that seals one's faith. It is this inward revelation, delivered in the life and teachings of Jesus and attested to by the sense of God's truth in our inmost being that grounds believers in faith. And while all things of God are not revealed, enough is for one to live in faith and hope. Our life together in the church is to nurture faithful listening to the inward Spirit who ever whispers God's care and touch to the ears of our hearts.

God does not hide. Life obscures. Humans muddle and confuse their thoughts. God reveals.

Unlikely Story

From its very beginning, Christianity has been a missionary religion. Christians have told others about their Lord. They continue to do so today all over the world. The last chapter of Matthew's Gospel tells us that the risen Jesus commissioned his followers to go and make disciples of all nations (Matthew 28:19-20). Part of the mission of Christian churches today is the same – to tell others, young and old, about the Lord.

But when one knows the context of the New Testaments texts – that is, the world and cultures in and to which these stories were written so long ago – one quickly realizes that sometimes the unusual and even strange aspects of the story are what give the story its credibility as well as make it seem unlikely.

In the ancient Jewish and Greco-Roman world that Christianity was born into, to share one's faith and conviction – to evangelize in Christian terms – required all sorts of explanations to make one's claims, especially the unlikely ones, worthy for someone to consider. This was especially necessary if one was claiming that a Jewish manual laborer who had been crucified by a Roman governor named Pilate had not only died an ignominious death but had also been raised from the dead, appeared to various persons, and was starting a new community of followers because his previous ones had all but abandoned hope.

The real sticking point for Jesus' followers in trying to convey their religion was that the culture of the Middle East at that time (and still today) was an honor and shame culture, and crucifixion was the most shameful way to die in that world. It was not seen as noble martyrdom of any sort. People in that world believed that the manner of one's death most revealed one's character. And on that basis, to tell the Jesus story would be to reveal him as a scoundrel, a man who committed treason against the state, a man who deserved the punishment used for slave revolts. The Romans called it "the extreme punishment," and no Roman citizen would be subjected to it. It was reserved for the lowliest criminal. Unlikely indeed, how does one convey Jesus as Lord when his death was shameful?

It wouldn't make sense to create a story about a crucified and risen man being the savior of the world – unless one actually believed it to be historically true. No one would make up a story like this because it just wouldn't sell. The instinctive reaction to such a message is exactly what Paul, the earliest New Testament writer, said it would be: It was a stumbling block or scandal to the Jews, and sheer nonsense to Gentiles (I Corinthians 1:23). A good illustration as to how scandalous such an account would be can be seen in the graffiti found in the pagan catacombs in Rome. One shows a donkey hanging on a cross, with a Roman kneeling below it with a sarcastic remark about "a man worshiping his god." That's how crazily this Christian message came across to many in that time (and still does to some today!).

There are some other odd things to consider that no one would use if it were desired to sell the Christian story in the first century. For example, if one wanted to start a world religion in a highly patriarchal world – a world where men dominate and women are secondary, one doesn't make up stories about all the male disciples abandoning Jesus and the women being chief witnesses. Women are last at the cross, first at the empty tomb, first to hear the angelic message "he is risen," first to see the risen Jesus and first to go and testify to the male disciples hunkered down behind locked doors in Jerusalem for fear of the Jewish authorities. The witness of women was considered suspect by most in that first-century world, and indeed, Luke 24:11 says that the male disciples thought it was an old wives' tale when the women came and breathlessly claimed the tomb was empty and Jesus was risen.

Add to that that the accounts of Jesus appearing after his resurrection feature women quite prominently – to Mary Magdalene, Mary, and the other women – and not to any of the Twelve.

So, if one is interested in making a story that others will buy, one wouldn't make up a story like the story of Jesus' arrest, trial, crucifixion and resurrection. And because it wouldn't fly in that world and one wouldn't just make up something like it because it wouldn't fly, it lends a great deal of credence to the fact that this story is quite real. These things happened, as unbelievable as it might seem to some, or no one would tell such a tale.

How is it that a band of defeated and depressed disciples, who had abandoned hope after the crucifixion of Jesus became galvanized and inspired enough to carry the good news of Jesus from Jerusalem to Rome and beyond? What happened that caused the deserters to become the martyrs, the deniers to become the confessors, and women to take a chance at being laughed out of court by telling the men that "he is risen and has appeared to us?" What stands between the terrible death and the disciples becoming a world-evangelizing group was something almost unbelievable to most minds - the appearance of the risen Jesus that they had seen. They believed that God's yes to life in the case of Jesus was louder than death's no. They had seen it. No matter how unlikely, it was real.

The story reaches its climax point as the disciples gather with Jesus in the upper room to celebrate the Passover. The deliverance God seeks to provide the world through claiming the hearts and minds of his people is foretold and enacted as Jesus broke the bread and shared the wine proclaiming that this was his body and blood crucified for them. In his promise to be with them beyond his death, he foreshadows each one's journey with the risen Lord in life and the resurrection to come for us all. This unlikely story is God's way of showing us the truth about himself and about us. It's an unlikely story because God's ways are not ours.

It's an unlikely story into which each one is invited for the sake of one's life.

Denial

I suspect we learn to deny ideas and things when we are very young. Maybe at first it is because of a mild case of a desire for self-preservation in the face of authority or superior power and, if not self-preservation, at least a desire for differentiation. It contributes to our ability to define ourselves as unique, independent people to some degree. It also serves as a means to move one to think for oneself rather than simply to accept blindly what is offered. From a young age we learn to deny, to be slow to accept at face value what is told to us. As such, a healthy bit of denial can lead us toward truth and clarity.

As one of the stages of the grieving process, denial, that sense of not being able to grasp the reality of a loved one's death at first, can serve as a kind of protection, like being in shock, for a time until one is able to process the reality of the loss of a loved one. Of course, to remain permanently in denial about the death of a loved one can block one's ability to move into the future healthily. In this sense, denial is a temporary aid, but not the end of the story.

The Bible has a number of ways of expressing denial. It can mean to refuse to consent to a claim or demand. In Acts 4:16, Peter and John have been hauled before the "rulers, elders, and scribes" of the Jewish Council to explain their preaching and marvelous deeds. After their explanations confessing (the opposite of denial) the coming of the Spirit and the significance of the death and resurrection of Jesus, the members of the Council were perplexed as to what to do with them. The people liked what they had been testifying to. The members of the Council said, "What will we do with them? For it is obvious to all who live in Jerusalem that a notable sign has been done through them; we cannot *deny* it." ("It is true no matter how we feel about it. Now what?")

The term *deny* is also used in the Bible to dispute an assertion that is nevertheless true. In the Gospel of John (1:19-20), some were questioning John the Baptist as to who he was (they feared he was claiming to be the Messiah). John confessed that he was not the Messiah and did not deny that confession.

More often, the term is used to repudiate, disown, or renounce someone or something as when Jesus famously said, "If any want to become my followers, let them deny themselves and take up their cross daily and follow me." The clear implication of this denial is to get the self and self-preservation out of the center so that discipleship (following) can take place. As important as this way of using denial in the Bible is, there are many New Testament occurrences which have to do with refusing to associate with Jesus or even in disowning him. Peter, of course, is famous for denying Jesus three times before the cock crowed on the night of Jesus' arrest. But Peter also preached, after his acceptance of the risen Lord, that the religion of the Jews had denied (rejected) "the Holy and Righteous One and asked to have a murderer [Barabbas] go free" (Acts 3:15).

It is certainly true that denial can be a way of protecting the self from uncomfortable issues or decisions as well as a way of limiting stress and confusion. It can also function as a shield from useful thinking and a desire to find what is true. As such, denial is no land to live in for long.

In considering the issues aroused by denial, I can think of two areas at present where much denial is taking place, neither of them very healthy.

The first is in the reality of Jesus as God's emissary to humanity to claim hearts and minds so that one's life and hope is defined by God's grace and love for a people as a basis for living and dying in our world. It appears that many in our time simply cannot accept this and some go to great links to deny it altogether. On the other hand, it also appears that many have co-opted the Jesus story and refashioned it into some form of Christian nationalism, mixing up Christianity as God's way of life with one's love and devotion for our country. As such, a form of denial has crept in by making Jesus an icon for our nation. Jesus is Lord over all nations.

The second is the prevailing spread of a denial of the fruits of science and of the facts of history. It appears that a great cloud of suspicion and denial has grown in our time particularly concerning the results of scientific studies about both the climate and the pandemic. Denial of proven facts concerning the results of the high use of carbon on our atmosphere with its resulting changes in weather patterns and temperature is rampant among many. Even more seriously for the moment are the vast number of illnesses and deaths that have resulted from the denial of solid science with regard to the efficacy of masks and vaccination. It's another example of political devotion leading to the denial of truth and the creation of "alternative facts" (which are no facts at all).

Jesus taught us that we are to seek the truth, follow the truth, and live in the truth. While the truth he promotes gathers around what God has revealed to us, it nevertheless includes what is true in all things. Jesus said, "Know the truth and the truth will make you free." So, here's to what is true, so needed in our time.

Blessing

The terms *Bless, Blessing, Blessed,* all have an important place in the lexicon of Christian people. While the terms speak often of things unseen, they also speak of things easily known and experienced. The origins of these terms are rooted in the experiences of ancient Israel and the early Christian Church. As such, they are theological terms expressing the experience of being connected to our God. On the one hand, that connection is sensed and believed (that's the unseen part); on the other hand, the evidence of such a connection is seen and experienced in one's life. Because of God's gifts, I can sense God's nearness; as I experience God's gifts I know my life to become blessed.

The unblessed person is one who may take part in the blessings God bestows (like beauty and the creation and acts of forgiveness by others to name a few) but does not sense any connection with the divine. That's probably a good definition of a secular person. A believer, however, revels in the sense of holiness and the connection with God as he or she participates in the blessings bestowed. It all has to do with our internal sensors, so to speak. Are we geared up to sense the divine in the ordinary by a willingness to take God at God's word that he loves us and moves among us on our behalf? That's the gift of faith and trust in the promises of God. Without such internal sensors, however, without a faith in God's promises, that which might draw one into God's presence simply becomes a good feeling, often fleeting.

Blessings may be discovered; they may be pronounced; and they may be lived. "What a blessing to have had children to raise and love," says the grateful parent, giving thanks to God for such a blessing (a lived blessing). "Go forth into the world as God's people; remember who you are and love one another, knowing God's blessing as you go," is a pronounced blessing given by one on behalf of God. "When I found that you really have forgiven me, I found hope once again" (a discovered blessing). But all three of these ways of knowing blessings in life are a connection with the divine. They are living evidence of God's Spirit in our midst. That's why the term "blessing" or "bless" is found over 600 times in the Old Testament alone. To be blessed in any way is to know God's touch.

After the people of Israel under Moses and Aaron had lingered in the wilderness for some time and Moses had gone up onto Mt. Sinai to receive (twice) the Ten Commandments, it was time for them to move on. They were a people now covenanted with God, being led to a new land. Upon the departure time from Sinai, Aaron, as priest to the people, gave a benediction (blessing) to them, a blessing that has marked God's people ever since:

The Lord spoke to Moses, saying: Speak to Aaron and his sons, saying, "Thus you shall bless the Israelites. You will say to them: **The Lord bless you and keep you; the Lord make his face to shine upon you, and be gracious to you; the Lord lift up his countenance upon you, and give you peace.** *So you shall put my name on the Israelites and I will bless them."*

In thinking about *blessing* in its several forms, it occurred to me that living as a blessed people, giving and receiving the fruits of God's blessings to and from others, and recognizing that it is God who "keeps" us along the way, can help us in this time of "cancel culture" and angered division. How's that, one might ask?

To bless generally means to speak good or to do good things for another. Perhaps remembering this each day as a blessed people might dissuade us from the impulse to strike out at those who frighten or anger us. This is because to be blessed is to seek to speak or do good for another. One of the things I like about being a part of a believing community of faith is that there is an intention to speak well to and about each other. Such an atmosphere among a church family breeds a strong sense of being blessed. As we gather for worship, it is with thankful hearts that we announce God's blessing in calling us to worship and then pronounce God's benediction (blessing) as we depart. It is the ground upon which we stand as we live out our calling each day. May God continue to bless us, each one.

Gradually, then Suddenly

As I listened to the comments made by the four Capitol officers about their frightening experiences during the insurrection at the US Capitol on January 6, one of the panel of members of Congress made a remark that has stuck in my mind. As she tried to account for how our nation ever got to such a place, she quoted Ernest Hemingway in his novel, <u>The Sun Also Rises</u>. The quote, three short words long, covers a vast territory: ***"Gradually, then suddenly."*** It struck me that this short sentence can be used to define so many things in our lives, including our lives as God's people.

For some, the sentence can apply to a whole host of habits, both good and bad. People don't become alcoholics overnight, it comes gradually, then one day one is painfully aware it's there. The same with gaining weight. Or learning to play an instrument. Or forming a relationship. Or gaining an education. Gradually, then suddenly!

Although often unnoticeable, gradually eventually leading to suddenly becomes a general principle in life. Gradually can build momentum. It can succumb to the compounding effect. While one coasts along doing one's thing, great and almost magical forces are at work using the effects of one's labor to fortify the foundation for future habits. These effects compound one's daily acts, both good and bad, into a grand result that sometimes can take one by surprise. The initial effects happen gradually. The first way is delayed consequences. One just doesn't notice gradually. One doesn't realize the gradual change occurring until it becomes something more profound or more dramatic. Then it becomes painfully obvious.

I think this is happening throughout the world with the pandemic. When Covid and its variants are gradually pushed out of mind and ignored, especially in not getting vaccinated, the compounding effect of its spread catches many by surprise with spikes and its dire effects on the unsuspecting, effects that can lead to death. Gradually becomes suddenly.

In Proverbs 6:12-15, the wisdom writers point out the way "gradually, then suddenly" works:

> *A scoundrel and a villain goes around with crooked speech,*
> *Winking the eyes, shuffling the feet,*
> *Pointing fingers,*
> *With perverted mind devising evil, continually sowing discord;*
> *On such a one calamity will descend suddenly;*
> *In a moment, damage beyond repair.*

Of course, "gradually, then suddenly" works for good as well as for evil. How often can one find references to God's gifts "suddenly" becoming known to those who have sought out his way and his will throughout the years? After 40 years of painful travel and almost constant travail where the people of Israel had to renew their trust in God over and over on the way, "suddenly" there was the Promised Land, there was the new future, realized by the years of trusting and renewing that trust in God.

Perhaps the Jesus story in the New Testament can be understood as another chapter in the "gradually, then suddenly" frame as well. For decades the prophets had been promising that God would send his Messiah ("Anointed One") to them to redeem them and lead them through heart and mind into the Kingdom of God. "How long, O Lord? Will you remember us not forever?" And then, suddenly, the angel songs burst out over the land, a star alights in the heavens and shines upon Bethlehem, and a child is born to change the hearts and minds of all who will follow him. "Gradually, then suddenly."

I think the Christian journey for each of us can be understood in the "gradually, then suddenly" frame as well. Through years of belief, prayer, worship, and trust (that's the gradual part), one has moments along the way where "suddenly" we realize that God is near, that sins are forgiven, that faith is real, and that life contains the rich hope of God himself. Such moments may come readily or sparingly, but whenever they come, they come "gradually, then suddenly."

In thinking about this for our daily lives, one might want to take some time and review how one spends each day. Where, we might ask, will the things we do every day or every hour or even every year take us? Where might we be when we get where we think we are going? More than most other things, the little things one does every day can determine what one becomes. Gradually will one day become suddenly.

Consequences

I think of the term *consequence* with a bit of fear and trembling. Widely used, sometimes feared (as in bad results), often offered up in order to motivate (as in giving encouragement and hope), occasionally used to warn (as in invoking fear), it is a term of, well, great consequence (as in importance). However the term is used, it always places an emphasis on results or rewards or conclusions. "The child is the father of the man," wrote Shakespeare, indicating that the grown person springs forth upon the seeds of his or her planting. Along the way in each person's life choices are offered, decisions are made, and consequences are resulted. It's a process taking place on many levels in each person's life, physically ("you are what you eat, etc."), emotionally ("be mindful and take time for yourself"), vocationally ("what do you want to do with your life?"), financially ("money and investment management"), and spiritually ("a cultivated faith deepens one's life"). No wonder the term *consequence* can invoke some fear to one's mind and not a little trembling. Our lives are ever intertwined in the consequences of our journeys.

What is the constant barrage of news reports received each day via the television or radio, via the internet or by word of mouth, but the recital of actions and consequences taking place like the swirling vortex of a major storm all about us at all times? Each day is filled with consequences, mine, yours, others, as well as that of nations and peoples. Often those consequences move us along in the process of living. Sometimes they swallow us up or empty the rooms of our lives of air. Sometimes they injure us or our loved ones or strangers or enemies, and people die.

The consequence of life lived away from God is pictured in the Bible as a life where the consequences are emptiness and hopelessness, racked by confusion about right and wrong, ravaged by the inability to see neighbors as sisters and brothers, and scrambling to hold on to life amid the fear of death. That's a good summary of St. Paul's statement to the Romans that *"the wages (consequences) of sin is death, but the free gift of God is eternal life in Christ Jesus our Lord"* (Romans 6:23). The consequences of such a life is a form of blindness about what is real and true in our world resulting in a kind of stumbling around in darkness, grasping first one thing or another to give one direction and hope, calling first this way of thought and then that way of thought as the truth as though one might make the truth what one wills.

Paul goes on and tells the Galatians (6:7-10) to remember who they are and that they should *"not be deceived; God is not mocked; for you reap whatever you sow* (consequences). *If you sow to your own flesh* (his term for life in the darkness of the self alone), *you will reap corruption from the flesh; but if you sow to the Spirit* (his term for submission to God's promises and way through Jesus Christ), *you will reap eternal life* (life in God's kingdom, under his rule, day by day) *from the Spirit."*

Consequences. A 13-foot Burmese python in Florida (one of those huge snakes that have taken over the Everglades), is recorded as killing and swallowing a 6-foot alligator. There are photographs of the dead snake with a huge bulge in its mid-section - the consequences of a grave miscalculation. In Cape Cod, a young man was arrested for shooting out the insulators on the electric poles on his street resulting in a black-out for the whole community for hours. Consequences, including his arrest. The good Lord gave us minds for thinking through our beliefs and actions in order to anticipate consequences. And he gave us the way and the truth as well as life in Christ to instill in us a certain kind of wisdom to guide us in our living.

I fear that not anticipating the consequences of fierce resistance to sound medical and moral advise pertaining to masking and vaccinations for the Coronavirus will continue to produce serious and sometimes deadly consequences in our land. This is second to the reasonable fears of the consequences of where the abundance of conspiracy theories about politics, the climate, and our national life are leading our nation and its civic life. I fear that a lack of focus on history, science, and facts as well as God's truth is resulting in damaging consequences for many of our brothers and sisters as well as for our society. But more than fear for those who seek God's truth and Christ's way is hope, the kind which comes from confidence in the God who lives among us. As the prophet Isaiah said so long ago (Isaiah40:10-11): *"See, the Lord God comes with might, and his arm rules for him; his reward* (consequence) *is with him, and his recompense* (consequence) *before him. He will feed his flock like a shepherd; he will gather the lambs in his arms, and carry them in his bosom, and gently lead the mother sheep."* In this troubled time, that's a consequence I pray for and seek.

Awe and Wonder

As I listened to several reports of the on-going Perseid meteor shower lighting up the midnight skies during this week, I couldn't help but hear a sense of awe and wonder in the words of those who observed it. It's the same sense of awe and wonder I've felt myself in regarding grand vistas in the mountains and the countryside or in observing particularly spectacular displays of the color and behavior of birds or in the deepening sense of the presence of God while singing in church. Watching a small child at play, or listening to the chatter of little ones in their activities evokes such wonder in me that I'm glad Jesus himself put his seal of approval on the wonder of children when he told those stiff-necked adults who gathered around him to "let the children come to me, for to such as these belongs the kingdom of heaven" (Matthew 10:14).

Wonder and awe are such "wonderful" experiences. It reminds the curious mind that there is a distinct difference between a problem and a mystery. A problem is outside the self. It does not directly involve the self. There is a final answer to every problem even if that answer eludes one. The mood for dealing with a problem is curiosity and in general most problems can be studied by just about anyone.

On the other hand, thinking about mystery involves the self and introspection. True mysteries are not solvable but, rather, are to be experienced. It is impossible to think about the mystery of death without thinking about one's own death. Such thought often evokes wonder. The same is true in thinking about freedom, the mystery of love, and the presence of God. Though one can go deeply in thought about a mystery, there is no final answer in the objective sense. Reflecting on mystery is a very personal activity creating its own moods. However, the mood in reflecting on mystery is not so much curiosity as it is awe and wonder. Awe and wonder might best be defined, then, as a heightened state of consciousness and emotion brought about by something singularly beautiful, rare, or unexpected – that is, by marvel. Awe experiences are what psychologists call self-transcendent: they shift our attention away from ourselves, make us feel like we are part of something greater than ourselves, change our perception of time, and even make us more generous toward others.

Rabbi Abraham Heschel once wrote concerning awe and wonder these emblematic words: *"Awe. . . is more than an emotion; it is a way of understanding. Awe is itself an act of insight into a meaning greater than ourselves. . . Awe enables us to perceive in the world intimations of the divine, to sense in small things the beginning of infinite significance, to sense the ultimate in the common and the simple."*

So it is with the common and simple things of life - to ponder them allows one to sense the mystery therein. To ponder them is to reflect on meaning and truth. Such pondering moves the heart outward. Experiencing a sense of awe often promotes altruism, loving-kindness, and magnanimous behavior.

The mystery of God known in three persons is awesome and wonderful – God experienced within, without, and above. The incarnation (being made flesh) of God's self in his Son is awesome and wonderful. That God has taken on human flesh out of love is awesome. That we can celebrate around the Lord's Table and in symbol and word experience the nearness of Christ is awesome and wonderful. That God loves each and every one of us, has created us out of love, and will never withdraw that love is awesome and wonderful. That through sanctifying grace we share our lives in the presence of God is awesome and wonderful. That the Holy Spirit is always present to us and trying to help us to be more like Christ is awesome and wonderful.

That whatever heaven is, whenever we experience it we will be united to God and reunited with our Loved ones who have died is awesome and wonderful. That when we meet God in heaven our deepest dreams and desires will be fulfilled is awesome and wonderful. That God has created every single one of us so that we can have an intimate loving relationship with God himself is awesome and wonderful. If we believe in the truths of Christian faith and do not find them awesome and wonderful then I wonder if we can find any truth awesome and wonderful.

One might ask during this perilous time of fear and disease whether it is possible to sense anything awesome or wonderful. Indeed, there is ample evidence that many are downtrodden and depressed over the ongoing stresses in our common lives. It has even led many to believe in fantasies and conspiracies and to hope for rescue. Of course, we must continue to use our best common sense and judgment in dealing with the problems lest they overwhelm us. But the deeper sense of life doesn't come in solving problems. It comes in the wonder built into life itself. We lose ourselves in problems. We can find ourselves as well as the wider vistas of our God-given lives in sensing the wonder in the ordinary, the awe found in the beautiful, and the presence of God himself in God's gifts scattered around us each new day.

Rest

According to a Greek legend, in ancient Athens a man noticed the great storyteller Aesop playing childish games with some little boys. He laughed and jeered at Aesop, asking him why he wasted his time in such frivolous activity. Aesop responded by picking up a bow, loosening its string, and placing it on the ground. Then he said to the critical Athenian, "Now, answer the riddle, if you can. Tell us what the unstrung bow implies."

The man looked at it for several moments but had no idea what point Aesop was trying to make. Aesop explained, "If you keep a bow always bent, it will break eventually. But if you let it go slack, it will be more fit for use when you want it."

People are also like that. That's why we all need to take time to rest.

The term "rest" can mean a number of things in general: When one takes time out, ceasing activity can be termed "rest." So can sleep. Peace of mind or spirit is often called rest because it doesn't allow outside forces to crowd one's life. And, of course, for centuries folks have viewed death as a time when one can "rest in peace." In music, a rest is a pause from sound and it even has its own symbol in the keyboard nomenclature. "Come on in and rest awhile," is a welcome invitation to most all of us.

The words translated in the Bible as "rest" appear 274 times in the Old Testament alone and another 52 times in the New Testament. It appears that "resting" of one kind or another is very important in our Scriptures. Aside from physical rest and the enlargement of that on the seventh day of the week (Sabbath = rest from labor), rest generally has to do with inner peace, freedom from anxiety, and an emotional state of being at ease within. It even includes the concept of security in that peace and is thus used by Israel to describe her anticipated life in the Promised Land (Joshua 1:13 – "Remember the word that Moses the servant of the Lord commanded you, saying, 'The Lord your God is providing you a place of rest and will give you this land.'").

The Bible also presents rest in terms of the future not only for Israel, but for believers. Both in the decisive forgiveness of their sins (Hebrews 10:14-23) and through entrance into the very presence of God at death (Hebrews 12:23), Christ's followers experience the ultimate blessings of true rest both in the "now" of this life and the "not yet" of the life to come.

Perhaps the most important mention of "rest" in the Bible is found in Matthew 11:27-28 (*"Come to me, all you that are weary and are carrying heavy burdens, and I will give you rest. Take my yoke upon you, and learn from me, for I am gentle and humble in heart, and you will find rest for your souls. For my yoke is easy, and my burden is light.").* This, of course, is the invitation made by God through his servant, Jesus, to enter into a kind of restful life which gets its defining point and its sustenance from one's deep spiritual relationship with Jesus. It's the kind of rest that "passes understanding," in that it depends upon trust in God through him.

Here one gets at the heart of the Christian faith. Our rest in Jesus is the very wellspring for Christian living. Believers are not compelled from outside the self to follow Jesus and to serve him. They are drawn into following Jesus and serving him from within. Such rest is the by-product of one's heart being directed towards God as revealed through Christ. Such rest infects attitude and behavior. It enables one to view time and event with a kind of dispassion, for "nothing can separate us from the love God through Christ Jesus our Lord" (Romans 8:39). It offers one a chance to hear more clearly and understand more deeply the sounds and sights of the world around us. Godly rest strikes at the heart of loneliness, renders others as neighbors, and soothes the anxious soul. "Coming to Jesus" is the way God provides for us to live boldly and creatively as God's people in an oft-darkened world. "Coming to Jesus" offers rest in the knowledge of who one is as a child of God as well as in the knowledge that this "rest" is the foretaste of the rest God provides for eternity. "Coming to Jesus" enables one to escape from the anxiety produced by sin and sin's many burdens as well as to renew life despite that sin because God's "rest" contains at its heart God's loving forgiveness of his children. From such a restful state of life, the words of Psalm 131:2 can become one's own words: "But I have calmed and quieted my soul, like a weaned child with its mother, my soul is like the weaned child that is with me."

I pray for this rest each day. Amid fears that some I love will be felled by the pandemic or by other means as well as anxieties related to the advance of time, my soul yearns to be at rest. In Christ, my soul is quieted anew and I rest.

Hills

In order to honor the oldest surviving sibling in our family of eight siblings (four of whom now survive) who turned 86 on Wednesday, I drove to Montreat, NC, to gather with the other three for celebration, memory, and thoughts about our respective journeys. As I have no doubt shared from time to time, as the distant hills and mountains came into view as I drove, with it a noticeable change of heart also came. There's something about driving into the hills and forested mountains that can soothe one's soul. Our celebration went well and the four of us departed with hopes that we can be together again sometimes in the near future.

In thinking about "the hills," I am reminded of how often some version of "heading for the hills" has been part of the human story. For some, there comes a yearning to flee – to get away – to head for the hills, either figuratively or actually. One wants to get away from it all, to be restored, made whole again, to regain one's balance, to get renewed, or, as often happened in former days, to find protection from enemies, to rediscover Gods comfort. I am reminded that the coves and hollows of our mountains in earlier times were not only places of refuge from enemies but were also areas of isolation and protection from the spread of disease. Some of the areas of the Smokey Mountains were settled by those seeking to escape diseases like cholera and diphtheria.

Maria sang, "The hills are alive with the sound of music," and we all sing with her for we know something of those songs the mountains sing to our hearts. We've been there. Heading for the hills may have been more for safety in the frontier days, but today it is more for peace and the help that peace can bring.

It was somewhat like that in Old Testament Israel too. They were a people of the hills and mountain valleys of that not so peaceful land. All through the Old Testament there are frequent references to the hills and the mountains.

No doubt in those days heading for the hills had a lot more to it than it does for us. First of all, it took far more work for them, for they had to do it on foot. They fled to the hills often to escape enemies. But in the oldest of days, they went there to worship, too.

Somehow the majesty of the mountains, the fact of being high and lifted up, and the refuge often found in the hills reminded them of God. One might remember that Moses went high up on Mount Sinai to meet with God, to hear and receive God's covenant, and to obtain the Ten Commandments. In the early days the clouds at the tops of the mountains and the noise and awesomeness of volcanic action convinced folks that God was enthroned on some mountains and that he could be found wherever there were mountains and hills.

It has always been very easy for one to assume, as perhaps some do today, that when one heads for the hills, one can find God.

But a wonderful discovery was made by the people of Israel as they continued their journey with God down through the years. And because of it, they broke with the prevailing view of most peoples in the world at that time. They were shown by God himself that God was not found in the hills or in nature at all. He was not in the trees, in the rivers, in the hills, or in the storms. These things were his handiwork all right, but they were not God and God was not living in them. Indeed, they discovered that God was above them and among them and that they in themselves did nothing to produce God for them. In other words, to head for the hills was not a primary way to find God.

There's that wonderful account in I Kings 20 to remind us of this discovery. The Syrians, like most peoples of that day, believed in localized gods, and felt that since Israel's God was a god "of the hills" and their gods were gods of the valleys and plains, that if they fought Israel in the valley they, the Syrians, would win. Of course, it didn't work out that way and we are given a glimpse of Israel's discovery – that God is not in the hills or in the plains – God is Lord of all places. And because one goes to the hills does not mean one will be nearer to God.

Now that's what is pointed out in the magnificent 121st Psalm. The psalmist, speaking for the pilgrim journeying to festival time in Jerusalem, says like we might say in our time of need, "I lift up my eyes to the hills. From whence does my help come?"

But the truth is, as Israel discovered, that if it's God's help we seek in the mountains, we don't find it there any more than in any other place we may be, for God is not in the mountains. The mountains do not contain God in some special measure or bring God any closer than anything else. This is why the psalmist continues on to get his perspective right: "My help comes from the Lord, maker of heaven and earth."

We may head for the hills in our times of need, but the hills do not produce God or God's help for us. To head for the hills may be for a get-away time, to find beauty and such, but it alone does not give us God.

Rather, God is to be found in the mystery of the interaction that takes place between the God who made all things and the receptive inner life of a person, wherever he or she may be.

Labor

Monday is Labor Day. To many it is a free day, open for relaxation, hot dogs and other such symbols of time off from work. Perhaps some will remember that the day was first celebrated in 1882 in New York and that following the deaths of 13 workers during the historic Pullman Strike in 1894, President Grover Cleveland made reconciliation with the labor movement a top political priority, and Labor Day became a federal holiday in that year. As such, its origins are in the labor movement toward unionizing and collective bargaining for worker's rights and amenities. As such, it is a remembrance of the collective decision made in our land that labor relations and rights are a vital part of creating a fair and safe workplace for all workers. Sounds like an important day of remembrance to me.

Most of us have worked in some fashion since we were adolescents. In order to have money to purchase both the necessities and the extras of growing up, young people have worked. Of course, that became a prelude to the necessity of work for our adult lives. Fewer and fewer adults in our society don't have some kind of paying job. Indeed, it takes two incomes generally for middle-class life to succeed in our land. Work is necessary, it is toll-taking, it is creative, and it is here to stay. Very few will reach a position where their labor is not necessary for living or for securing their future.

The Bible has a whole lot to say about work and workers. The usual words found in the Bible are "labor" and "laborers." In studying the ancient world one can discover a great contrast between the Greek (and Roman) and the Hebrew (and Christian) attitudes toward work. To the Greeks work was something to be left to slaves or mechanics (I'm afraid that attitude persists among some today). Aristotle's Perfect Man will not soil his hands with it. It has been suggested that this attitude towards manual labor is one of the reasons why the Greeks made little progress in natural science as contrasted with their achievement in philosophy or mathematics. The Hebrews, on the other hand, regarded work as a divine command from which no person was exempted. To be created by God was to be placed in the world of labor. However, that purpose was tempered by the requirement also to rest. Thus, it is written in the Ten Commandments "Six days shall you labor, and do all your work" (Exodus 20:9). In 1 Samuel 11:5, King Saul plows a field in order to enhance his royal dignity – work becomes being human, even for kings! The idle rich were frowned upon in the Bible. Among the Jews, even rabbis were to work as a sign of the dignity of worthy labor. Paul, the Christian missionary, carried this tradition forward as a tentmaker who earned his way while on his missionary journeys.

Sometimes we hear that work is a curse placed upon humankind because of sin. Indeed, the expulsion from the Garden in Genesis and the subsequent work for the man and the woman are conceived by some as pointing to work as a curse for sin. This is a distortion. Work is a divine ordinance for humankind throughout the Bible even apart from disobedience. In the earliest chapters of Genesis, the creation of the man and the woman was to "replenish the earth and subdue it and have dominion over all living things."(Gen. 1:28). They are placed in the Garden to "till it and keep it." In Psalm 104:19-23, work is the normal, natural and healthy routine of human living; it is obvious and regular an activity as that the sun should rise or that lions should hunt: "People go out to their work and to their labor until the evening."

Thus, the Biblical point of view is that labor as such is neither a curse nor a punishment but is an integral part of God's original intention in the creation of the world. Nevertheless, like every other aspect of human existence, it has fallen under the curse which is the consequence of human sin. Perhaps that's why there is such disparity in earning ability, wages, working conditions, benefits, and satisfaction. While work is necessary and wholesome for humanity, provided for us by our God, it is nevertheless not the whole of it. Nor is it our most important endeavor. As the Westminster Catechism puts it, "The chief end of humankind is to enjoy God and to serve God forever. This means at work and at rest.

Sorrow

I can think of a number of words that immediately evoke feelings in me upon hearing them. I get a peaceful feeling when something is described as *lovely*. There's a bit of cringe that comes over me when something is described as *cruel*. The term *shudder* makes be draw back a little in my mind, while the word *ecstatic* seems to prepare me inwardly to dance. I suppose everyone has words which trigger various emotions or thoughts unbidden except for the very words themselves. One such word for me as I write today is *sorrow*. To me, the word feels heavy, like a weight on my mind.

Saturday, September 11, marks the 20th anniversary of the terrorist attack on our country by their flying planes into the Twin Towers at the World Trade Center in New York City as well as into the Pentagon in Washington. A fourth plane crashed in the Pennsylvania countryside due to a takeover of the plane at the last moments by valiant passengers, thus keeping the U.S. Capital safe. Altogether, 2,997 citizens were killed while 19 hijackers committed murder-suicide. The term "9/11" produces a sense of profound sorrow in most of us and has for these last twenty years.

Sorrow is a feeling of deep distress caused by loss, disappointment, or other misfortune suffered by oneself or others. As such, it is an emotion, feeling, or sentiment. As one writer has put it, sorrow "is more intense than sadness. . . it implies a long-term state. At the same time 'sorrow – but not unhappiness - suggests a degree of resignation which lends sorrow its peculiar air of dignity."

That air of dignity which accompanies sorrow is what marks the loss as very significant in one's experience. The losses of 9/11 have gained in dignity as the nation pulled together, as the accounts of extreme heroism came out of the rubble, and as the massive response by so many to help, to heal, and to work for things hopeful streamed forth – even to this day. Adrian Rogers has a little rhyme that captures that sense of dignity borne by such sorrow:

> *I walked a mile with pleasure, she chatted all the way*
> *but left me none the wiser with all she had to say.*
> *I walked with sorrow, and not a word said she,*
> *but oh the things I learned from her when sorrow walked with me.*

There's a lot about *sorrow* in the Bible. The primary term used for it in the Old Testament is found fourteen times in Genesis, Psalms, Isaiah, Jeremiah, Ezekiel, and Esther. The word is typically associated with death, exile, or being attacked by an enemy. Sorrow is the opposite of happiness and is thought to be something that others, either human or divine, imposes upon a person or group. It can be a punishment imposed by God (Ezekiel 23:33). Life can be lived in sorrow (Jeremiah 20:18). It can be experienced empathically because of how others are treated (Jeremiah 8:18). Death can be experienced in sorrow though this is undesirable and not necessary. Sorrow can be remedied and God is known to turn sorrow into happiness (Jeremiah 31:13). In the Psalms appeals are made to God to deliver people from sorrow (Psalm 31:9-10) because it is believed that God can and will do so. Also in the Psalms, sorrow is experienced when one is suffering knowing that God can bring relief but does not (Psalm 13:2). In the New Testament, John 16:6 and Romans 9:2 provide the location of sorrow, which is given as the heart. In John 16:6, Jesus causes sorrow in the hearts of his followers by telling them that they will suffer in the future. In Romans, Paul speaks about the sorrow in his own heart. In 2 Corinthians 2:7 forgiveness is mandated so that an erring person is not overwhelmed by sorrow.

Many today are filled with sorrow at the hundreds of thousands deaths that have taken place due to the Covid pandemic. Sometimes loved ones left behind have had to work very hard to keep their sorrow from turning into anger – anger at the one who died for not being vaccinated, anger at the society for not doing more to protect our citizens, anger at those who continue to promote falsehoods and misinformation about the pandemic and the remedies we have at hand.

Today there are numerous areas of life that are producing sorrow among us beyond the pandemic and its issues. Worries about climate change produce sorrow in the feelings of helplessness many have in the face of the massive destruction brought on by extreme weather, colossal forest fires, and the diminishing natural world. The political world we live in produces sorrow when it seems that we just can't get to solutions and answers needed. Some are sorrowful over social issues which impact life – gender roles, marriage issues, and the continuing issues pertaining to parenthood and childbirth. The burdens attached to this little word, *sorrow,* weigh heavily on so many.

Though accused by non-believers as being pollyannish, Christian folk know what to do with the burdens brought on by our sorrows. We vitalize (make alive) our walk with our God as made known to us through our Lord, Jesus Christ. When Isaiah prophesied that the suffering servant would "bear our infirmities" and that by "his bruises we are healed," (Isaiah 53) he wasn't whistling in the wind. He was reminding us of God's offer through his Son to bear our burdens with us. On this basis, Christians have learned to sense hope in all things. It is such that in faith, sorrows lead us with hearts joined with our Lord into avenues of hope and, thus, into renewed life beyond the sorrows we bear. We are living beyond 9/11 now. We shall be living beyond this pandemic. And we shall adapt and live in the face of the changes in our climate and culture. Such hope gives true dignity to our sorrow.

Laughter

There's actor Ed Wynn bouncing off the ceiling as he is convulsed in laughter. As he began to laugh he also began to rise up (floating) until he reaches the ceiling where he remained for as long as he laughed. Watching and listening to him laugh away cannot fail to draw forth one's own laughter. That scene from the movie, <u>Mary Poppins,</u> is indicative of what *laughter* can do for a person. It can literally make one "rise up" from whatever mental or emotional state one is in. We even use the expression, "He's bouncing off the walls" to indicate the effect of laughter in charging the atmosphere with a hefty amount of the stuff. And laughter has a cleansing effect as well. An old Jewish proverb puts it like this: "As soap is to the body, so laughter is to the soul." The Irish poets have many blessings for the important occasions in life, most of them including laughter, seeing laughter as a true blessing for one's day and one's life.

> *May love and laughter light your days, and warm your heart and home.*
> *May good and faithful friends be yours, wherever you may roam.*
> *May peace and plenty bless your world with joy that long endures.*
> *May all life's passing seasons bring the best to you and yours.*

It is interesting that in addition to enabling one to "rise up" from whatever state one might be in, laughter is seen as providing "light" for the day and "warmth" for the heart. Pretty good stuff, this laughter! So good, that hundreds of writers advocate "laughter as the best medicine:"

> *Take time to laugh. It is the music of the soul.*
> *Take time to think. It is the source of power.*
> *Take time to play. It is the source of perpetual youth.*
> *Take time to read. It is the greatest power on earth.*
> *Take time to love and be loved. It is a God-given privileged.*
> *Take time to be friendly. It is the road to happiness.*
> *Take time to give. It is too short a day to be selfish.*
> *Take time to work. It is the price of success.* (Anonymous)

And chief among these is laughter!

In thinking about laughter, how we use the term, and what comes to mind when the term is used, it would be easy to conclude that laughter is solely a state of amusement. While there is much amusement in the use of the term, the meaning of laughter is much broader than that. In the Bible, for instance, laughter denotes amusement only some of the time in its use. The ancient world viewed life and reality differently that we do today, and the Bible reflects a more Eastern view of life than it does a Western view. Most of the uses of *laughter* in the Bible are unpleasant. Though the writer of Ecclesiastes does admit that there is "a time for laughter" (3:4), he frowns upon it (2:3; 7:3). Some of the Psalms denote joy (and laughter) at good fortune (cf. Psalm 126:2), but more frequently Biblical writers use *laughter* to denote surprised incredulity (Genesis 17:17; 18:12; 21: 6) as when Abraham and Sarah laugh in disbelief when told they would have a child in their old age. Some of the Psalms and Prophets speak of scornful laughter and derision of the wicked or the enemies of Israel who make fun of Israel's one God and the emphasis on living by the Law. In a list of blessings and woes found in the Gospel of Luke, we hear Jesus say, "Woe to you who are full now, for you will be hungry. Woe to you who are laughing now, for you will mourn and weep (6:25)." This is not laughing in amusement, but laughing foolishly as they continue in folly. The opposite of that is found in vs.

21 where he states, "Blessed are you who weep now, for you will laugh," indicating that life in God's Kingdom transforms weeping in new life, something well worth laughing about. Using anthropomorphisms (describing God in human images), God is sometimes characterized in the Bible as "laughing" at wicked or the proud, not in amusement, but with a kind of righteous scorn (as in Psalm 2:4 – "He who sits in the heavens laughs; for the Lord has them in derision" – the wicked, that is. In the Bible, unbelief, pride, blasphemy and irreligion are objects of ridicule because they are so patently things which only a fool would consider.

So, there are different kinds of laughter. It seems that the laughter of scorn is well-practiced in our time. It is used to put away what one doesn't understand or like. However, such scornful laughter surely does little to help one rise up amid the circumstances of life. Nor does derision or scorn offer any sort of cleansing effect or give anyone a blessing. God's people are invited into the kind of laughter which can celebrate God's good gifts and God's good ways which lie at the heart of the life of the faithful. Just maybe one can reach the ceiling with that kind of laughter.

All In The Same Boat

Our family home was in a small town (Dunedin) on the west coast of Florida. We lived a block from the bayfront (St. Joseph's Sound/Clearwater Harbor) where we kept our boats (one sailing and one motor). Among the members of our large family there are a number of stories about times when sailing various ones were caught in squaws, had equipment failures, ran aground, or became becalmed. While each of those stories had its own points, high and low, they all had one thing in common: whoever was there on any of those boat excursions were "all in the same boat." If we ran aground, we ran aground together. If we were caught in a lightning storm, we were all caught together. If we were becalmed, we were becalmed together. Stories abound throughout nautical history of groups of people who faced threatening circumstances together all the way from my own local sailing stories to the terrible tragedy of the sinking of the Titanic.

There are numerous accounts in the Bible of similar "all in the same boat" incidents, some metaphorical and some historical. One can remember Paul on his fourth missionary journey, the one where he is a prisoner of the Romans, being shipwrecked on the island of Malta in the Mediterranean Sea. He and the two hundred seventy-six people on board of this merchant and prisoner ship all faced storms, being grounded on a reef, the breaking apart of their ship, and the desperate swim to shore in common. Literally they had all "been in the same boat" (Acts 27). The same can be said for Jesus and his disciples in that famous account in Mark 4 where they were crossing the Sea of Galilee to get to the other side and away from the crowds when a great storm blew up seriously threatening to swamp the boat. Jesus, one might remember, was asleep in the stern until awakened by his frightened disciples. They were all in the same boat to be sure, even in the calm that came after Jesus' command, "Peace! Be still!" Here we get a vision of all of us in this same boat of life being there with our Lord, the Lord of the wind and waves of life.

The expression, "all in the same boat" alludes to the risks shared by all those present in a small boat at sea. It dates from the time of the ancient Greeks and has been used figuratively for many centuries. One uses the phrase to indicate that one and one's companions or contemporaries are experiencing the same conditions or taking part in the same situation. Zac Brown's lyrics capture the expression in verse:

> We're all in the same boat
> Fishing in the same hole
> Wondering where the same time goes
> And money too
> Tryna fix the same broke hearts

Wishing on the same stars
We're all hoping hope floats
And we're all in the same boat.

There's little doubt but that we are all in the same boat in numerous circumstances. One might mention the Covid-19 pandemic, traversing the whole world, rendering all vulnerable to one degree or another. Interestingly, some cannot accept the sense that we're all in this together, much to the detriment of us all. The same might be said for the reality of climate change and its effect on weather, wind and wave. It affects us all in one way or another. Here again, denial of this as a common reality affecting all of us in the boat, is giving rise to more struggle and fear in the boat. One could say similar things about a whole host of other issues that affect us all. Perhaps the reality of racism, the downplaying of rational thought, and the continuing propensity for sin could be other examples of us all being in the same boat.

Christians have long known that the propensity for sin, for self-preservation in its many forms, has always been a kind of denial that we're all in the same boat and that what is continually needed are means for helping us all as we drift along. It is at this point of realization that one can hear the eternal command of our Lord for peace among us in the boat as well as his provision for us in enlightening our minds, claiming our hearts, and expanding our vision and hopes in order to give us hope for the day and insight into how to address the tomorrows of our common journey in the sea of life. There is more than fear in this boat, thank God! - Pastor Rich

Trouble

Among the more memorable words which come to us from Jesus are the words found in the 14th chapter of the Gospel of John: *"Let not your hearts be troubled, believe in God, believe also in me."* These words are often the words heard at funerals for they can draw us into another way of viewing things when the time of death arrives. They can also draw us that way when any pain troubles us. They were first spoken long ago to Jesus' disciples and friends on the eve of his arrest and crucifixion. While the disciples did not yet know what was in store for Jesus, nevertheless the moment was a moment of parting, of that they knew. So, their hearts were troubled.

How many echoes of the reality of troubles and troubled lives in our time can we name, comes the question? And the answer is the echoes which reverberate all around us. Many today can sing, *"Nobody knows the trouble I've seen...."* The Christian focus doesn't stop there, however. *"In the world you will have trouble, but take heart! I have overcome the world,"* Jesus tells his disciples in John 16.

And to add to his admonition that their hearts not be troubled, Jesus told them that there were other troubles ahead of them. The bright and light-filled days of his ministry among the people were over. Something ominous was at hand. They felt it intuitively. Their small world was shaking into pieces; ahead lay change. And that change was seen as darkness rather than light. They were certainly right. A time of trouble was at hand. And in so many ways, it has ever been so since. *"Let not your hearts be troubled."* Sounds a little simple, doesn't it? Surely, if we could help it, none of us would let our hearts be troubled ever. The problem is that we cannot stop our hearts from being troubled, for troubles abound in each and every life at one time or another.

It occurs to me that there are two things to be said concerning Jesus' words to his disciples. The first is that he was in as deep as they, deeper as a matter of fact. Whatever black cloud hovered overhead would break upon his head as well as upon theirs. In fact, he would be at the center of it.

Secondly, the advice that he gave, *"Let not your hearts be troubled,"* was not just a cheery word of positive thinking left hanging in the air like the common phrase, "Have a good day!" It was not a chin-up, carry on, give it the old college try, kind of encouragement. One has to take the whole thing in its context. *"Let not your hearts be troubled,"* he said, and immediately following upon that was the basis for saying it: *"Believe in God, believe in me."* His invitation not to fear was tied to what they already knew, what they had experienced in those months together with him. He was not just saying, *"Don't worry, boys! Everything will turn out all right."* He was reminding them of a life of commitment to God and God's ways through him. He was saying, *"Don't collapse now, for Heaven's sake. Because you know from the past you've reason not to. Remember God. Remember me. Remember that I have shown you the way, the truth, and the life."* William Barclay translates it: **"Don't let your hearts be distressed; keep on believing in God and keep on believing in me."** Jesus, then, is setting the handling of this time of trouble in the context of a whole lifetime of faith, and said in effect, *"Keep it there; that's where it belongs."*

This is can be a real problem can't it? Sometimes Christian folks fail to see the continuity of life. One wants to fragment it, to separate it into segments and divisions. One doesn't just believe once and be done with it. One doesn't just believe when the crises come. Jesus is reminding them that the God of the sunny hills of Galilee was the God of the dark upper room on the city street in Jerusalem, that the God of the flowers and the springtime was still God amid the winter snows. The God who walked with them and filled their hearts in the time of health and happiness was also the God of the time of pandemic, economic and political unrest, and great stress.

What he said and taught and lived out was far more than any intuitive reflex or any faint hope. What he said and taught and lived-out grew from a full-orbed life and a total way of being which had its source in the indwelling of God's Spirit in his life.

Dietrich Bonhoeffer wrote once, *"No one's life flows on such an even course that it does not sometimes come up against a dam and whirl round and round, or somebody throws a stone into the clear water. Something happens to everyone - and he must take care that the water stays clear and that heaven and earth are reflected into it' - when you've said that, you've really said everything."*

Thus, Jesus' way of handling trouble revolves around the evident inner awareness that God was not just to be called upon at the last minute, summoned for a deathbed scene, as it were.

George MacDonald, a great Scots preacher and novelist of the 1800's, had a long struggle with poverty, ill health, and bitter grief. He wrote on one occasion toward the end of it, *"My heart withers. Health, my means to live, all things seem to be rushing straight into the dark. But the dark still is God. Am I not a spark of him who is the Light?"* That's a great sentence when one thinks of it. *"The dark is still God."* This is no frenzied last-minute faith. MacDonald could say it because of a lifetime of experience with God. Thus, the faith and trust one nurtures throughout one's days becomes the vehicle for assurance and God's peace for the troubled heart in troubled times.

On Giants and Grasshoppers

Recently I got to thinking about the Bible stories I had heard and learned as I was growing up. Not only did I hear many of the more familiar ones about Moses and Abraham and Jacob and Joseph in my Sunday School classes, but in those days when one could promote religion in public schools, I had a teacher for both first and third grade (same teacher) who started each day's class with stories from the Bible. She made them come alive and today I can still see the same pictures of them that I had in my mind while I was little. The stories had quite an impact on me.

I have never forgotten the little tale of Joshua sending out spies into the Promised Land to see what was there before the Children of Israel, fresh out of forty years wandering in the wilderness, would venture forth into that new land. The story can be found in Numbers 13.

According to this account, Moses selected twelve men and sent them to spy out the land of Canaan and to report their findings to him and the people. And so, they went. They snuck through the whole land, noting with joy how fertile it was and how pleasant for living. Yet they encountered many other tribes living there including the sons of Anak, a legendary people who were related to the Nephilim, giants of an older time who seemed to grow bigger in the passing down of tales about them. The point is that these spies saw the inhabitants as giants, terrifying to the diminutive Hebrews (average height about five feet).

As one might surmise, when the spies returned to Moses they told what they had seen and ten of the twelve spies were ready to abandon their plans to enter the Promised Land right then and there. However, there were two spies, Joshua (of "fought the battle of Jericho" fame) and Caleb who saw it differently, saying to Moses and the people that they could enter the land and settle there despite the Anak.

The ten cowering spies had said: "We were no bigger than grasshoppers." They were afraid and the reality of that situation looked impossible to them. Their cries were countered by what Caleb and Joshua reported: "The land, which we passed through to spy out, is an exceedingly good land. If the Lord delights in us, he will bring us into this land and give it to us . . . do not fear the people of the land, for they are bread for us; their protection is removed from them, and the Lord is with us; do not fear them!"

How often, as we spy out the land around us, the world, the time, that is set before us, have God's people seen the giants and felt like grasshoppers, figuratively speaking? It's a question worth pondering in a time where the pandemic, the results of climate change, the unrest throughout the world, the mass movements of people seeking a better or more secure life, as well as the battles raging over truth versus conspiracy theories, the issues of the unborn, and the issues regarding the real inclusion of the various ethnic groups around us into our society, loom as giants before us.

In the Biblical story, sad to say, the people listened to the ten spies rather than Joshua and Caleb. They had spent forty years wandering the wilderness for those fears, for they were much afflicted with the "grasshopper complex." The revelation found in this ancient story is very much apropos for our age – that there are always what appear to be giants out there, that there are always things to fear. Indeed, in every age there are those who exploit the fears for their own gain – like political power or financial power. But as God's people have learned over and again throughout history, the future and its benefits lies with the Calebs and the Joshuas rather than with those who see themselves as grasshoppers and huddle down in enclaves of ignorance and distortion, resisting truth and the kind of forward-looking living that has marked God's folks throughout time.

At the heart of this issue of viewing the forces of our time as giants and ourselves as grasshoppers, helpless in the face of the force of power, is the question of truth. And if there is anything present within our grasp today to help us see the truth, trust the truth, and decide based on truth, it is the life we may have in our journey with our Lord Jesus Christ. When power is used to mask care for the planet, care for others, care for the marginalized, and care for fancy rather than fact, submitting oneself to the leadership of Jesus and his ways, can show us truthfully that those "giants" out there are truly the grasshoppers, and that we can live forward without fear of their having the last word.

Dreams

Dreams. We sure use the term in a number of ways; "I had a dream last night". . . "You are a dream come true". . . "I dream of the day when race and class no longer divide us into mistrustful tribes". . . "Joseph had a dream and an angel of the Lord spoke to him". . . "Life is about fulfilling your dreams." There are waking dreams which shower forth from our imaginations and there are sleeping dreams which tell stories or show events which entertain us but just don't fit right into the order of things. It's a wonderful term which can be employed in many useful and some imaginative ways.

In the Bible, as in the history of religions in general, dreams sometimes served as scenes of what is called "theophany" – a revelation from God. Great pains must be taken to distinguish those dreams which may bear God's word to one from those which are deceitful or represent the wiles of evil forces. This was true in the ancient world as well as now. Unfortunately, many dreams are so ambiguous that one can be enticed into interpretations fraught with evil. Perhaps that is the weakness of current conspiracy theories. What are they but someone's dreams which in reality are fraught with evil meaning and intent. In the ancient world, such dreams needed interpretation lest they steer the people wrongly. But the process was so imprecise that some, like the prophet Jeremiah, rejected dreaming altogether as a source of revelation from God. Nevertheless, there is a tradition in the Bible of selected persons (e.g. Joseph – both Joseph, Jacob's son, and Joseph, Mary's husband, and Daniel) who had the ability to interpret certain dreams that reveal God's intent. Those days appear to be gone.

We don't do such dream interpretation much today. The recognition is widespread that dreams are too reflective of one's psyche and experience rather than a foretaste of what is to come. Psychiatrists and other specialists can use dreams as gateways into a person's inner self in order to help one deal with inner conflict and pain.

Nonetheless, the term "dream" is a magnificent term when it denotes hopes, plans, schemes, projects, visions, and guiding lights. Where would one be without a picture in one's mind (and heart) of where one was going? What would happen to us if there was no vision? We find that thought echoed in the Proverbs (29:18) – "Where there is no vision, the people perish. . . ." And it is true. If one does not have any thought about where one is going, one will probably end up someplace else. We are guided by our visions, by our dreams.

On a personal level, we surely are a dreaming people, trying to figure out the next move in whatever current direction our lives are traveling. Most of us have short-term goals or dreams, making new ones as time moves on. And some of us have pictures (visions) of our lives that guide those short-term goals. I wonder how each of us would describe our dreams for our lives?

Does God have dreams for us? It would most certainly seem so if the insights found in the Scriptures are true (and they are).

There appear to be three aspects to God's dream for his creation and especially for his creatures. These aspects of God's dream are found all over the Scriptures. Each one is envisioned as vital for our lives and for the earth itself.

First, there are those passages which focus on God and our right relationship with God. In Genesis 3 there is that classic question being asked of Cain who represents us all in hiding and avoiding God: "Where are you?" (in your attention to living with God).

Secondly, there is the question also asked of Cain with regard to his brother Abel - "Where is your brother?" (in your attention to living with others).

These two aspects of a right relationship with God are echoed over and over in Scripture. Jesus himself put it into words when challenged as to what the greatest commandment was: "You shall love the Lord your God with all your heart, with all your soul, and with all your mind. . . and your neighbor as yourself" (Matthew 22:34-40). At the heart of God's dream for his human creatures are these two vital relationships.

The third aspect of God's dream is for the earth itself. Passage after passage in the Scriptures have to do with God's care for and focus on his created order, on the earth. God's dream is for the earth to supply our needs, and for it to do so bountifully. I found that the term "earth" is used 886 times in the Bible. No small subject! Let's let the Psalmist tell us how God's dream includes the earth: (Psalm 104; vss. 24-30):

"O Lord, how manifold are thy works! In wisdom hast thou made them all; the earth is full of thy creatures.

Yonder is the sea, great and wide, which teems with things innumerable, living things both small and great.

These all look to thee to give them their food in due season. When thou givest to them, they gather it up; when thou openest thy hand, they are filled with good things.

When thou hidest thy face, they are dismayed; when thou takest away their breath, they die and return to their dust.

When thou sendest forth thy Spirit, they are created; and thou renewest the face of the ground."

In other words, the earth is the Lord's and all that is within it. It is made for him and he has placed us in his earth to be a part of it. There is great celebration over the creation throughout the Bible. And human creatures are exhorted to exercise wise rule and tender caring over the earth and all its creatures. The earth is God's gift for us to treasure. That is part of God's dream.

Remembering

Remembering. Yes, that blessed gift of the mind wherein we transverse time and space into a kind of alternative reality with pictures, sounds, and familiar words transporting us otherward. I love to remember, though sometimes it brings sadness and even dread. Mostly, though, remembering is a comfort and adds to the sense of the ongoing-ness of a full life.

The sixtieth high school reunion, recently attended in Florida (and thus missing writing a devotional last week), was a time of remembering – remembering past experiences and events from long ago once again. And people – seeing many for the first or second time in 60 years, yet picking up in some cases where we left off, remembering how important some of them were to me and are even now. What are reunions if not a time for remembering? I also attended the 150th anniversary celebration of my home church in Dunedin while in Florida, remembering how my growing up in that congregation and later serving as Associate Minister there have contributed greatly to that room in my mind called "remember."

Here we are into November already, a month with special days of remembrance – Elections, Veterans Day, Thanksgiving – each one entailing important memories. Indeed, our calendars are marked with special days throughout the year – days for remembering. Such special days serve as reminders that people love to remember. Perhaps it can be said that one of the marks of being human is that remembering is a vital component to our lives.

It is also vital to Christians faith, remembering is. The word is found all over the Bible, forty-five times in the Psalms alone. It is the Biblical term that is most linked with the Covenants God has made with his people, first with Israel, then with humanity through the New Covenant in Jesus Christ. Indeed, without the agency of memory, there would be little to say about the content of our faith.

What is Christian faith other than remembering that we are born in God's time, nurtured through gifts God provides, gifted ourselves with talents, interests and memories galore? What is life in Christ but a movement of remembrance through his birth, ministry, journey, teachings, death and resurrection? Could there be any substance to the Christ who journeys with us throughout life without remembering the Christ who was? It is in that remembrance that the One who was becomes for us the One who is among us as Lord.

The word [remembering] often occurs in the Old Testament in laments crying out to God to remember them (Psalm 25:7), and also in gratitude that God has remembered them (Psalm 78:39). In Isaiah, the prophet speaks of both remembering and not remembering, putting emphasis on awaiting the new things God will do rather than focusing on the past (not remembering) and at the same time anticipating in faith and hope because of their remembering God's faithfulness in the past (cf. Isaiah 43:14-21 and 46:8-11).

In the New Testament, proclaiming the significance of Jesus through story and reflection depends upon remembering the Covenants God has made with Israel in the Old Testament. Mary sings to God "in remembrance of his mercy, "and Zechariah states that God "has remembered his holy covenant" (Luke 1:72). The followers of Jesus remember his words (Luke 24:6-8; Acts 20:35) and the things prophesied about him (John 12:16). Remembering becomes the basis of the tradition "handed down" (1 Corinthians 11:2).

"The uses of the word *remember* in both the Old Testament and the New Testament suggest that remembering is about more than the mind; remembering is about covenant and requires response. In the Old Testament, the instructions for observing the Passover state: "Remember this day on which you came out of Egypt" (Exodus 13:3); "This day shall be a day of remembrance for you" (12:14). Luke 22:19 and 1 Corinthians 11:24-25 describe the purpose of the Lord's Supper as a remembrance of Jesus and his new covenant: "Do this in remembrance of me." Remembering is depicted not simply as a "bringing to mind," but as an active, participatory event, in which God and people somehow mysteriously interact." [The Interpreter's Dictionary of the Bible, Vol. 4, p. 761]

To my mind, remembering is also an important element of prayer. We don't pray to a vague idea. Rather, we pray to One who has made himself known to humanity and to us in the midst of history and our lives. We remember who God is and what God has done. As we join God in that memory, especially as we join him in the Jesus story, we can draw those memories forward into our lives as pictures and intimations of God's will for us today. Perhaps remembering in faith is one of the most important things we can do.

Thanksgiving (2)

There is one job that Christianity hopes to help each person do well - and that is to see more deeply into life than to what happens on the surface. When one sees a child, one may see more than an offspring or a noisy imp. One may see God's child - a person, learning, growing, and trying out life, and pointing to the potential that is ever present.

When one sees a birth, one may see more than a biological event. God's miracle of life may be seen before one's very eyes. When one sees a death, one may see more than a dead body and a tragic event. There to see is also hope, a miracle of God, caught up in the mystery and gift of resurrection. When one sees the church, there is much more to see than committees and duties and budgets. There in the midst of ordinary things one might see a community of imperfect people, caught up in the process of sharing life, love, hope and service together, bound in their worship of God. And when believers talk of Jesus, they are talking about much more than a superior man who lived long ago, dazzling folks with his words and power. No, there to be seen in story and word is God with us, beckoning one to live with him and through him.

Now is the time of thanksgiving in our land – a time to pause and reflect on how we see life and its many assets. And to talk about Thanksgiving is to go beyond the surface as well. I'm sure folks could talk about all the things, the gifts and gadgets, the goodies which surround us and which we're glad to have. That's what our children often think they're to do - be thankful for the stuff. I guess we have to do that some, so that they get a good start on learning how to deal with each other. But when we deal with thanksgiving, it appears that one diminishes it if one never gets beyond the goodies.

The Bible, our frame of reference for dealing with life with God, is filled from beginning to end with an interlocking of a sense of the graciousness of living and the response of gratitude. It appears that this interlocking may be difficult for some to grasp - which is why the Bible might be hard for some people to deal with. But Biblical folks, those often-ordinary people of the Bible, for the most part, were able to see beyond the ordinary for something which held true despite the vagaries of existence, something which was true no matter the challenges and changes.

They sensed that under the surface there was a "givenness" to life - a sense that there were gifts given to us that remained in spite of struggle, in spite of war or suffering or death.

The natural world pointed them to this givenness. No matter what happened, the rhythms of the seasons, the beauty of the day, the laws which governed life and death, and the sheer miracle of rebirth year after year shouted that something is behind it providing for its operation and scope.

Human relationships pointed to is as well. Watch the children and one can tell that there is a sense in them that life is a gift joyfully expected and received, bringing delight to their eyes. The taste of close ties in families which stand together, the sense of loyalty, tradition, pride and love which comes with dependable life together is felt to be provided rather than earned in life. The fierce joy of close friendships, the overwhelming warmth of love and marriage, the pride of community, the strong sense of identity which comes with belonging - all of it points to the givenness which is built into life. Biblical folks wrote about this, prayed about this, and sought to live in its light. And as the Biblical person sensed the movement of history in positive ways, even in the face of evil and setbacks, and as he or she tasted the deep "givens" of life that were neither earned or deserved, there grew up among God's people this awareness of life as a gift, an act of grace, and they called it the graciousness of life.

Small wonder, then, when Israel was delivered from the Egyptians she saw this as a part of the gift of life, of graciousness. Small wonder that she was able to praise God throughout her tumultuous history as though there was always more to see that met the eye.

But she didn't stop there. She went on and recognized that this graciousness wasn't just a philosophical interpretation of life, offered as a balm to ease whatever pain was there, that it came from somewhere – that it came from someone - that God was the giver, that the God they were learning to trust was a gracious God! And no one else had ever known that before.

So it was no wonder when some men and women, taught and loved by a wandering Rabbi named Jesus, saw in his teachings and in his life this same deeper consciousness of living - this graciousness of life in spite of all its troubles, that they adopted this stance for themselves. So, they followed him. And later, when they saw him die for his stance on life, and experienced the wonder of his resurrection, God's overthrow of death through him, they knew that this deeper level of life was true - that it was no illusion. They became people of the gift - people shaped by God's graciousness through Jesus Christ.

Indeed, at the center of their growing faith stood the sense of the gifts of life. God revealed in Jesus that he loves humanity deeply, that he doesn't hold our sins irreconcilably against us, that he desires our fellowship each day, that he shows us the key to gracious living in the teachings of Jesus, and that life on this deeper level can indeed be abundant, even in a badly broken and scarred world.

The Biblical person sensed life on a deeper, a gracious level. It has ever been the stance on life for believers.

And thanksgiving is therefore not a duty because one ought to be thankful. It is what one does when one has sensed this gracious level of life. It's the response to life which blesses those who hold it dear.

As one Christian has put it, faith in God is not simply belief in God, or in the existence of God. It is a "bringing together into one great motivating power for living, the interlocking of grace and gratitude - of gift and thanksgiving."

Bread

Come To Bethlehem and Be Nourished

On Sunday next the Christian world begins its yearly cycle marking the year with seasons denoting the basic story of God's work in coming among us in Jesus Christ. The first Sunday of Advent this year is November 28 and for the four weeks following, the Advent theme of Christ's coming into our world for our sake will be celebrated throughout the Christian world. Advent means *coming* and the celebration of Advent marks the fact that he *has* come, that he *is coming*, and that he *will come again*. Of course, we are talking in both an historical and a metaphorical sense here. For Christians, Jesus Christ and his life and ministry is an historical fact. And he is also revealed to us as God with us (Immanuel) in that we have and do sense in him God's presence and truth with us now. To complete our understanding of him and his promises to us, we are encouraged to trust that in God's good time, Christ will return when God completes his Kingdom in full. So perhaps it should be stressed that the Advent time for believers is a time to remember that Jesus was among us in real time, that we can accept him again and again in our personal time, and that whatever else lies in the distant future, that the story ends with Christ's return in the creation of a new heaven and a new earth. Just as the beginning of the drama of the universe begins with God, so it ends with God as well.

One way of thinking about Christ's coming, past, present, and future, is to think about the nourishment that life in Christ, life with Christ, provides. Such nourishment leads us to one of the richest symbols of Christ's coming among us - the symbol of *bread*. BREAD – you know, the stuff we almost don't think about but count on being present at most meals. Indeed, bread is such a common food that we often fail to marvel at it – unless, of course, you've come in after a long day and you're so famished that boiled fish-scales sound tempting. And then you sit at the table where hot fresh rolls have been placed before you, and bread becomes an instant marvel, an answer to prayers, the focus of attention, an almost living reality wafting into your senses and declaring itself to be the very staff of life that it's cracked up to be. And it has been this way since before recorded history. Bread – better than chocolate, better than deviled eggs, better than steak, chief among the finest things of life!

It's quite understandable, therefore, that something as important and as common as bread would be talked about in the common languages of the world not only in a literal sense, but in a metaphorical sense too. As the staff of life, bread can symbolize many other forms of life's essentials as well.

In the Lord's Prayer Jesus teaches us to pray, "Give us this day the bread for tomorrow" - that's the literal translation - bread enough for one day at a time.

Yet the bread being prayed for here is far more than simply the hot rolls used to assuage the famished stomach. The richness of the whole Biblical story is found in this simple term - *bread* – which, of course, has several levels of meaning.

One meaning, of course, is that bread means bread - that cooked grain which gives butter most of its reason to be. But as a word for this basic food, it stands as a word which points to all those things one needs to survive in this world - food, shelter, love, security, and warmth, those elements which nourish us in life and for life. *Bread* is a word for the necessities of life. It is important to point out that all through the Scriptures we see vivid scenes which let us know that God is very concerned with these small things, the physical things that give life its stability. Jesus says to pray for the bread one will need for the next day. And by doing so one will first of all be acknowledging what some people have such a hard time admitting to themselves or to others - that humans are dependent creatures, limited in so many ways. Without a very well-balanced natural world which can depended upon. humankind will perish - for humans are far more the users of what has been provided in this world than they are the creators who can cast off dependence upon food or warmth or the creation which provides them at will.

To pray for daily bread is to say there are limits to what we can do for ourselves - and thus, this prayer is a way to keep us from the sin of pride which assumes that we are the complete masters of all things human and earthly. That's the first level of our understanding about bread: to pray for the things we need for life because we know that we have little to do with their being given. Come, Lord Jesus, and show us again our dependence upon God's provision for life together and nourish us for our journey with you.

Yet, even as we admit that food is essentially provided, that we are not the creator of the stuff by which folks live, we are drawn into the awareness that it is in the ordinary things of life that one can discern the presence of God, every bit as much as in the great events and experiences. To pray for daily bread says something about the way we see God.

Do you remember the Old Testament picture of the children of Israel wandering through the wilderness for a generation prior to their coming into the promised land? What did they eat? You remember. They ate manna, sent by God himself, and each day they gathered enough for the day to come. This, of course, is the way the Bible tries to say that in spite of our work, our skill, our abilities, our cleverness, that all things come from God. God's providence can be seen in all that is left here for our use. All things show his handiwork.

To pray for daily bread is to ask for a sense of the givenness of life and a sense of the one who gives it in all things. It is an important dimension, for it enables us to gain insight each new day into the God who stands behind our bread, our families, our lives, and this very world and all that is in it. It is the key dimension which separates those who sense the nearness of God from those who don't. It is what God promises to provide for those who trust him - who seek to live in fellowship with him. Remember Jesus' words:

> *"Ask, and it will be given to you; seek, and you will find; knock, and it will be opened to you. For every one who asks receives, and he who seeks finds, and to him who knocks it will be opened. Or what man of you, if his son asks for bread, will give him a stone? . . . If you, then . . . know how to give good gifts to your children, how much more will your Father who is in heaven give good things to those who ask him?"*
> (Matthew 7:7-12)

Daily Bread

I have been much reminded of my high school days of late since I was recently able to take part in the 60th reunion of my high school class in Florida. One of the memories that has come to mind as I reminisced about those precious days was that of bread. Not bread as fresh rolls on Sundays, not bread as homemade biscuits hot out of the oven, and not Greek bread from the bakery in Tarpon Springs, though all three of those forms of bread were much appreciated in those days (as well as now). No, what of bread from those high school days of long ago that has come to mind is my coming home from school and raiding the bread box for the fresh loaf of Sunbeam white bread that was always there. It was one the more primitive joys of my adolescence to take seven or eight slices of that bread and eat it, feeling the soft texture of its freshness, while I read the daily newspaper. It was such a super delight that ever since, when I read any newspaper, I feel something is missing if I don't have a half a loaf of fresh bread to devour (diabetes has tempered this behavior somewhat).

The last devotional dealt with bread, one of the most common substances in the world. As such, it should come as no surprise that because of its universal need and use that the term has taken on multiple connotations both in the secular world and in the church. We spoke of bread as an apt metaphor for the necessities of life and noted that we have been encouraged by no less than Jesus himself to pray for bread, noting in doing so that God is the ultimate provider of what is needed for us to live. To pray for "daily bread" is to acknowledge that as we work and carry out our responsibilities for caring for our lives and that of others, we are drawing upon that rich provision which is both given and sustained by God. Were there no God, there would be no provision, no bread, in all its forms. Thus, to pray for daily bread is to acknowledge our God and God's provision in the midst of life.

However, a caution has been added in the Biblical narrative to our focus on bread. We are urged to remember that, like most of what has been provided for our lives, one must take care not to overdo the focus on the necessities of life. One can do that, you know.

In the New Testament we are told that Jesus himself spoke that word of caution when he said to the tempter who was trying to bait him into disobedience, that "One does not live by bread alone." And that is certainly true. That which makes a person fully human is more than food and shelter, more than physical safety, more than the physical necessities of life.

So as we ponder the petition in the Lord's Prayer which invites us to pray for our "daily bread," our horizons are broadened when we realize that in the New Testament Jesus is himself called bread. Perhaps our lives are deepened when we can see beyond the loaf before us or the real needs of daily living and can see behind them the figure of the One who can fill the inward places of our hearts and minds with purpose and joy.

In John's gospel, after Jesus fed the great crowds with the boy's five barley loaves, the crowds settled down on the mountainside and went to bed. The next morning they set out after Jesus and found him on the other side of the Sea of Galilee, and they said to him, "Rabbi, when did you come here?"

Jesus' reply was blunt and candid:

> *"Truly, I say to you, you seek me, not because you saw signs, but because you ate your fill of the loaves. Do not labor for food which perishes, but for the food which endures to life with the eternal one, which the Son of Man will give to you. For the bread of God is that which came down from heaven, and gives life to the world."*
> *They said to him, "Lord, give us this bread always." And Jesus answered: "I am the bread of life; he who comes to me shall not hunger, and he who believes **in me shall never thirst."** (John 6:22-26; 33-35)*

To pray for bread enough for the next day is to acknowledge that a cosmic event - an event that changes the whole structure of reality - has taken place in the life, death, and resurrection of Jesus Christ. It is to ask God to help us (through active faith and trust) to make this fact be a real part of our way of living and seeing. To pray for daily bread is to pray for the ability to see each new day from the perspective of what God has done in Jesus Christ. It is to receive the living Christ into our minds, into our hearts, and into our daily lives as an essential part of us. So this deeper level of understanding bread points us directly to Jesus Christ, God's bread for us that we might truly live.

Reading the newspaper with this kind of bread, brings insight, assurance, and great hope — just the kind of things the Advent of Jesus was given us to provide.

Now/Not Yet

The season of Advent underscores a "now/not yet" aspect of Christian belief, something that at first glance can seem a bit puzzling to some. Christians believe that Jesus Christ has come into this world as "God with us" (the "now" aspect); he continues to live among us as seen where faith is alive (Paul's continuing prayer was "Come, Lord Jesus." This is also the "now" aspect), but his coming is not yet complete and there is more to come (the "not yet" aspect). These are the "comings" of Christ that the Advent season points to as preparation for our celebration of Christ's birth at Christmas: Christ has come, Christ is coming where there is faith, and Christ will come again. Puzzling, perhaps, but with a certain grandeur as well.

I remember as a boy sensing the change in the atmosphere around our home when December began and the Christmas decorations went up. It was as though Christmas had already come into our home (the now aspect). But the "Day" hadn't arrived yet and there was much yearning, anticipating, counting, making lists, buying presents, doing Christmasy things, and living in vital anticipation of the Christmas that was already among us (the now aspect) and that which was still to come (the not yet aspect). While the not yet aspect was still ahead, I was living in anticipation as though it, too, were now here among us. Something like that is just the way the New Testament presents the three aspects of Christ's coming into our world and, subsequently, the three aspects of the Advent season we are celebrating in the Christian community.

We have been discussing the prayer request in the Lord's Prayer, "Give us this day our daily bread," as a way of understanding this movement of thought in this Advent time. We looked at the notion of bread being an apt symbol for the daily necessities for our lives, something God cares about for us as individuals and us as a community (the now aspect). We also looked at the notion of bread as pointing to Jesus himself as the "bread of life," providing spiritual sustenance for us on a daily basis (the now aspect). And to complete the picture, it seems apparent that we might seek to understand the daily bread we pray for as encompassing the "not yet" portion of the picture as well.

Bread in the New Testament is a word which can point to the future (the not yet aspect). There are images all through the New Testament which picture the future as a banquet at which the risen Lord is host and we are his fellow party-goers. It's something akin to the 23rd Psalm's gentle words: "The Lord is my Shepherd, I shall not want . . . He prepares a table before me . . . he anoints my head with oil. . . my cup overflows."

To pray "give us this day our daily bread" is to acknowledge that the future is ultimately in God's hands - that this is our Father's world, our Father's history, and that the direction the future is heading in is under God's control and not ours. And it is to trust God's promises, portrayed for us in the New Testament, that that which we sense now in faith will not be wasted, but will be completed and fulfilled in good time. Just as at the beginning stood the Word, and during time the Word was made flesh, so too, at the end, will be God's final word: Jesus, the bread of life.

To pray for daily bread, then, is a way of saying, "Lord, help me have the trust for tomorrow which enables me to give the events of that day to you - to see it as one more day in which your Lordship over all things, even to the end of time, is continually valid. Lord, help me to taste the bread of life which lasts."

And there you have it. To pray for daily bread is to acknowledge our limitations and dependence. It is to ask that we be enabled to see God's hand in every aspect of the new day. It is to ask that our perspective be informed by the life, death, and resurrection of Jesus Christ. And it is to ask for a day filled with hope.

All four of these insights simply and profoundly point to Jesus' statements to his followers: "Do not be anxious about the future." By taking a day at a time, knowing that God is walking into the future with us - indeed, God is out in front of us drawing believers to him each new day — we are given the ground on which we may travel and a true sense of the One who travels with us. That is the essence of the Advent of Christ. To pray for daily bread is to entrust each new day to God, trusting that God will provide for us. To pray for daily bread is not to know about the next day except, as Paul says, that in it nothing can separate us from God's purposes or God's love - "neither death, nor life, nor angels, nor principalities . . . nothing in all creation." It is to trust that in all things God is working for good with those who love him. In our time with such fear-mongering and distortions of what is true and real, daily bread such as this will see us through. May we have a happy and faithful Advent season together.

Christmas

William Shakespeare is supposed to have said, *"Oft expectation fails and most oft where it promises."* I doubt Shakespeare intended that to apply to God's promises. For God's fulfillments may be better than our expectations – certainly better than our limited human understanding of God's promises. Long centuries ago, God promised to send his Messiah. When the Messiah finally did come, he promised to come again and again. And the witness of 2100 years of Christianity is that he has come, that he does come, and that he will come.

He comes to us in times we do not expect. Jesus visits us in what seems to us the strangest places. He speaks amidst the most peculiar surroundings to those with ears to hear. He appears in the most unusual settings to those with eyes to see.

The great Russian novelist, Alexander Sozehenitsyn, describes how the baby Jesus was born anew in a location no one would expect. At the beginning of his novel, <u>The First Circle</u>, he described a Christmas celebration that took place in the bleak, barren and cold atmosphere of a Russian prison camp - a gulag. The scene was desperate and depressing. But in the midst of it is an amazing element of hope and light:

Their Christmas tree was a sprig of pine wedged into a crack in the stool. A braid of small, low voltage, colored lights on milky plastic-covered wires wound around it twice and dropped to a battery on the floor.

The stool stood in a corner of the room, between double bunks, and one of the upper mattresses shielded the whole corner and the tiny Christmas tree from the glare of the ceiling lights.

Six men in thick, dark-blue parachutists' coveralls stood together near the Christmas tree and listened, heads bowed, while one of them, swarthy, thin-faced Max Rictman, recited a Protestant Christmas prayer.

So it was with the first Christmas. The birth of Jesus happened in a place one would hardly have expected. Rather than being born in a royal setting, his birth would hardly have been noticed. As Phillips Brooks wrote in that most perfect of Christmas carols: *How silently, how silently, the wondrous gift is given.* How humbly, too! How surprisingly humble the place, the people, the gift itself.

Would you be startled if I told you the place for the birth of God's Messiah was apparently chosen by politicians! William Barclay quotes the government edict that caused Mary and Joseph to be in Bethlehem when Jesus was born:

Gaius Vivius Maximus, Prefect of Egypt orders: "Seeing that the time has come for the house to house census, it is necessary to compel all those who for any cause whatsoever are residing outside their districts to return to their own homes, that they may both carry out the regular order of the census, and may also diligently attend to the cultivation of their allotments."

Joseph and Mary were required by law to return to their own hometown for the census. Since scholars know from other sources that such censuses were taken periodically, they have calculated that Jesus was probably born in the year 6 or 4 BC. And, since the weather was such that sheep were still out in the fields, we can conclude reasonably that the birth probably occurred sometime between April and November.

Whatever the precise date, the schedule was God's. Government officials had nothing to do with that. You may have noticed that I said the politicians "apparently" determined the place of Jesus' birth. One of the commentaries comes closer to the truth when it says: *"By the decree of Augustus, the Messiah was born where God had chosen."* Bethlehem is the place prophets had been predicting for a long time. Politicians and officials may have thought they were responsible. But God did the picking. Prefects, Procurators, and Emperors were only the unwitting instruments of God's will. God did it God's way for God's own unfathomable reasons. For reasons not fully understood by us, God picked a humble, crude setting in a small backwater town.

That's the way of God, you know. In his providence God is always working his will in and through the events brought on by the choices of men and women. Modern people tied blindly to the rules of cause and effect may have a hard time with such reasoning, but it is the nature of believing hearts to recognize that cause and effect does not tell us everything about reality. If God is God indeed it is neither ignorance nor a suspension of reality to see God's hand in the common ventures of life.

And the human failures that caused the baby to be born where he was may have special significance as well. The fact that Mary, Joseph, and the baby found no room in the inn has long been appreciated as a profound symbol. Those human reasons why the Lord was born in the animal shed rather than in the sleeping portion of the inn may have particular meaning for us.

One obvious reason is that others had taken the available space. It has been imagined that the innkeeper was harried and rushed with the crowd that thronged the little town. One can imagine that he was tired and short on patience. One wonders whether this is a parable of our condition at Christmas time. How does the Lord find his people when he comes to them? How will the Lord find us this year? Will we be too tired and too much caught up in holiday frenzy to care? Is the inn of our hearts too filled and preoccupied with other "guests?" Is our encounter with this ancient account received only as nostalgia? Or can we sense here at this pivotal moment in history the extraordinary in that which is ordinary? That is the way always to receive the gifts of God, you see.

The other reason the Lord ended up being born the way he was is that nobody knew Joseph and Mary were coming. And, no one recognized their importance. Unless the innkeeper had carefully read the prophecies and been a spiritually sensitive person, he would not have known for whom or what to look. Unless he had been specifically looking, longing, and waiting for God's Messiah, he would not have any chance at all of recognizing the wondrous event he relegated to his cow pen.

Can we see the parallel? Unless we have taken the pains to be spiritually sensitive, he will probably once again be excluded from the place in our lives that ought to be reserved for such a special guest. Unless we take that bold and unscientific step of believing that God is true to his word and moving about even now in the midst of ordinary things, then we may be unaware that the Lord is knocking at the door of our hearts, seeking admission.

The fact that Jesus, the Savior, was born in Bethlehem may have been a very great surprise and totally unlike the way one might expect. But that unique event in that unusual place is the most amazing "good news" ever to fall on human ears. In the words of the angel:

Be not afraid; for behold, I bring you good news of great joy which will come to all the people; for to you is born this day in the city of David a Savior, who is Christ the Lord. And this will be a sign for you: you will find a babe wrapped in swaddling cloths and lying in a manger.

How tremendously important that fear and good news are juxtaposed in the same announcement. How exceedingly significant that the ordinary and sublime are intertwined in the birth of this child. The connection is so crucial for us to understand. Fear has to be banished before good news can be heard and responded to. I mean very specifically the baseless fear that if we allow Jesus the Lord into our lives, that he will spoil the party for us, asking more of us than we'd like.

For to receive this Christ again and again in our hearts and minds, whether we welcome him in birth, or weep for him in death, or spring forth with him in new life, is to mingle God's grace with our need in such a way that we discover his holiness and truth in the midst of our lives. Rather than diminishing us, such encounters always lift us up, transforming the ordinary into something holy.

The good news is that the Son of God seeks admission into the inns of our hearts. If he finds his place in us, he will bring more joy than we can imagine. The early poets expressed it by saying that when he comes to us, the angels will sing within.

So, today, in these days before Christmas, let us let go of any fears that will distract us from what he provides. And I urge each of us to get ready once again for God's gift – in our celebrations, in our prayers, in our homes, around our tables, to get ready to receive. Hear again amidst sight and sound the good news that our Savior and Lord has come! Let us welcome him. Enjoy him. Seek him. Live with him. And let him lead us even further toward abundant life. In this sense I bid you a merry Christmas!

Light in the Darkness

Arise, shine; for your light has come,
and the glory of the Lord has risen upon you.
For darkness shall cover the earth,
and thick darkness the peoples;
but the Lord will arise upon you,
and his glory will appear over you.
Nations shall come to your light,
and kings to the brightness of your dawn.

Isaiah 60:1-3

It is in the school of darkness where we learn to love the light. This has been true about humanity ever since we climbed out of the caves. Was it not in darkness and suffering that we learned to climb at last that which the poet called "*. . . the great world's altar-stairs/ That slope thro' darkness up to God?*"

In the old language of Clement of Alexandria, written many centuries ago, early Christians are described as "*holding festival . . . in our life; persuaded that God is altogether on every side present, we cultivate our field praising, we sail the sea, hymning.*" You see, the ancient Christian message is good news indeed. In the darkness there is always God's light. Always.

The mighty aircraft carrier was sailing through heavy seas in the South Pacific. Night came, but one plane was still up there somewhere, searching for the ship, its only landing place. Enemy submarines were also in the area. Any light aboard was forbidden. Only the captain could give the order, which he did. "*Light up the ship.*" At what terrible risk the missing was saved. Even so, Christ came, the Light of the world. But at great risk as well.

"*Darkness shall cover the earth, and gross darkness the people,*" chanted Isaiah long ago. Yet you and I know that this is present fact and persistent history as well. But in Advent and Christmastide, we remember something else too. We remember that there is light - God's light.

Darkness can be very personal. If anyone persists in insisting that God's glory cannot come to earth, that there is nothing to provide light to a darkened world, that persistence is respected by God. We are not compelled to see or believe the light. Frozen unbelief may plead: "*Come not in darkness, come not in light,*" for some changes would have to be made. The change from confident unbelief can be painful before it is blessing. Ptolemaic astronomy made the earth the center of the universe, and thus all its conclusions about the universe were wrong. Yet that's the way people lived and believed for many centuries.

Likewise when anything or any person other than Jesus Christ is made the center of the universe, or the center of the church, or the center of one's life, God's order of reality is missed. Darkness holds sway. It's an old story. And it can be very personal.

Scripture holds that women and men prefer darkness rather than light because they like their evil deeds. True enough, but often many do not prefer darkness. Many just find the light too good to be true. When darkness is the rule, it appears to make little sense to talk about light as a possibility. We can hardly believe that such a thing is there for us. An American long ago told an Oriental that back in his country it gets so cold in winter that one could walk on the water. The Oriental who was of limited exposure to a wider world resolved right then and there never to talk with so demented a tourist again, for that was impossible in his worldview. This is quaint and costless ignorance. But how much more when we consider the terrible words of the New Testament: *"If the light that is in you be darkness, how great is that darkness."* Often many don't prefer darkness, they just don't believe that there really is light.

We read, *"Nations shall come to your light, and kings to the brightness of your rising."* These words are ablaze with expectations. Yet there are few that are known for their sheer delight in belonging to the light. Could it be that many have not truly embraced the revelation that God is giving us in the Christ? The excitement and joy of connection with the holy escapes because the revelation doesn't fit rational expectations. Many want final truth to be good logic, or provable in some way, socially acceptable and politically correct. But what we are given that brings God's light into our world is a small face, born of a woman, in a drafty cowshed, under these ordinary skies, long, long ago. Is this truly light? So asks many in every generation.

The struggle between darkness and light is the history of the world. That is good philosophy. The real struggle, though, is between human darkness and the commandments of God. That is religion. Then came the Advent of Jesus Christ, God's light to the world. That is Christianity.

"Darkness shall cover the earth, and gross darkness the people." While true, who needs one more dreary cataloging of the world's darkness? From one's door to the end of the earth and back, our spirits faint because darkness is there indeed. Amid the fierce outcroppings of evils of our time, we have joined the cry of those who saw their children killed at the hand of Herod the Great so long ago. Our cries come because of failed dreams, rampant darkness bannered each day in the news, and because, in the words of Exodus, the world has in it a *"darkness which may be felt."*

There is a world in darkness, and there always has been. Sometimes in the history of humanity, it has been only slightly shadowy. At other times, it is all midnight. Even within us this is true. Who among us has never been touched by the dark night of the soul, moments when we see no light at all? This swirling planet has never known a day without oppression and hunger, without massive greed and grave suffering. The cynic says that on any clear day the view is terrible. It has always been so. Some days are less dark than others, of course. But there are tragic themes in the human story that are present always and are always dark. Isaiah was right.

"Darkness shall cover the earth." Notice that the verb is future tense. But notice, too, that in the darkness, even the darkness that is to come, there is the promise and the reality that light arises. In the darkness of Egypt . . . Moses. In the darkness of Babylon . . . Isaiah. In the darkness of Christ's death . . . resurrection. In the darkness of the early church . . . Paul. In the darkness of the Roman Empire . . . Augustine. In the darkness of slavery . . . Lincoln. On and on the drama is spelled out for us right before our eyes . . . right in the midst of our own hearts and minds. In the darkness of our own day, whether it be political, economic, or personal; whether it be national or international; whether it be near or far away, God continues to provide light. He continues to raise up his Church. He continues to call folks like you and me. And that's light. Indeed, God's people do not deny the darkness, they find the light God is always sending in its midst. Like the poet says: *"Ring the bells that can still be ringed, there is no perfect offering. There is a crack in everything. That's how the light gets through."*

The light that came at the advent of Jesus Christ acts as a solvent for the darkness at any time. That is, Christ does not take away our problems. What he does, even through the Church, even through you and me, is to illumine our pathway, and walk with us along the way giving us insight, hope, and good company. He can claim our inner selves and strengthen the fibers of hope and trust. He can stir the heart of one into fervent action on the behalf of others. In this manner, we find meaning even amidst darkness. We find joy in sharing the journey together even along darkened paths. We sing the songs of salvation at the light that shines in the darkness that the darkness cannot overcome.

So we celebrate the Christmas. And in our celebrations we acknowledge the central truth of the universe. That is, we know it if we know and trust that Christ is God's light for the world. It is in that knowledge that we can celebrate Isaiah's other word to us at this Christmas time: *"Arise, shine, for the glory of the Lord is risen upon thee."*

Keeping Christmas

I hope King David of a thousand years before Christ will forgive us if we borrow his words from a passage in 1 Chronicles and point out that what he said in that passage is what we have been doing for the last few days. David and his men were encamped in the desert outside Bethlehem while the Philistines were garrisoned in Bethlehem itself. As is recorded (1 Chronicles 11:7), "David said longingly, *'O that someone would give me water to drink from the well of Bethlehem that is by the gate!'*" He was in the desert and longed for the fresh water of Bethlehem.

In a way we believers have been drinking from the "water of the well of Bethlehem" ourselves during these last few days. Hopefully, we have been spiritually refreshed by the reminder of what happened in that little town so long ago. We've been to the manger during this time. We have joined in the angel's song. We have heard the words of peace and goodwill. We have found our thirst for a richer sense of reality in some degree satisfied by the water of life that is drawn from that deep well which is for us the Gospel that came with Jesus Christ.

Bethlehem has become for the Christian more than just a point on a map where Jesus was born. Our annual visit to Bethlehem reminds us and refreshes us in some potentially powerful ways. For our visit there each Christmas draws us once again into the promises of God and into the power of God. And for a few days at least, love gets its way in unexpected places, joy comes peeking through the curtains of our anxieties, and peace seems not such an impossible dream. Some drops from the water of the well of Bethlehem have fallen on our thirsty lips during our Christmas celebrations. I certainly hope this is the case.

The question is – and it always is as we leave the Christmas celebration behind us – how do we keep Christmas? Now I don't mean how can we keep on celebrating Christmas. What I have in mind is the meaning of the word "keep" that is found in that lovely verse that tells us of the response of Jesus' mother to all that happened at Bethlehem. We read that *"Mary kept all these things and pondered them in her heart."* She didn't say, *"Well all that stuff around the manger was sure exciting – and now, back to the kitchen at Nazareth."* Nor should we. When the last tree has been dismantled, and the last Christmas card examined and put away, one wonders if we are liable to dismiss what we call the Christmas spirit until another year rolls by. But, like Mary, maybe we shall "keep all these things" only if we "ponder them in our hearts." And that is what we have the opportunity to do in the days ahead. That is what we can do to keep Christmas.

You and I know that there is a little yearning, a smidgeon of longing, a bit of thirsting which Christmas evokes in most of us. Some nerve or feeling is touched within most of us during this time of celebration and warmth. It shows up in the music or the lights or the story or the intimacy with others. Something is touched that connects with the holy. One might wonder just how deep it might go for us. Is it simply nostalgia for what seems to have been better times? Is it just the fleeting hope that the decent instincts of humans really are more basic and lasting than the suspicions and selfishness which often can grip us? Is it an escape away from the realities of our world oft-gripped in the fear of terror? Or is it a half-belief that there is something to this notion that Christ is the true center of our lives, the One in whom God and sinners are truly reconciled? At its best, is it simply an illusion found momentarily believable in the music, lights and sounds of the Advent time? Or can there be more for us?

You see, the first step for keeping Christmas has to be going beneath the surface happiness of such a time to that which truly satisfies our souls. The only thing which lies beneath our good feelings of Christmas that really gives Christmas its foundation and meaning is the Word of God which is addressed to the world and to each of us. Christians are those people who at their better moments can sense the might, majesty, and purposes of God in the Christmas celebration, and who know that only this Word of God can truly permeate our lives and satisfy our inner places. Only this Word can last for us throughout the year and within the movements of time and effort we each experience. For there is within us all a thirst for an intimate connection with the divine, with the one by whose very power and love the universe is sustained and who alone grasps his people in both life and death. There is as a part of the nature of our being human a hunger for an intimate knowledge of the God who made us, for the grace that takes our unworthiness, our sin, and throws it into the oblivion of divine forgiveness, and for a refreshing and renewing Spirit that can release in us the man or woman we are meant to be.

We shall be keeping Christmas if we let that longing loose in us, nurturing it, pondering it and recognizing that it is no passing dream but the cry of a wandering child for the Father's home. We may keep Christmas insofar as we keep before us and within us the Christ in whom these longings find their endless satisfaction.

Beginnings

Many have found events and activities observed in the natural world to be suggestive of elements of life in the human world. A beautiful sunset, with clouds multi-colored and spacious, can lift one's spirits and paint elements of hope into one's heart. Pictures of the first snowfall covering everything within sight with the purest white can calm the mind and draw one into quiet places. So it seems, I'm glad to say.

Loren Eiseley, the late anthropologist and naturalist, has written many reflective articles about his experiences with the natural world. None surpass a brief reflection upon a scene he happened upon in the forest one day (The Immense Journey). I've quoted it many times.

Eiseley was asleep in a small clearing in the woods when a commotion awakened him: a raven had taken a baby bird from its nest and held it firmly in its beak. The racket which had awakened him was being made by the parents of the baby bird which flitted around the raven making alarm calls. Before long, other birds joined in the protest so that the forest was filled with their scolding and cries. Eiseley said that it seemed as if a cry of complaint had arisen among the birds. Whatever the bird emotions might have been, the noise awoke him and with his naturalist's eye he observed the scene. While the parent birds and the others flew at the great raven, none dared attack such a large opponent. Their complaints registered their inbred alarm, but Eiseley noted that there appeared to be more: *"There was a dim intangible ethic he [the raven] had violated, that they [the birds] knew. He was a bird of death. And he, the murderer, the black bird at the heart of life, sat there, glistening in the common light, formidable, unmoving, unperturbed, untouchable."*

Eiseley went on: *The sighing died. It was then I saw the judgment. It was the judgment of life against death. I will never see it again so forcefully presented. I will never hear it again in notes so tragically prolonged. For in the midst of protest, they forgot the violence. There, in that clearing, the crystal note of a song sparrow lifted hesitantly in the hush. And finally, after painful fluttering, another took the song and then another, the song passing from one bird to another, doubtfully at first, as though some evil thing were being slowly forgotten. Till suddenly they took heart and sang from many throats joyously together as birds are known to sing. They sang because life is sweet and sunlight beautiful. They sang under the brooding shadow of the raven. In simple truth, they had forgotten the raven, for they were the singers of life, and not of death."*

They began again.

Life offers many opportunities for new beginnings. Time and nature are shaped that way. So is God who is truly a God of new beginnings so far as humanity

185

is concerned. It's as if the designer of life knew that humans would never make it unless renewal, going beyond the old, escaping that which decays, and beginning again, were possible. We begin again when we reach adulthood, when we choose a vocation or change vocations. We begin again when we recover from illness or an accident, or when we recover from an argument. On and on – new beginnings and the possibility thereof built into the fabric of the life God has given us. New beginnings mark us if we are to live.

For believers, God began again on behalf of the world amid all its complaints and ruckus when Jesus was born among us. That new beginning was sealed into reality when Jesus was baptized by John the Baptist in the River Jordan (see the Scripture for the Day printed below) and, as the writers affirm, the Holy Spirit, the very presence of God, was upon him as power and truth. And the world has never been the same since.

Here we are at the beginning of the year 2022 – that's 2022 years, so to speak, from that new beginning there on the banks of the River Jordan. During the intervening years, many black birds of evil have done their deeds, many a ruckus has been raised, and many have begun again and again and again. Would we have it any other way as we seek to make our way through the days and nights that are given us? Of late we have been ravaged by a pandemic, forces of authoritarianism have been unleashed both here at home and throughout the world, cherished understandings of basic principles are being challenged and rejected, and there are numerous ones who hold portions of our lives in their beaks threatening the days ahead. But listen carefully, for the plaintive note of the song sparrow sings and the marvelous recounting of God's continuing action among us and for us can hold us, and we have, each day, the opportunity to begin again, learning much from whence we've come and from the One who holds us, as we move into the new year as "singers of life" and not of death or of evil or of the darkness.

Eyes

Having recently gone through cataract surgery, I have been more keenly aware of my eyes and how they see. Without belaboring the point, I see so much more and so much better since the surgery. Colors are more alive, the landscape more distinct, and the sky shines more brightly. I see birds more distinctly and can catch their movement among the trees more readily. Eyes and the accompaniment of ears connect us with others and with the world. I wouldn't have it any other way.

It should not therefore be unusual for such a vital ability such as seeing to be used in a myriad of ways to express various aspects of our lives. How common such expressions are. One need not interpret them, so connected are they with the vitality of seeing. A random list of the use of "eyes" as metaphor ranges wide and deep in our usage. The eyes are: "the window of the soul." We say that "her eyes screamed in silence," or he has "eyes that are deep;" or that the child's eyes were "open in wonder." Who do you know whose eyes "tell a story," or who has eyes "that sparkle with amusement?" If one has an "Eye of the Tiger" that one is fierce looking while the one who has "Eagle eyes" doesn't miss much around him or her. Some folks seem to have "eyes in the back of their head" and others are so bold that they can "look death in the eye" and live on. In thinking about what the eye does, one might remember that one's eyes are "the mirror of the soul" reflecting what one is feeling or thinking. Metaphysically, the right eye in some ways of thinking represent seeing clearly what one wants (the will) whereas the left eye (the spirit) represents seeing clearly what one feels. Some folks don't see very clearly, "blinded" to facts often, or "cross-eyed" in their views. The eye sure gives us ample means of expression because of its vital role in our lives.

Not surprisingly, the Bible uses "eyes" and related words in a number of ways as well. Remember Adam and Eve whose "eyes were opened" (Genesis 3:7) after eating the forbidden fruit? They became aware of their vulnerability when they could see more clearly. Job expresses his extreme sorrow and pain by pouring out "tears to the Lord" (Job 16:20). The Psalmist prays that God would "keep me as the apple of the eye," nor worrying about the mixing of metaphors at all (Psalm 17:8). The Preacher in Ecclesiastes expresses the fact that he does not understand fully nor is satisfied with what he understands by mentioning that "the eye is not satisfied with seeing" (Ecclesiastes 1:8). The eye is often mentioned in the physical sense: "his eye was not dim" (Deuteronomy 34:7); the "speck that is in your brother's eye" (Matthew 7:3). Jesus even used the eye metaphorically when he amusingly said that "it is easier for a camel to go through the eye of a needle than for someone who is rich to enter the kingdom of God" (Matthew 19:24). And, as one might think, the eye becomes an apt picture for presenting God's way of "overseeing" the world:

"The eyes of the Lord are in every place, keeping watch on the evil and the good" (Proverbs 15:3). How bereft our communication would be if we had not the eye as such a versatile metaphor!

There is one way that "eyes" are used in the Bible that I wish to underscore. It is found in 2 Chronicles 16:9. In expressing the profound faith of Judah/Israel, a seer told King Asa after some military action to keep on trusting God in the midst of the situation. The seer expressed it this way: *"For the eyes of the Lord range throughout the entire earth, to strengthen those whose heart is true to him."* Rather than ducking out of sight for fear that God might be watching us and therefore might object to us, the basic faith of Israel (and the church) is that God is watching *over* us! One need not fear God's eyes on us. In a simple way, this trust is in a God who cares for his creation and his creatures. And it is not a passive care, but a particular care which includes his eyes on each of his people for the purpose of "strengthening" them for their lives. Of course, this is not magic or automatic, this strengthening. It comes as the result of one's "trust" (another word for "faith") in God. That's the connection for one's confidence in God's care and purpose and is the vehicle for insight and revelation into God's will. The promise is that God watches over us all. The benefit comes through our trust in him and his ways. So it is not at all unusual for the Biblical writers to include admonitions for believers to respond to this promise of God. The prophet Jeremiah puts it like this: *"Call to me and I will answer you, and will tell you great and hidden things that you did not know."* Because God watches over us all, it is resoundingly possible for us through the "eyes" of faith to "see" God in our lives as well. At this point metaphor becomes reality. And we can see.

Hands

Have you ever taken a close look at your hands, or the hands of anyone else for that matter? Simply viewed dispassionately and objectively, they are rather strange looking, I'd say. An irregularly flattened palm, smooth on one side, dimpled with the shapes of tendons and vessels on the other, with dangling things attached; what poetry can turn that into beauty? Of course, they lose such observation and any conclusion that they are rather unattractive on their own when they belong to someone. Hands become personal when they belong to the self or to another. And when one notes what hands can do and how they can be adorned with color and jewel one can see them anew as implements of beauty and purpose. Notice the smooth hands of the dentist or the surgeon. Recall the delicate and tender hands of a baby. Watch the hands of the musician at the piano or the banjo or the harp and hands become objects of admiration and appreciation. Feel the warmth of a hand holding one's own or extended to one in friendship or love and hands can touch the soul.

So central to our lives are our hands, both functionally and symbolically, that we use the term and the pictures it can draw in countless ways to express many things. We regard those who come alongside to help us as "helping hands." Teachers hold students to the thought or study "at hand." Economists have described the phenomenon of market forces controlling the economy as "an invisible hand." Royalty was shown obeisance by the "kissing the hand" by underlings. We speak hand-language by saying things like "hand it to me," "Look, no hands," that's 'hand's off," and "hand-deliver." We all know what those expressions mean without anyone telling us. That's how ubiquitous and familiar the many ways "hand" can be used and understood are. "Hand me that book," "how can we handle it?" "keep your hands off," and "caught red-handed" are often used and need no explanation (By the way, "red-handed" was first used in 15th century Scotland for those caught with "blood on their hands" from cattle-rustling or murder. Today, it means "obviously guilty.").

Perhaps the tenderest uses of "hand" come when we are talking about the connection of one's hand to another's. Vera Nazarian opines "Sometimes, reaching out and taking someone's hand is the beginning of a journey." And Richelle E. Goodrich echoes her sentiment by saying, "Nothing in this world compares to the comfort and security of having someone just hold your hand." Countless witnesses have attested to the significance of holding the hand of the ill and dying. Hand-holding joins hearts, connects sentiments, and speaks of love. One writer puts it in personal terms: "Even though my brain was a mess, what kept my soul whole was the warmth of the hands holding mine on both sides" (Won-pyung Sohn). So powerful is hand-holding that children know they are safe when holding the hand of a parent and lovers know they are connected when their hands are joined.

Should it surprise us to learn that the Bible, ever the book of folks like us, uses hand-language as well? It uses "hand" in some of the ways we use it in ordinary parlance. And it uses it to advantage in describing ties to God, or rather, God's ties to us. *"O sing to the Lord a new song, for he has done marvelous things. His right hand and his holy arm have gotten him victory."* (The "right hand" is seen in the ancient world as the "good" hand whereas the left less so. It's still used that way today.) -so says the Psalmist (98:1). But not only is God righteously active, God holds the earth and all that is within it in his hands (*"For the Lord is a great God, and a great King above all gods. In his hand are the depths of the earth, the heights of the mountains are his also."* – Psalm 95:3-4). This is the big-picture view of God in the ancient mind. Ours, too. Closer at hand (no pun intended) is the notion that God's care for the earth and its people, especially those who honor him, is actually God holding them in his hand. Isaiah speaks for God in saying to his people, *"For I, the Lord your God, hold your right hand; it is I who say to you, 'Do not fear, I will help you'"* (Isaiah 41:13). 1 Peter stretches that out even more by adding *"Humble yourselves therefore under the mighty hand of God, so that he may exalt you in due time. Cast all your anxiety on him, because he cares for you"* (1 Peter 5:6-7).

This is no magical view. God's hands hold the world and all within it. God's purposes are always at work. None of this is totally objective. God's ways are discerned in faith, God's love is revealed through trust, and God's victories are not the same as the world's, but are more profound and essential to our being. It is in seeking to live with God that we come to know the touch of his hand. It is in following God's ways that our journeys are held in his hands. It is in submitting ourselves to God in trust and love that we know our lives are in his hands. Therefore, a prayer for believers might well echo the words of a wonderful old hymn and we can sing such words because God truly holds us in his hands.

Precious Lord, take my hand, Lead me on, help me stand.
I am tired, I am weak, I am worn.
Through the storm, through the night,
Lead me on to the light.
Take my hand, precious Lord; lead me home.
When my way grows drear, Precious Lord, linger near
When my life is almost gone.
Hear my cry, hear my call,
Hold my hand lest I fall.
Take my hand, precious Lord; lead me home. -Thomas A. Dorsey

Way

Back in the late 50's not everyone knew the "way" to jump start a car with a dead battery. This was particularly true for the fellow teacher who lived in the same boarding house as did my brother, John, in the small town of Bardstown, KY, where both taught in the local high school. My brother had a 1954 Renault, the tiny car with the engine in the back. His car battery was weak and one day he walked to his parking place in front of the boarding house and tried to crank her up – but, to no avail. What to do? The only other person around was his fellow teacher whom he implored to come with her car to give him a push until he could jump start the car. She was willing, but the problem was that she said she had never done such a thing before and didn't know the "way" to do it. John told her to bring her car around from behind the boarding house and to come up behind his car, getting them up to about thirty miles an hour when he would pop the clutch and his car would start. Fine and dandy! Off she went to get her car. Brother John sat in his Renault and in his mirror saw her round the corner and begin toward him – at thirty miles an hour! Oh, no! John began to wave his arm outside the window to get her to slow down. She thought it meant to "come on." Then came the moment when time stood still and John's body clutched up and she hit that Renault right in the rear at thirty miles an hour! His little car lurched forward some but, then, she hit him again! John began to laugh and wave his arms in a desperate attempt to have her back off, but on she came, again and again, bumping him forward until, at last, he coasted down the hill and rolled into an abandoned lot. The rear end of his Renault was smashed in, motor damaged, and the car unable to run. John said that he left it there in the lot and never went back (I don't know if that part is true!). The other teacher was certainly correct in saying that she did not know the "way" to jump start a car!

Remembering this story (I laugh with it every time I think of it) got me to thinking about the many "ways" that little word "way" is used, particularly in our Bible and faith.

In general, a "way" can mean a direction or pathway ("Take NC 101 to Havelock, then US 70 West."). It may refer to the description of how to get somewhere (Go until you see a white house with green shutters. The lot behind the house is what you are looking for."). It is also used to indicate the method one might use to accomplish something ("Here's the way to build a good campfire."). In philosophy and religion it can indicate a particular direction of one's thought or one's belief ("The way to inner peace is through quiet moments of prayer."). We use the word almost effortlessly: "I don't see things that way;" "Don't get in my way;" "The house is way down there." When we use it for roadway or path it can be both literally or metaphorically such as in "the road less travelled." In the account of my brother and his dead battery, the "way" to jump start a car refers to the method to be used. On and on.

Aside from the normal ways of using the term, the Bible also uses the term "way" in metaphorical "ways" as well. The customary or habitual behavior of an animal or a person can be described as a "way" (*"Go to the ant, you lazybones; consider its ways, and be wise,"* Proverbs 6:6). This can be expanded to include the moral action of groups or individuals, both negative and positive. Positive: *"For John came to you in the way of righteousness and you did not believe him . . ."* (Matthew 21:32). Negative: *"Their feet are swift to shed blood; ruin and misery are in the paths, and the way of peace they have not known"* (Romans 3:15-17). And because life is often conceived of as a journey, the way or path may refer generally to the course of one's life (*"The God who has girded me with strength has opened wide my path"* (2 Samuel 22:33); *"Their ways prosper at all time; your judgments are on high, out of their sight. ."* (Psalm 10:5).

In many places in the Bible, God's actions or habits are referred to as "God's ways" (Exodus 33:13; Psalms 25:10; Hebrews 3:10; Revelation 15:3). That God's ways are beyond human understanding is emphasized (Job 26:14; Romans 11:33) and are contrasted with human ways (Isaiah 55:8-9: "my ways" vs. "your ways."). Yet God's ways are always made available to humans as they follow God's law. In Deuteronomy 13:5, God's commands are known as *"the way in which the Lord your God commanded you to walk."* Following the logic of these uses, those who do not live according to God's law or wisdom *"turn from the way"* (Deuteronomy 9:12).

The New Testament writers often understood Jesus' "way" as replacing the Old Testament way to God. Better put, Jesus "enfleshes" that way, lives it out as example. The Old Testament way of the law is not put aside in the New Testament as the way to God, but is enhanced and made more real in Jesus. When John the Baptist begins his ministry with the words, *"Prepare the way of the Lord,"* he is using an Old Testament quote as pointing to Jesus as a continuation of the Old Testament "way" (Isaiah 40:3 and Matthew 3:3). Thus, the way of the Lord that had been known to Israel is present in the person of Jesus. When Jesus says that he is "the way, the truth, and the life" he is offering himself and giving an invitation to following him as the fulfillment of the way revealed in the Old Testament (John 14:6). In Acts (9:2), the early church described itself as "the way." This is broadened in Acts 18:26 to indicate (*"the way of God"*) that this way which was shown to the people in the Old Testament is now embodied in those who follow Jesus. This is surely echoed in Paul's words (1 Corinthians 12:31), *"But strive for the greater gifts. And I will show you a still more excellent way."*

Perhaps the deeper learning from this discussion is that Christianity is more than momentary assent. It is more than a legalistic approach that focuses on stringent laws. And it is more than entertainment as a means of feeling good. It is a "way." Or, as in indicated in the Scriptures, it THE way to life with our God. And at the heart of that "way" is the man sent from God, Jesus of Nazareth, whose way with us and among us reveals him to be the Christ, the Anointed One of God. Following him truly leads us on a sure pathway. Drawing near to him in our minds and hearts surely opens the way for us more clearly. Knowing him as we journey, surely gives clarity to each step along the way. Trusting him surely enables insight into where the way is leading us. And living with him day by day surely allows us "a still more excellent way." When someone asks what Christianity is, an appropriate answer is that it is the way for life both now and for eternity.

Sounds

It's hard to do, I know, but in your mind's eye try to wander back to the very beginning of the creation of this universe. If you can imagine it, you find that there is nothing there. The empty black reaches of void – no stars, no planets, no galaxies, no light, no radiation, nothing. And it is very quiet. There are no sounds being made and no ears to hear them if there were. There is nothing at all, eternal, dark, void, and silent nothing.

As science has been able to show us, it was out of this primeval state of nothingness that the first flickers of the beginning of the universe were born. In the beginning where there were still no ears to hear, out of stillness and silence came what we call the Big Bang – a chemical and nuclear reaction that shattered the silence and began a propulsion of energy some 15 to 20 billion years ago that has resulted in the universe as we know it.

The sounds were there all right, billions of years before ears could hear, and to the sounds of an expanding and changing universe were other sounds added along the way to the present. And to those who now have ears to hear, the question the sounds raise and all the things that make the sounds is why? Why is it here? What is it for? Where does it lead? What is it that we are a part of?

Since that time so very long ago, the universe has continued to expand and is still rapidly doing so. Our astrophysicists can even measure the rate of expansion. By mathematics they can calculate where the edge of the universe is. And because it takes millions of light years for light from the edges to reach the earth, what astronomers see goes back in time to the beginning. The new James Webb space telescope will be able to peer back to those early days as we have never been able to do before. The vastness is staggering. We cannot readily conceive of it, so great it is. But its meaning for us has not – nor cannot – come from science alone.

In a little corner, tucked away as it were, willy-nilly, picture the earth. For the earth is product of this expanding universe – indeed, we are its child. And while exceedingly small on the universal scale, out of the elements of this place called earth has come all living things of which we know. Oh, the laws of probability point us to the thought that there must be other living things out there somewhere. Maybe – maybe not. But the truth of this day is that so far we know of nothing else alive but that which is here in this little place we call earth.

But the sounds of living things, at least here, have been added to the sounds of the universe. And to those who have ears to hear there are many sounds around us now. There are cosmic sounds brought to us by our radio telescopes. There are the sounds of the continuing process of creation throughout the universe. And there are the sounds of earth – the sounds of the natural world and the sounds of human beings. Attention to one without the other robs us of a sense of perspective about it all. The sounds here are the most commanding: the sounds of industrious human beings scampering around like ants on an anthill. The sounds of joy. The sounds of sorrow. The sounds of sin and the results of sin. A jumble of sounds it is and to many a source of confusion. Interpretations abound as to its meaning. We are the pawns of powerful outside forces say some. The ancient religions of the world began with this theme. The quest for meaning among them therefore pushed them to find those forces and placate them lest they destroy us. And so, gods and goddesses of one sort or another were invented. To others, especially in our time, there are no reasons, no hidden meanings, no overarching purposes or forces or structures out there holding it all together. We are here simply because we are here – to do with our existence what we will. Except for each other, we are alone. And to still others all reasons are tied to genetics and to the determinative laws of cause and effect. Learn those laws and live with them aiding you, we are told; there is no God beyond them.

But you and I are part of a strange group of human beings – ones who hear more than just the sounds of confusion or the sounds of threat. And we have faced those who limit all sounds to things either cosmic or earthly alone and have challenged them with the conviction that some sounds in this universe may just be divine.

A little over 4,000 years ago, out of the jumble of sounds, a new sound began to emerge among us. Compared to other sounds it was strange indeed. For it was a sound of joy – a positive sound. It was a sound that acknowledged that behind and within all creation there was someone – someone who cares. The new sound was the sound of praise. – for meaning was found in the jumble and the praise pointed to that meaning. Indeed, the answer to the question of the meaning of creation and all its sounds was seen in giving praise to this one. The purpose of humans was found to be in honoring him with our sounds and with our lives.

The sounds of praise to Almighty God, the one God of the universe, were born in Israel. It did not represent yet another religion bent on placating the forces or in mesmerizing the self. It represented the conviction that all things seen and heard belong to the creator as we do ourselves. Praise was the affirmation of the people who knew to whom they belonged and why. And the sounds of that praise grew and spread through the years until it reached new understanding and new insight and hope in the man, Jesus, through his life, death, and resurrection. God was now seen as not only there behind it all but here with us through it all, suffering and joy alike. And the sounds of praise pointed to the kind of God he was – the sounds were positive – an affirmation – a "yes" even amid the terrible limitations of life.

God came to us in the dimness of history and the praise began. He created a people and the praise increased. God sent his chosen one to signal how seriously he took our suffering and death and how graciously he overpowers it all for us and in us. And God has called you and me to add our voices and our lives to this throng for we know that God has called his people to add to this praise in each succeeding generation. Throughout of days one might reflect on how the sounds of our lives add to this praise of the eternal God.

Whispers

The license plate on the back of my truck is encased with a frame that has the words "Bird Whisperer" on it. It was given to me by a good friend in recognition of my passion for birding. And, of course, it is a take-off on the more familiar expression "horse whisperer" made famous by the book and movie of that title. Made me feel right good to be thought of as a bird whisperer, though I had no idea what that might mean. In addition, I wondered what in the world might a horse whisperer or a dog whisperer be as well. Visions of the whisperer having quiet and whispered words to speak into the eager ears of whatever animal he or she might be the whisperer of came to mind. So, I looked it up and I found this: "A horse whisperer is an expert who uses horse whispering techniques to create a sound basis of cooperation between human and beast. Contrary to popular belief, horse whispering has little to do with quiet talking and more with observation and non-verbal communication." And there, in black and white, was the key to the idea bandied around by believers for, lo, these many centuries about the "whispers of God" as the primary way God uses to get his word to his people.

The notion of the "whispers of God" is not clearly spelled out in the Scriptures very well, though there are strong intimations of it scattered throughout. The four direct references to "whispers" in the Bible break down into two speaking about hearing God's whispers (Job 4:12, Job 26:14) and two which speak of whispers of other identities (Psalm 41:7, Isaiah 29:4). Of these four, the Job 26:14 passage points to our devotional discussion. The setting is Job's thoughts on how God has shown his great power in the parting of the sea and delivering the Hebrews from Egypt – *"By his power he churned up the sea; by his wisdom he cut Rahab (the legendary sea monster and figure of the sea itself) to pieces,"* that is, divided the waters. But, then, he goes on to spell out the more essential way of God's revelation to us. Referring to such mighty acts, he adds in verse 14, *"And these are but the outer fringe of his works; how faint the whisper we hear of him!"* God's revelations often come in "whispers!!" And the meaning is more kin to the notion of "hint" or "trace" of the divine. That's often what we get from our God as has been attested to rigorously down through the ages: the intimations, the traces, the hints, the whispers of God.

I don't know about most others, but numerous fellow believers have shared with me how this notion of the "whispers of God" rings true in their experiences. As one writer has put it (Becky Toews), "Sometimes the voice of the Lord seems almost audible. We pick up the Bible and it's as if certain words are italicized. We hear a preacher and conclude God must have told him or her our secrets. The message comes across clear, direct, unmistakable. Other times, in order to hear the Lord speak, it's necessary to lean in, to come closer. Because he is whispering."

This notion is echoed in one of the more famous Old Testament accounts where Elijah, when he was fleeing the wrath of Jezebel who was dead-set on killing him for his prophecies against her rule (along with Ahab) of Israel, fled to the wilderness (in the Old Testament, the foreboding nature of the wilderness was also frequently the setting of hearing the whispers of God). The prophet had hoped God would speak through mighty acts, through shock and awe such as a howling wind or an earthquake or through fire. But he didn't. Instead God spoke "in a still small voice" – a whisper for goodness sake! Maybe Elijah had to silence his expectations of how God would speak before he was ready to listen! Perhaps one's expectations of how God should speak may cause one to miss God's whispers as well – it's worth pondering. This is because predetermined expectations as to how God wants to speak can cause a believer to miss God's whispers.

In remembering that the essence of "horse whispering" has more to do with "observation and non-verbal communication" one can identify with Elijah's experience in this account. And it can be instructive for us as well. The Psalmist reminds us of this need for observation and deep listening when he quotes what he has learned from God: *"Be still and know that I am God"* (Psalm 46:10). It's difficult to catch such whispers in a noisy environment. It's hard to focus on the non-verbal when our world of internet and phone prevents us from quiet reflection. The voice from our endless to-do list shouts that we don't have time for quiet. The worries of life and the living of life in the immediate scream for our attention. Before long, listening for God in the earthquake and fire become difficult much less listening for God's still small voice, God's whispers.

In inviting us into deeper observation of the world in which we find ourselves and into a more intuitive, non-verbal frame of mind, God's seeks to whisper to our hearts and minds every day. While I am not truly a bird-whisperer, through God's constant seeking after me, I am learning something of what being a God-whisperer can be—Pastor Rich

Coming Home

I recently attended the funeral of a friend of mine. It was an affirming and hopeful time of worship and appreciation for a life well-lived. Most funerals I attend are ones I myself conduct as the officiant, so attending one as a worshipper was a good experience and underscored for me once again the richness of the Christian hope in the face of death. The familiar words of Scripture held out to me images of hope in the face of the reality of death - words of comfort reminding us that God was near at all times, words of hope that God strengthens us in both life and death, and words of promise that our journeys' final destination is into the loving arms of our God. I was strengthened by the words and the presence they conveyed.

Living as we do in a time where the very value of religious hope in the face of both life and death is being severely challenged from numerous angles, I came away from the funeral and commendation with much reflection. I had read in a recent book a discussion that in the continuing development of the human race that religion is but one of several mythologies by which humans have sought to make sense of life. As I read, I realized that while the writer found the mythologies helpful for many lives on the practical level he also stated that these belief systems are not rooted in fact or objective truth in any way. This got me to thinking about the veracity of what I had just heard and participated in at the funeral. The funeral presented in numerous ways that living or dying we are in God's hands, that in our Father's house there are many rooms, even one prepared for each of us when we die. We heard Paul's great words to the Thessalonians that we should not grieve like the others who have no hope, for *"since we believe that Jesus died and rose again, even so, through Jesus, God will bring with him those who have died"* (1 Thesalonians 4:13). The worship service was thoroughly rooted in the promises of God revealed to us in the life, death, and resurrection of Jesus Christ. The way the author of the book I read used the term "mythology" was to note that mythologies are frameworks, stories, systems, and or beliefs that help humans organize and understand life and its mysteries, but that they also are mental constructs, ways of thinking often in story form to soothe anxieties and provide comfort and (possibly) hope in the face of the unknown. As the writer affirms, humans need such mythologies to make sense of life and death, but as Sigmund Freud wrote years ago, they are also primarily "wishful thinking." I think not.

One of the ministers in his prayer for those of us who knew and loved the deceased used a phrase that stood out to me grandly. He prayed that God's claim on us in life and death would "swing low and carry us" into the confidence and hope of the reality of God's promises and the *"place prepared for us"* as we deal with death, our loved ones' and our own. Yes, I thought, finding my heart touched by the assurance that the "mythology" by which I lived and preached, being rooted in history (the ministry, death, and resurrection of Jesus), included God's coming and taking me "home." I remembered Paul's words to the Corinthians, *"If for this life only we have hoped in Christ, we are of all people most to be pitied."* (1 Corinthians 15:19) So, the minister's prayer that God would "swing low and carry us" was more than apt; it conveyed a grand vision using human pictures to convey the reality of God's promise to us that *"neither death nor life. . . nor anything else in all creation can separate us from the love of God in Christ Jesus our Lord"* (Romans 8:39). And the minister conveyed it with the words of the familiar spiritual:

Swing low, sweet chariot, Comin' for to carry me home;
Swing low, sweet chariot, Coming for to carry me home.

I looked over Jordan, And what did I see, Comin' for to carry me home,
A band of angels comin' after me, Comin' for to carry me home.

If you get there before I do, Comin' for to carry me home,
Tell all my friends I'm comin' too, Comin' for to carry me home.

Sometimes I'm up, sometimes I'm down, Comin' for to carry me home.
But still my soul feels heavenly bound, Comin' for to carry me home.

Swing low, sweet chariot, Comin' for to carry me home;
Swing low, sweet chariot, Comin' for to carry me home.

While this spiritual had its origins in slavery as the slaves yearned for God's chariot of righteousness to deliver them from bondage, it also began to take on spiritual meanings in the face of death. Using Biblical images of God's might and power being illustrated by "chariots" and remembering how Elijah was reportedly carried off into heaven by "chariots of fire" (2 Kings 6:17), the spiritual underscores that our hope and our deliverance in the face of death is provided by our God. To believers this is fact. Mythological way of speaking or not, I have great confidence that at my end God's chariot of love and power will be "comin' for to carry me home." I've been humming and singing that spiritual ever since that funeral.

Fear

Everybody gets afraid at some time or other. Like right now with war clouds swirling in Eastern Europe and a tyrant sending thousands of troops into Ukraine and threatening the world with the use of nuclear weapons. We can imagine the fear of those who are fleeing their homes as well as those who are putting up a defensive fight. And we can feel the fear, the dread even, when the unthinkable is imagined – a nuclear war.

There are many kinds of fear, I suppose, though at rock bottom, they may all seem somewhat alike. As one man put it, *"We are so largely the playthings of Fate in our fears. To one, fear of the dark; to another, of physical pain; to a third, of public ridicule; to a fourth, poverty; to a fifth, of loneliness – for all of us our particular creature lurks in ambush."* (Hugh Walpole) And to all of us, the fears brought on by the prospect of and realty of war.

We all know the instinctive kind of fear that makes us jump back from a speeding car. We have learned to be cautious around infectious diseases, enraged animals – or people, and perhaps when we are tempted to do something wrong, it is the fear of the consequences that keeps us on the right track. These are some of the normal fears of life – and they are important for they keep us from danger.

Sometimes, however, we are the victims of fears that are exaggerated and irrational, that we know are overdone, but from which we cannot free ourselves. Elevators frighten some of us – or flying – or high places. Some of us suffer from fears sent up to our consciousness by emotional conflicts, memories, or other factors buried so deep in the mind that the sufferer knows that he is afraid but may not know why. I have had several close calls with lightning, even seen people killed by lightning, and I can feel myself tense up whenever a thunderstorm approaches, particularly if I am exposed in any way.

There are hundreds of fears like that – fears of going to a new school or class, or of taking a course, fear of having to go upstairs when it is dark up there, fear of failure, fear of someone leaving us, fear of losing people we love, of meeting people we don't know, fears of illness, old age, and death. It is the fear that in our minds turns every root, every stick, into a snake when we walk a wooded path in the dark. And such fears take on grim personalities of their own in our minds when they come upon us.

Indeed, our fears, large and small, complicate life for us – and may even destroy it.

The Bible, our source of God's word and ways, has a great deal to say about people who are afraid. Just about every fear imaginable to people of those times can be found in the Bible. However, the presence of fear is not necessarily evidence of the absence of faith for there actually is much to fear in our world. We might well remember when Jesus was in the garden of Gethsemane. One translator puts it like this: *"he began to feel appalled and agitated."* Another scholar suggests that these words mean the distress that follows a great shock. And when we hear some pious souls say that Christians ought to be serene in the face of fear, we might wonder more deeply how serene Jesus was when, *"being in agony of mind his sweat became as it were drops of blood falling down on the ground."*

To be told, then, that to be afraid makes us unfaithful only deepens whatever despair may already be there. Many of our fears have such deep roots that we cannot control them, and to rebuke or blame someone for having them is like rebuking someone for having cancer. Jesus, you will remember, never once had harsh words for anyone who was afraid. He gave them only words of assurance. He never claimed that a fearful person only imagined his malady. He never advised them, as we so often do: "The thing you really ought to do is to try to pull yourself together." He recognized the presence of fear as something quite common. I do not think it any accident that the very first words his followers heard after Jesus' resurrection were, *"Fear not!"*

But, let's be more specific in our dealing with fear as Christians. The 118th Psalm is an excellent place to look for help in the Bible when it comes to being afraid.

Psalm 118 was Martin Luther's favorite Psalm. Listen to what he says about it: *This is my Psalm, my chosen Psalm. I love them all. I love all Holy Scripture, which is my consolation and my life. But this Psalm is nearest my heart, and I have a familiar right to call it mine. It has saved me from many a pressing danger from which neither emperor, nor king, nor sages, nor saints could have saved me. It is my friend, dearer to me than all the honors and power of earth.*

Luther loved this Psalm for many reasons, I'm sure, but none so much as for a theme that occurs over and over in it – four times in the first four verses and once again at the last. It is the one thing the Psalmist would have all of the people to know and trust. It is the one thing believers have known, have trusted, have dared to believe in the face of all our fears. It's a simple phrase and it is a great phrase, one we might carry with us always: **His steadfast love endures forever.** It is the antiphonal shout of the people of God gathered to praise their God. You Jews sing it, the Psalmist says; now you priests sing it; then you people who stand in awe of God sing it. **His steadfast love endures forever.** (Now, you say it: "His steadfast love endures forever!") This is given as the focal point for our life with God. *"Therefore, we will not fear thought* *the mountains shake in the heart of the sea; though its waters roar and foam, though the mountains tremble with its tumult,"* says another psalmist (Psalm 46). *"The nations rage, the kingdoms totter . . . [but] the Lord of hosts is with us; the God of Jacob is our refuge."* There is one thing you can count on no matter what else happens in life. And you can build life and hope upon this one thing: **His steadfast love endures forever.**

If there are any proclamations in the New Testament that offer us hope in the face of such fears, the New Testament proclamation concerning death is certainly chief among them. Paul, echoing the sentiments of the 118th Psalm, says in the 8th chapter of Romans, *"We know that in everything God works for good with those who love him."* And he goes on . . . *"What shall we say to this? If God is for us, who can be against us? . . . Who shall separate us from the love of God in Christ Jesus?"* Nothing can so separate us, he says, not even death. *"I go to prepare a place for you,"* said Jesus, *"and when I come,"* (Not *if* I come) *"when I come again, I will receive you to myself, that where I am you may be also."* Can you hear the echo of *"His steadfast love endures forever"* in his promise? The whole Bible is built around it.

It is the promise of the resurrection, that even in death we are not alone, not unvalued, not through. It is no wonder, then, that Jesus' words on that Easter morn were words to all of us as we deal with death or the fear of death or any other fear for that matter. *"Fear not,"* he said, *"for I am with you always, even to the close of the age."*

Don't be afraid. His steadfast loves endures forever! Such assurance provides balance in the face of every fear. It is the sure antidote to all of our fears.

He Leadeth Me

Psalm 23. The Lord is my shepherd, I shall not want.
He makes me lie down in green pastures;
He leads me beside still waters;
He restores my soul.
He leads me in right paths for his name's sake.
Even though I walk through the darkest valley, I fear no evil;
For you are with me;
Your rod and your staff – they comfort me.
You prepare a table before me
In the presence of my enemies;
You anoint my head with oil;
My cup overflows.
Surely goodness and mercy shall follow me
All the days of my life,
And I shall dwell in the house of the Lord
My whole life long.

I love this Psalm. It has become a standard word of God for the church and for many others in moments when there is need for reminding of the belief that God is with us as a source of hope and comfort as well as truth. Now with both the threat and reality of war staring us in the face, I find it well to reflect on where basic hope, comfort, and truth may be found.

I suppose there are some who do not find much in this Psalm to comfort or encourage them, perhaps because of the belief in some kind of a diminutive or magical God. But these words have stood the test of time and I would wager that many can recite this Psalm from memory.

The 23rd Psalm touches us because it pronounces a tremendous expression of the relationship between God and humanity in the midst of real life.

As is found in all of the Psalms, the language and figures of speech of the common folk are here used to convey the awareness that though evil, disappointment, failure, threat, war, and even death itself lurk on the journeys of life, that the actual experience of life in its fullest is found less in immediate solutions and more in a living connection with the God of the universe. This theme is recounted over and over throughout the Bible and throughout Jewish and Christian history.

This Psalm is a Psalm of confidence, moving directly from the past through the present and concluding in the future.

The language of the first section finds its roots during the time when the Jews were in captivity (exile) in Babylon during the 6th century BC. During that period and thereafter Israel had no king. The nation was a vassal nation of whatever prevailing conquerors were around at the time. So, they built upon their rich faith and theology to evoke a poignant picture of what was real for them, what they could count on throughout the many changes they were experiencing. Always a people who saw their earthly king as a regent for the rule of God, they found ways to look to God as their true King. No matter the upheavals, God was always there. God was always their king. *Shepherd* is used here as one of their King-words. God was called shepherd because he was known to the Jews, and to believers to this day, as the one who delivers, the one who leads to the resting place – the green pastures, the one who shows them the still oasis waters in the desert land, even when threat and death surrounded them. And they knew him to be one who maintained his relationship with them, not abandoning them, staying with them on the right paths. They had experienced this as they were finally returned to their land through the desert and wilderness from exile in Babylon.

Now, one can also hear in this part of the Psalm the faint echoes of the sons and daughters of Israel as they look back to a prior deliverance - their deliverance from Egypt through the desert and wilderness to the Promised Land when Moses was their leader. One can hear here the confidence of someone speaking who knows no philosophical God, no made up God, no God of sentiment or wishful thinking, no God of never-never land far off someplace – but rather a God who has done something among the people throughout their past.

This then is the character of the shepherd God: he delivers his people. He brings them through the wilderness. He doesn't drive the wilderness away but goes with them through the wilderness. He establishes a home with them. He offers them authentic life in the face of great threat. He quiets their fears. He guides them along right paths. Small wonder then that the Psalmist can say, "I shall not want."

This brings us to the present, to the second part of the Psalm. A transformation has taken place in the writing. The psalmist has switched from the third person ("The Lord is my shepherd . . . he makes me lie down . . . he leads me . . .") into the second person ("I will fear no evil for you are with me . . . your rod and staff comfort me, you prepare a table for me . . . .").

It is out of the confidence based on what God has done that the psalmist can turn to his present need and express confidence that God will deliver him and make things whole again here as well. The point stands out clearly that the confidence in what God has done in the past is the ground whereby "he" becomes "you." This, of course, is the central theme of our lives in God's great drama of redemption. He has done his thing on our behalf that we might know him, belong to him, live with him and in him day by day. And in living with him, we can readily sense his presence and his movement in the events of our lives.

The last stanza of the psalm makes the movement from past to future complete. Here we find the confidence he has expressed in terms of past events and present needs becoming the frame of reference for his movement into the future – into each new day. To dwell in the house of the Lord is the underscoring to the fact that living and meaning are not found solely in what happens to us, but are found in terms of in what or in whom we have confidence. Confidence in God in the common ventures of life provides a hopeful way into the future.

This little psalm, so powerful in its images, serves to remind us of what God has done with power and authority in the past on our behalf, particularly in the life, death, resurrection, and presence of Jesus Christ, so that we might have confidence in him in our present moments and on into whatever futures we face. I'm so glad that we have this reminder as well as the God it points us to through Jesus Christ our Lord. Use this Psalm. Treasure this Psalm. It points us toward hope.

Face

As a professional wordsmith, I am attuned to the variety of words I hear each day. I often ponder their origin and various uses, and, occasionally, their misuses. Sometimes I am surprised at how common words and expressions are used in so many different ways. Take the word "face" for example.

People use the term as a kind of descriptive short-cut to communicate some things about the character or nature of a person. *"He has the face of a saint,"* one says about persons who strikes him as being pure and good. Those who are deceptive or duplicitous in their dealings with others people often say are *"two-faced."* For someone who is seeking to cover up a mistake the term used is *"saving face."* And when one talks about the lack of personal identity the term *"faceless,"* as in a faceless crowd, comes to mind.

There are other uses, too. One doesn't want it to be said of her that *"she has a face only a mother could love."* It isn't often that one runs into a person who can *"face down"* a crowd. And who hasn't been greeted somewhere each week with a smiley face or some other emoji seeking to cheer one up!

What we can do with our faces is to show truth or fiction, character or personality. It is perhaps our chief agent of communication. I am reminded of a story told by a Scottish preacher in St. Andrews, Scotland. He was telling young ministers a thing or two about preaching. He said, with a twinkle in his eye, *"When you are speaking of heaven, let your face shine with glory and joy! On the other hand, when you are speaking of hell, your ordinary face will do."*

Joking aside, faces are an important and serious subject. One has only to look at the dour expression on Mr. Putin's face to visualize a man who is in conflict with what is right. On the other hand, the face President Zalensky has shown to his people as well as to the world is a face of a resolve to remain steadfast in the defense of democracy and freedom. Faces reflect many truths, most of them rather important, especially the one found in the account of Jesus heading toward Jerusalem and certain death. One reads in Luke 9:51: "**When the days drew near for him to be taken up, he set his face toward Jerusalem.**"

When Jesus *"set his face"* to Jerusalem, he was setting his face toward his death as well as toward God's salvation for all the world. The expression *"to set one's face"* is found in several places in the Bible. It is a way of saying that one has strong determination, a determination that cannot be turned aside. And it is reflective of the fact that Jesus was in motion, moving from something and then toward something. In his case, he was moving from a ministry of teaching where he prepared many to follow him even as he declared to them that God was at work in him to transform the world. He was moving from this time of preparation and teaching to a climax that would forever mark human life with the seal and ways of God. He was setting his face toward that climax, knowing that it would be death, a death in reality certainly, but a death enacting God's redemption of humanity from endless darkness and confusion. As the writer, John, portrays it, *"What has come into being in him was life, and the life was the light of all people. The light shines in the darkness, and the darkness did not overcome it"* (John 1:4-5).

We are in the season of Lent in the Christian churches. It is the time for one to reflect and prepare the heart for the meaning of the crucifixion of Jesus. That crucifixion is the historical way the eternal God bent low to show what love truly looks like as well as to offer believers the sure way human sin and rebellion may be transformed by that love. For folks who doubt that God ever does anything about the evil in our world and in the hearts of each one, here is presented God's answer: God through him is loving the world so that the world of people might not be perishing but journey with Christ through life into eternity. In the life, death and resurrection of Jesus we are brought *"face to face"* with God. Which leaves us to face ourselves.

One is drawn to ask, then, whether he or she has seen in the mind's eye the glorious "face of God," looking at us across the ages, showing us in countless ways his deepest love for us? In what ways has one watched the face of Jesus as he smiled at little children, reached out to lepers and outcasts, and gently enfolded all kinds of people into his embrace? In what ways has one seen the face of God in Jesus' parables – on the father of the prodigal son as he rushed to restore him, on the face of the vineyard owner as he paid his workers out of generosity rather than their merit, and on the face of the Good Samaritan as he willingly bound up the man on the side of the road? Has God's face shone forth to us when we hear Jesus' words, *"Come to me all you who are weary and overburdened and I will give you rest,"* or his words of invitation, *"Behold, I stand at the door and knock. If anyone opens the door, I will come in to him and eat this him, and he with me?"*

With this kind of face-showing by our God, one must ask about the kind of faces are being made in each one's life. To what has each one's face been set? Together, God is calling his people to set one's face like Jesus toward him in one's life. And in response, perhaps we can hear our God speaking as he did to those of old: *"The Lord bless you and keep you. The Lord make his face to shine upon you and be gracious to you. The Lord lift up his countenance upon you and give you peace"* (Numbers 6:24).

Blessing

Scripture for the Day: Genesis 32:22-32.

The same night he got up and took his two wives, his two maids, and his eleven children, and crossed the ford of the Jabbok. He took them and sent them across the stream, and likewise everything that he had. Jacob was left alone; and a man wrestled with him until daybreak. When the man saw that he did not prevail against Jacob, he struck him on the hip socket; and Jacob's hip was put out of joint as he wrestled with him. Then he said, "Let me go, for the day is breaking." But Jacob said, "I will not let you go, unless you bless me." So he said to him, "What is your name?" And he said, "Jacob." Then the man said, "You shall no longer be called Jacob, but Israel, for you have striven with God and with humans, and have prevailed." Then Jacob asked him, "Please tell me your name." But he said, "Why is it that you ask my name?" And there he blessed him. So Jacob called the place Peniel, saying, "For I have seen God face to face, and yet my life is preserved." The sun rose upon him as he passed Penuel, limping because of his hip. Therefore, to this day the Israelites do not eat the thigh muscle that is on the hip socket, because he struck Jacob on the hip socket at the thigh muscle.

*****

Some years ago both a book and a TV production entitled <u>Holocaust</u> captured the nation's attention. It's goal was to present the absolute horror of the systematic annihilation of six million Jews by the Nazis. There was a scene in the story that has stuck in my mind over the years: Karl Weiss, the gifted Jewish artist, was being kept in the Nazi show-prison at Theresienstadt. His Christian wife, Inga, was there too. Karl had been beaten savagely and repeatedly by the Nazis, trying to get him to tell where pictures he had drawn of the horrors of the death camps were being hidden. In the last meeting he had with his wife before he was taken to Auschwitz to be gassed, Inga told him she was pregnant with his child. Ironically, Karl said she should destroy the child as he would be scarred forever by being raised in such a camp. He told her, "If you love me, end its life before it opens its eyes in this damned place." But Inga said something that's so vital for life. She said, "No, I won't. I want your blessing. I want you to sanctify its life."

How well Inga speaks for us all! How much like all of us she is in seeking a blessing for her child. For if there is anything characteristic among human beings, it is a desire, a need really, to be blessed, if one is live a well-grounded life.

In the story of Jacob wrestling with God in the Genesis passage listed above, the same theme is central. Jacob hangs on to his adversary for dear life saying, "I will not let you go, unless you bless me."

The desire for blessing is deeply stamped in each one. One wants to know if he or she is okay, is loved, is affirmed, is valuable. One seeks to know that one's life is significant and important to others. And at its deepest level, one wants to know that in the larger scheme of things, one has a place of value, especially to the Creator who is above all. To put it another way, one wants a connection with the divine, with God. It's deeply imbedded in each one to want validation of one's existence as well as notice of one's life. Perhaps this is why some seek to make so many different things in life ultimate. Perhaps the desire to be blessed is at the root of both the marvelous things humans have done as well as that which is destructive and mean. As meaning-seeking creatures, humans seek the deeper meanings through connections, through blessings both local and divine.

The personal history of each person one knows could be written in terms of each one's need for and search for whatever is perceived to be a blessing. It could be the blessings of material things - long life, food and possessions, or peace. Or, more likely, it could be the more intangible blessing that Inga sought - approval and worth, validity for being alive.

Our friend, Jacob, though he had stolen the blessing of his father and his brother and was running for his life, still sought a blessing in that gray dawn there on the banks of the River Jabbok. We can read of his fierce determination to cling to his nighttime adversary until such a blessing was given. Here is a picture of a person who was unfilled by all he had maneuvered himself into in life and who finally gave in to the need to find his value in his place in the universe, to find himself grounded because of his place with God. It underscores the fact that folks who don't fully feel or know the blessing of our heavenly Father are ever seeking to fill that void with other things. Jacob learned this through his fierce struggle as a parable for us all. For us, in encountering Jesus throughout one's life, one cannot but hear his many words of blessing that God has for his people, words like, "I am with you," "Fear not," You are God's people," "Come to me all you who labor and are overburdened and I will give you rest," and "Neither death nor life can separate you from the love of God in Christ Jesus our Lord." There is no darkness nor struggle but that these words of promise may hold us and bless us.

We are moving our way through the Lenten Season with Eastertide fast approaching. And what is Easter but a poignant reminder that God has provided the ultimate blessing for the world in coming to it in personal and loving terms, seeking through one's trust in him to provide the ultimate blessing for each one for both life and eternity? Inga was right to want her child blessed. God seeks to provide the same for us all.

Palm Sunday

Can you see it – the little donkey's hooves kicking up spurts of dust along the city streets? The crowd, following along or dancing ahead, is ecstatic in its enthusiasm. "Make way! Make way!" some officious looking, bearded men cry out as they press closer to the donkey and its rider. The children, who love a parade whatever the cause, are gleeful. "Make way! Make way! Here he comes!" the officious looking men cry out again. The rider sits loosely to his mount, his gaze wandering out over the crowd and over the street scene of which he is the center. Easy rider! Taking things as they come. Not fighting against the current. Easy rider! Unknown to the crowds - on his way to cross and crown.

Yet, looking closely at him, one is aware that the rider is detached from all of that exuberance. He seems almost pensive, withdrawn, not struggling, not directing events but riding with them. He seems . . . the only way to say it is he seems lonesome in the midst of the crowd, as if he knows that they don't truly get it. They shout, they wave their branches, they throw down their garments, their attention is on him, riding that little donkey. They crowd around him, some running alongside. Yet he remains a lonesome rider in the sun. Lonesome rider through a crowd that doesn't seem to get it. Lonesome rider on his way to a high noon rendezvous with destiny, not his destiny alone but the destiny of humankind. Lonesome rider, moving toward a cross and a crown, a rider in the sun. Jesus is his name. The strangest king the world has ever seen.

This is a king of peace. But everyone knows few kings are for peace. Kings are for power. Kings are for war. They ride in majesty and in pomp under the sun. They carry swords, wear crowns of precious stones. They sit astride proud horses that prance and toss their manes. They are accompanied by brilliantly garbed courtiers. Not this king! He comes in peace. He carries no sword. The only crown that he will ever wear will be a crown of thorns pressed upon his head. He carries no emblems of authority. His feet locked beneath the belly of the little donkey almost drag the ground. He rides alone. His attendants follow along on foot, dusty, sweaty men of the soil and the sea. A strange, strange king on his donkey in the sun.

And this king wept. ***"And when he drew near and saw the city he wept over it, saying, 'Would that even today you knew the things that make for peace.'"*** A king who weeps? Kings do not weep! Kings are hard-eyed and firm-jawed. They do not dare to weep. Tears may be thought signs of weakness. Kings make no public display of tenderness. To be tender is to be thought soft. Kings are not soft. They cannot be soft. Kings are hard, hard as the wood from which crosses are made, hard as hand-tearing nails.

But not this king! He saw the city, and he wept. He wept for a world of men and women, for a time-haunted, death-taunted world of men and women. He wept for their pain and their promise. He wept for their blind, stumbling despair and their eager hopes. He wept for the carefree and careworn, for the caring and the callous, for their foolish, fumbling failures and their splendid achievements. He wept because they did not know enough to weep for themselves. They just didn't get it. Strange king, this one, with tears on his face, riding in the sun.

Where is he heading? Toward Friday when he will ride no longer but will walk, carrying a cross. Toward Friday and a green hill with a fresh unused gallows and the hot stab of nails in his wrists. Toward Friday and beyond. Toward Friday and on into history.

Thus, our question is, do we get it? Do we get what God was and is up to in sending this man, this lonesome rider in the sun? How shall one speak for peace when cities are being bombed and citizens of Ukraine are being brutalized and annihilated and the world is in an uproar about a wicked king and what he is about?

Yet Palm Sunday is just around the corner and here he comes again in our collective memories, this lonesome rider. The dust is stirred by the hooves of his donkey. The sun is hot, the sky in blue. What will happen this time? The same repetitive reenactment in our minds of a past event with no present memory? Will he ride on down the street again until the dust settles, and the shouts hang hollow on the empty air? Will we see him as he is presenting himself? Will we hear him as he presents God's will to the world?

Perhaps. Perhaps there is something new. There is always the potential in our world of humanity for something new. There is always God's Spirit stirring the dust. And who knows? Out of the jangle of our age, something new may emerge. The turmoil of our time may be a sign of potential vigor. God works in history and in individual lives, but he works in his own strange fashion. And we, too, like those long ago citizens of Jerusalem, see and hear and yet may know not his coming.

Yet he keeps coming again in our minds and hearts, in our lives, in our worship and prayers, in our hopes, in the events which surround us. Note that Jesus said, "Would that even today you knew . . . ." It is never too late to know. Jesus still rides among us. (with gratitude to the late Dr. Kenneth Phifer whose words are adapted here)

Easter (2)

Maybe you remember the Irving Berlin song of years ago about an Easter parade. As best I remember, the words went something like this:

In your Easter bonnet,
With all the frills upon it,
You'll be the grandest lady in the Easter parade.

That, it seems to me, has a kind of swing to it and the tune is catchy enough to play through your mind over and over after you've heard it. Even the words stay with one:

On the avenue, Fifth Avenue,
The photographers will snap us,
And you'll find that you're in the rotogravure.

The words are catchy all right, but theologically it is seriously lacking as an Easter song, to say the least.

I'll be all in clover
When they look you over.
I'll be the proudest fellow in the Easter parade.

Isn't it strange how meaningful customs can become trivialized? This is not to speak against bonnets or clothes or warm songs. They have their places. But I am remarking on how attention can so easily be shifted from the sublime to the surface, especially when it comes to God's actions among us.

In early Christianity, there were new clothes at Easter, but hardly of the kind we think of today. Their new clothes were the white robes that were worn by the learners in the early church for their baptisms which took place on Easter Sunday. The original Easter parade was not down Central Avenue, but a planned dispersal from the worship service to hospitals and orphanages and homes of the poor on errands of kindness and mercy after the Easter service was complete. It was all in the spirit of Paul's words to the Romans: **"As Christ was raised from the dead by the glory of the Father, we, too, might walk in the newness of life."** That's what the resurrection is all about, a walk into the newness of life. As one man asked: "How might one respond to Easter? Paul's answer was that we start walking, not talking." **"As Christ was raised from the dead . . . we too might walk in the newness of life."** That's the real Easter parade.

Many years ago writer John Mansfield wrote a play entitled "The Trial of Jesus." In the play Longinus, the Roman Centurion who was in charge of the crucifixion after having reported to Pontius Pilate the governor, is detained by Pilate's wife, Procula, for further questioning. She asks for the details of the crucifixion.

Longinus: *He was a fine young fellow, my lady, not past the middle age.*

And he was all alone and defied all the Jews and all the Romans,

and when we had done with him he was a poor broken-down

thing, dead on a cross.

Procula: *Do you think he is dead?*

Longinus: *No, lady, I don't.*

Procula: *Then, where is he?*

Longinus: *Let loose in the world, lady, where neither Roman nor Jew*

can stop his truth.

"Let loose in the world." Those are words to ponder. For so it has proven over and over through the centuries. Time and again in these twenty-one centuries, he has been written off, sometimes in rather superficial fashion. D.H. Lawrence, writing to Katherine Mansfield said, *"Cheer up, Katie, Jesus is a back number."* How many times has he been so dismissed? Thomas Carlyle, gazing gloomily upon a crucifix outside a parish church, saying with a shake of his head sadly, *"It's all very well, old fellow, but you've had your day."* Many today, seeing what some groups of Christians say and do in Christ's name which are hard-hearted and politically motivated, have decided to have none of this Jesus, at least the Jesus they see portrayed. Yet, throughout history and throughout our lives just when folks pass this kind of judgment on him, gleefully or sorrowfully, he emerges with the same extravagant claim upon human life, giving us the something more we need.

For over four thousand years, the things of God have entered the human realm, unpredictably yet continually. Jesus who represents uniquely the things of God just won't stay dead any more than God doesn't stay out of human affairs. Jesus just won't go away. Neither for history nor for individual lives. If one wants proof of the Resurrection, this is the only kind of proof one will ever get – his turning up throughout history. Turning up to Mary Magdalene weeping in the garden, turning up to those two forlorn souls on their way to

Emmaus, turning up to his disciples hidden in fear, turning up to Paul on his way to Damascus where he went to stamp out the Jesus movement. Turning up in the lives of men and women throughout two millennia, even here in the lives of you and me. Turning up and turning lives around. Turning up and renewing spirits, forgiving sins, arming the heart against evil, and deepening the spirit so one can love. *"Let loose in the world,"* as Longinus put it. **"Let loose in the world."** I think that is as vivid and as accurate a description as one will find anywhere of the Resurrection. That was the heart of the preaching of the early church. Not "follow the leader and be good," but "Jesus is risen." God has raised him from the dead. He is here. Be not afraid. He abides among us, still turning up, turning up often when and where one least expects him, turning up and turning lives around. Happy Easter!

Shadows

I live in the shadow of those who have been and are important in my life – home, wife, children, and others. By this, I mean that their influence provides a shadow of influence which shapes much of the way I see and believe. In most cases, the shadows cast by those folks and their works provide a refreshing and nourishing place for my living and being. Where would I be without the shadow of my mother's love of reading, of writing, and of music? What kind of faith would I have were it not for the shade provided me by my church and its ministers and people? These are shadows where I love to dwell. And where would any of us be without the overshadowing of our lives by those champions of life and purpose who continue even in old age to provide the shade necessary for life away from the blistering sun?

In the Bible, *shadow* is sometimes used figuratively for something protective (like the king's or God's shadow – cf. Psalm 91:1-2 – *"You who live in the shelter of the Most High, who abide in the shadow of the Almighty, will say to the Lord, 'My refuge and my fortress; my God, in whom I trust.'"*). Further, human life is sometimes depicted as a shadow that moves and eventually disappears, denoting the transitory nature of life. The days of life are like an evening shadow in Psalm 102:11, and those in poor health compare themselves to waning shadows in Psalm 109:23. In the New Testament, *shadow* occurs in Old Testament quotations denoting that much of life is under "the shadow of death and that the coming of Jesus is to provide light for those *"who sit in darkness and in the shadow of death"* (Luke 1:79). A wonderful picture of the role God plays in the lives of those who trust him is seen in Luke 1:35 where the angel told Mary that the Most High would overshadow her, and she would become pregnant and bear a child. Somewhat akin to this use is the picture depicted in Acts 5:15 where Jerusalemites carried the sick out into the street hoping that Peter's shadow would fall on them when he passed by with the result that they would be healed.

As we journey through the Eastertide, I am reminded that the news of the resurrection began with Jesus in the shadows. Mary Magdalene went to the tomb, and after she discovered it was empty, she ran to the disciples and told them the news. Then she and Peter "ran" to the tomb. While Peter went into the tomb with all its revelation of resurrection, Mary Magdalene stood outside where in the dim morning mist she was confronted by two angels in white. Her grief was deep on the fear that someone had carried Jesus' body away. According to John's gospel, upon hearing her name called there in the shadows, she recognized Jesus, calling out "Rabbouni!" (which means Teacher). While I have always been a fan of "the light shining in the darkness and Jesus as the light of the world," nevertheless, there is something almost up front and personal for me in realizing that for Mary Magdalene (and for

216

countless thousands of others), Jesus has been known in the shadows. In so many cases, what God does through his Son is to encounter us in the shadows of life, as it were. And there are a number of ways we can sense him/know him in the shadows.

In the sense that we are not alone no matter the shadows which have come upon us, Jesus is known as God with us. In the sense that there is more to come, that this present time is not the final word, Jesus is known as God among us. The map makers of the sixteenth century used to produce maps of the known world. When they reached the limits of their knowledge, especially at sea, they would print *"Here be dragons."* The unknown and the future can be quite frightening. Our light is simply not bright enough to see what is down the road, but we can be and are given the sense within which there is enough to go on. Paul, writing out of resurrection faith, put this sense into Christian language for us when he said, *"We know that in everything God works for good with those who love him, who are called according to his purpose."* That is the sense that there is more to come from God.

Jesus may be beckoning to us wherever there arises in us a deep sense of right and wrong. Right out of the shadows of the evil we witness, our hearts can be turned toward mercy and righteousness by Jesus in the shadows. Sometimes that beckoning is a still, small voice, whispering from the shadows an assuring word or a commanding word or a word of hope. Elijah heard that voice in the shadow of violence, a voice not to be drowned out by earthquake wind or fire (I Kings 19:12). Jesus' word of forgiveness was uttered in the shadow of death, wind, and storm. I can think of no more profound voice from the shadows of life than that of Jesus given to us which forgives us our foolishness and folly, arms us with a way of life, and promises to journey with us into the unknown. Truly, the shadows of life are not to be feared or dreaded. Jesus is there, in the shadows, truly an Easter message.

Water

Susan and I have a half an acre of lovely property just off the waterfront in Beaufort, NC. It is property that has come to Susan from her parents and her aunt that has been in Susan's family since 1850. It's a grand place to live. It also affords us the opportunity to abundantly festoon the land with trees, shrubs, and flowers, both annuals and perennials. Aided by three towering 100 year-old pecan trees and gathered at the feet of a 200 year-old Live Oak, pathways wind throughout the azaleas, camellias, hydrangeas, roses, Turks Caps, lilies of several types, and a couple of dozen other types of plants. Hedges and plantings separate the land into "rooms," each of which has its own special selection of plants and shrubs. A fishpond supports the usual families of frogs and toads as well as a supply of goldfish which do very well except when the Great Blue Heron visits for a snack. Birds are abundant and the garden is visited regularly by raccoons, possums, foxes, and rabbits, coyotes, and turtles. 144 species of birds have been recorded either in, over, or heard from this special place. The garden is ablaze in color at this springtime and it is a delight to our eyes and to our hearts. One thing, though, the garden needs plenty of water.

As the land sits very close to the shore (saltwater Taylor's Creek), the land is very sandy. Some dirt has been brought it, but the sandy nature of the land makes it very thirsty as it does not hold moisture for long. Fortunately, we have two wells which pump ground water through a network of hoses with which we water the land. And I mean "water the land" since rainfall, while often plentiful, is not consistent. Susan has become a mistress of hoses and spends considerable time making sure the plants and shrubs are watered. Without water, the garden would wither.

That, of course, is an apt metaphor for many aspects of life.

One writer has seen water metaphorically by extolling its virtues and inviting readers to "Be like water" ("Be Like Water, by Russell Jeung, Christian Century, May 4, 2022). By this he notes that water is **clear** especially if it is still. So, the invitation is given to be still so that life and its many aspects can be more clear. Noting that water is **humble**, he underscores the reality that water does not force its own way but follows the most likely path. Perhaps this is what Jesus meant when he said the "meek" were to be blessed. However, Jeung notes that water is not passive but **persistent**. This is a good note for any who may tire of Christian faith and practice, for persistence can "wear away obstacles over time" especially in the land of Christian faith and practice. A final note about water for believers is that water is **restorative**. Who hasn't been thoroughly refreshed on a hot day by a fine glass of cold water or a dip in the swimming pool? Christian faith can and does have this restorative quality about it for those live in faith. Prayer allows one to purge the soul, identify the crossroads of one's life, and allow God's grace to envelope both heart and mind. I would call that restorative. The use of water as metaphor for so many parts of life and experience appear to be limitless.

This is especially true in the Bible. The Old Testament writers often used water metaphors to express the close link between the creator and sustainer God. Showers of rain reminded those folks of arid landscape of God's blessings (cf. Ezekiel 34:26). Conversely, the lack of rain was often seen by the prophets as a sign of some breach of the covenant by which they lived. Water was seen as one of God's gifts in the creation and when the Hebrews were wandering in the wilderness and alarmed by the lack of water, the provision of water (Exodus 15:25; 17:1-6) when Moses struck the rock underscores the creation gift of water given by God. This theme is picked up by the New Testament where Jesus describes himself as the divine water giver (John 4:10, 13-14). This "living water" provided by Jesus (a metaphor for a living faith) transforms the one partaking of it from within and becomes a "spring of water gushing up to eternal life" (John 4:14).

Interestingly, the New Testament ends with Revelation 22:1 echoing the creation by describing the river of the water of life, which seems to be an echo of the stream that went out of Eden (Genesis 2:10). In the metaphor, this river of the water of life emanates from the throne of God and the Lamb located in the city of God, again highlighting that God is not only the creator but also the sustainer of life, even and especially to eternal life. In a further echo of Jesus' dialogue with the Samaritan woman in John 4, the final invitation of the last book of the New Testament concerns access for those thirsty for the water of life to come and receive this water for free (Revelation 22:17). Isn't it most fitting that the symbol for entering the new life God calls us to in Christ is the water of baptism?

Without water, life on earth would die. That's reality and dozens of metaphors underscore its veracity. Likewise, without the "water" God provides through creation and redemption, the spirit within each one becomes parched and lessens the ability to live fully. Without water, whatever "garden" we are in cannot live for long. Pastor Rich.

Breath

Other than one's heartbeat supplying blood to brain and body I suppose that breathing is the most essential function of our bodies for staying alive. As one who is dealing daily with asthma and nightly with apnea, I give more attention to the way I breathe than ever before. Not only does breathing furnish the blood with needed oxygen, but one's brain cannot function without the refreshment given through one's breathing. And, one's sleep cannot refresh if breathing is impaired so that deep sleep (REM) is not reached.

So essential is breathing that phrases concerning breathing have crept into the vernacular as a means of expressing some important things. "Shortness of breath" is not only a physical condition, but it and "run out of breath" often denote lacking the strength to "go on." "To catch one's breath" can indicate the need to stop for a few moments to retool or refresh. Likewise, to be "out of breath" indicates that one has no more energy or desire to move on. To "breathe fire" is a very clear expression of fierce anger and when one is "scorched" by such anger, it is a powerful motivator. When one has an overwhelmingly negative experience, one might put it succinctly by saying that it "knocked the breath (or wind) out of me." Having adequate breath is essential for living, both literally and figuratively.

Interestingly, those practitioners of Yoga and meditative therapies place great focus on breathing and breath. They see a deep connection between breathing and peace of mind. Slow and deep breathing relaxes the mind as well as the body and allows for turning inward in thought and feeling. It also allows for relaxation both physically and mentally. Spiritual counselors often begin their sessions with clients with a period of deep breathing.

The root word for "breath" in the Bible can be translated in three ways: wind, breath, and spirit. When one translates Biblical passages with this word, one meaning may dominate, but the other two are usually in the background. In the Old Testament, the divine activities of judgment and creation are described in terms of "breath." In Genesis, the "wind" (breath/Spirit) of God swept over the waters of chaos and divided the waters so that the world was created. When the early church was formed (cf. Acts 2), we read that "a violent wind (Spirit/breath) filled the entire house where they were sitting," and "All of them were filled with the Holy Spirit' (wind, breath). God's anger is expressed in 2 Samuel 22:16 as being a "blast of breath from his nostrils." God's creative and purposeful power is clearly seen early on in Genesis when we're told that the Lord "breathed" into Adam's nostrils the breath of life and he became a living being." Any student of the Old Testament can remember that great scene in Ezekiel 37 where God takes the prophet out into the wilderness to see the "valley of the dry bones" and how those bones revived and became live once again because the Lord said: "Come from the four winds, O breath, and breathe upon these slain, that they may live." God's breath is God's power and purpose and it is expressed in wind, breath, and spirit. One might also remember that in John's Gospel, he emphasizes the overt act of Jesus breathing on his disciples telling them to receive the Spirit – a new creation. As God created life in Genesis 2:7, in the same way Jesus creates eternal life by breathing on his disciples after he is raised from the dead. One's spiritual life is a life animated by God's Spirit/breath/wind.

There was a moment when Moses had asked God what his name was. God was gracious enough to answer, and the name he gave is recorded in the original Hebrew as YHWH (Yahweh). Scholars and rabbis have noted that the letters YHWH represent breathing sounds, or aspirated consonants. When pronounced without intervening vowels, it actually sounds like breathing, YH (inhale), WH (exhale).

So a baby's first cry, her first breath, speaks the name of God. A deep sigh call God's name – or a groan or gasp that is too heavy for mere words. Even an atheist would speak God's name unaware that his or her very breath is giving constant acknowledgement to God. Likewise, a person leaves this earth with a last breath, when God's name is no longer filling the lungs.

Does this mean that when I can't utter anything else, that my cry is calling out God's name?

Being alive means that I speak God's name constantly as I breathe. Is it heard the loudest when I am quietest? In sadness, one breathes heavy sighs (Paul speak of "sighs too deep for words" in Romans 8:26). In joy, our lungs feel almost like they will burst. In fear we hold our breath and have to be told to breathe slowly to help us calm down. When we're about to do something hard, we take a deep breath to find our courage.

In thinking about it, breathing is a way of giving God praise. Even in the hardest moments!

This has really captured my imagination and broadened my awareness. Just think of it: God chose to give himself a name that we can't help but speak every moment we're alive. All of us, always, everywhere. Waking, sleeping, breathing, with the name of God on our lips. Just as we're invited to do in the last word of the last Psalm: "Let everything that breathes praise the Lord!" (Psalm 150:6).

Sit

My earliest memory of the instruction "to sit" comes from about the time I turned two years of age. Being of active mind and body, my early childhood was filled with discovery, action, learning, and mischief. All well and good except that the mischief part often resulted in my being banished from normal activity to serve out a sentence of "sitting on the stairs." The stairs to the second floor of the house were in the center of the house and, thus, a convenient place where Mother could keep an eye on me as I sat out my punishment. "Sit on the stairs" was reserved for special moments. But for an active child, they were painful in the way that limiting activity can be for one whose style was motion. "Sit on the stairs" was a frequent sentence, to be sure, but "sit still" was an even more frequent admonition to the active life of one such as I. It continues to be a useful goal to this day, however.

The Bible is filled with statements about "sitting," "sit," "dwell," and being "enthroned," all translations of the same root words. Indeed, there are 1,088 references to the words in the Old Testament alone. Of course, the regular meaning of "sit" and "sitting" is used often: "Moses sat down by a well" (Exodus 2:15) being an easy example. Solomon's prayer of dedication as he became the king of Israel includes comments about him "sitting on the throne of Israel" (1 Kings 8:25). "Sitting at the city gate" is used to indicate working or participating in the marketplace or, in some incidences, sitting in the place of judgement by members of the city rulers which usually took place at the gate of the city. Phrases like "sitting in ambush," "sit and beg," "dwelling in a land of deep darkness," and "sitting at the right hand" of a king or ruler are sprinkled throughout the Old Testament. To "sit at the right hand" indicates a place of special honor and authority. The phrase is even used in the Apostles' Creed where Jesus is depicted as "sitting on the right hand of God." One of the advantages of sitting is that one must be still usually. Sitting in this way is much admired in the Old Testament as one can come close to God in such a way ("Be still and know that I am God" – Psalm 46:10). The Old Testament writers envisioned God with human terms as they wrote. Thus, they could say that God "sits enthroned in righteous judgment" (Psalm 9:4). Indeed, the picture of God "sitting" on a throne continues to have a place in our mental pictures to this day. The terms are perhaps the best we can use to indicate that God dwells among us and above us and is enthroned over us. And when God is so envisioned, the vision is of God "sitting."

The New Testament continues with both literal and metaphorical uses of "sit" and "sitting" and other variations. When some of the folks asked Jesus who had sinned, a blind man or his parents that he had been born blind, they noted that he survived by "sitting and begging" (John 9:8) – the common way the term is used. Likewise, when Jesus was teaching the Disciples about riches, he comments on the future by saying, "When the Son of Man is seated on the throne of his glory" (Matthew 19:28). The term is used metaphorically in numerous places illustrated by its use in Zechariah's prophesy in Luke 1:78-79 (*"By the tender mercy of our God, the dawn from on high will break upon us, to give light to those who sit in darkness and in the shadow of death, to guide our feet into the way of peace."*) Through the ages, countless many have known something of what "sitting in darkness and in the shadow of death" implies.

"Sit" and "Sitting" as well as its cousins, "dwell" and "enthroned" are not terms limited to the poetry and narrative of the Bible. Our common language is filled with metaphors using the terms. And they are most apt. To wit: "sitting in the catbird seat," "like a sitting duck," fence-sitting," "come sit a spell," "sit back and let it happen," "taking part in a sit-in," "sitting on the edge of one's seat," "all at one sitting," "sat bolt upright," "sitting beneath the salt"(an old expression from Medieval times denoting sitting at a lower table than the nobles – the salt was at the nobles' table which was higher than the others), and "footprints in the sand of time are not made in one sitting." That's just a few.

All this brings to mind thoughts about Psalm 1, a Psalm which sets the tone for the hymnbook of Israel as well as helping believers think through just where they are "sitting" in their spiritual lives:

> *Happy are those who do not follow the advice of the wicked,*
> *or take the path that sinners tread,*
> *or sit in the seat of scoffers; but their delight is in the law of the Lord,*
> *and on his law they meditate day and night.*

> *They are like trees planted by streams of water,*
> *which yield their fruit in its season,*
> *and their leaves do not wither.*

> *In all they do, they prosper.*
> *The wicked are not so, but are like chaff that the wind drives away.*
> *Therefore the wicked will not stand in the judgment, nor sinners in the congregation of the*
> *righteous, But the way of the wicked will perish.*

In other words, where does one sit as one moves through life? To the Hebrews, one sat with the Law as revealed to them through Moses and the prophets. That Law guided them in righteousness. To Christians, one sits within the grace of the Lord given in Jesus Christ and lived out in the kind of righteousness as revealed in both Old and New Testaments . For both, life is more than "sitting on the stairs" or "fence-sitting" or even "sitting back and letting it happen." It is confident dwelling with our God.

Secret

One of my favorite church stories is about the pastor who was talking with one of his parishioners who hadn't been in church worship in a long time. Said the pastor: "If you are in the army of the Lord, how come I haven't seen you in church in a while?" The quick-witted parishioner replied without a blink of the eye, "I'm in the Secret Service!" And so he was in a manner of speaking. Many folks these days have joined him there in the Secret Service as well it appears, especially since and because of the interruptions the Coronavirus has placed upon us. Our church attendance is at present about 50 per cent of what it was before the pandemic came among us.

We use the term "secret" frequently. "Secret Santa" shows up at Christmas. Some of us remember the program "I've Got A Secret." We are hearing a good bit at present about our Secret Service. In many places "secret" is interspersed with "hidden" and "disguised." In today's world, it is interspersed with "classified" and "top secret" and "restricted." Sometimes it is used to denote the pivotal knowledge around which all else revolves or is influenced by, such as the "secret to life" or the "secret to understanding" one's teenager or the politics of our time. "Secret" sometimes means known only by a few, or as something that should remain hidden from others. I have loved the book "The Secret Garden" with its redemptive theme attached to the secret. One goes to school to learn the secret of good writing or good welding or good anything else. There are many secrets in our lives.

This got me to thinking about that term "secret" and how it has to do with our Christian faith. And as I looked into it, I found that it has a lot to do with our Christian faith. Indeed, things secret or hidden are mentioned in a number of ways throughout the Bible.

In some places "secret" denotes those things which are hidden from others – the normal way the word is used. In Proverbs 11:13 gossip is said to be the telling of secrets and the verse implores one to be trustworthy in keeping secrets. In Exodus 7:11, the *"secret arts of sorcerers"* are mentioned denoting that they keep their methods from others. These are normal uses of the term.

Elsewhere, "secret" points to those things which are to be hidden from others but which are beneficial to some as in Proverbs 21:14 where the teacher tells us *"A gift in secret averts anger."* But perhaps more importantly, there are numerous places where those things which are hidden from others but are beneficial for one's life with God are spelled out as in Jesus' Sermon on the Mount (cf. Matthew 6 where one is to give alms in secret, to pray in secret, and to fast in secret so that only God is aware). This is seen as moving away from pride and conceit and toward humility. Many of Jesus' parables are told by that master storyteller to open believers up to the "secrets of the Kingdom of God." In Mark 4:11 we find, *"And he said to them, 'To you has been given the secret of the kingdom of God, but for those outside, everything comes in parables.'"* Throughout the New Testament there is an emphasis on the faithful who can know the secrets of God while the rebellious cannot. Add to this the testimony of Jeremiah (23:23-24) that God is near and not so far off that one can hide from him: *"Am I a God nearby, says the Lord, and not a God far off? Who can hide in secret places so that I cannot see them? says the Lord."*

The Apostle Paul (Philippians 4:12-13) tells us after describing the suffering he has gone through for the sake of the Gospel that he has learned the secrets of perseverance: *"I know what it is to have little, and I know what it is to have plenty. In any and all circumstances I have learned the secret of being well-fed and of going hungry . . . I can do all things through him who strengthens me."*

So, while there is much about God who is in secret and humans who cannot have secrets from God, one finds much emphasis on God's will to reveal the "secret things" to his people so that they might prosper in life and have confidence in the face of death. In Deuteronomy 29:29 the writer states that *"The secret things belong to the Lord our God, but the revealed things belong to us and to our children forever, to observe all the words of his law."* Unlike many of the pagan religions of the ancient world, God is not hidden in secrets, but is revealed by his care for his people. God's wisdom and truth is known by the faithful because God reveals them through his life with Israel, through the life, death, and resurrection of Jesus, and through his continuing presence in the Holy Spirit. That's one reason we have regular worship as a church: to give witness and testimony to God's revelation to us for our lives. The Apostle Paul underscores this again and again: *"Now to God who is able to strengthen you according to my gospel and the proclamation of Jesus Christ, according to the revelation of the mystery that was kept secret for long ages but is now disclosed. . . ."* (Romans 16:25). Indeed, Pauls' ministry, echoing the revelation of the entire Bible is caught up in the words he wrote to the Corinthians: *"Yet among the mature we do speak wisdom though it is not a wisdom of this age, who are doomed to perish. But we speak God's wisdom, secret and hidden, which God decreed before the ages for our glory . . . ."* (I Corinthians 2:6-7). That's the kind of Secret Service into which we are invited to live.

Sufficient

One wonders if there truly is anything like self-sufficiency in this life. For many it is a goal: not to have to depend on anyone or anything, generating all that one needs on one's own, depending on the self to provide all that is needed. Perhaps that is the drive for those who have trekked into the wild lands to go off the grid and live providing all one needs by oneself. To have to depend on others for living for some seems burdensome and, at times, even intrusive. I suppose most everyone has feelings and thoughts about not being so dependent on others and on the utilities and staples of life. Let the power go off for a while and one wishes he or she didn't have to depend upon it to live a normal life. Let a relationship begin to show cracks or fail and one thinks that being alone is the better way. One of the heart hungers in life for many is more or less to be self-sufficient.

Of course, no one can ever be completely self-sufficient, ever. It's an illusion to believe that one can be. Yes, there are degrees of sufficiency, I suppose. Some people can get along with less dependence on others and the resources of life than others. But no one is completely and always self-sufficient. One of the two definitions of *sufficient* is *enough* or *adequate*, and it is true that many can find a place in life where there is enough for their living. Indeed, most folks I know have developed their lives so that they have enough to feel sufficient. Perhaps that is why when inflation rears its ugly head or there is a gas shortage or there aren't enough vaccines to go around or a fearsome illness comes along or some deranged person invades a school and kills teachers and children the fear of not having enough or being sufficient in daily living rears its own unattractive head. In cases like these, sufficiency is dependent upon outside forces and it doesn't take much to create the fear that there won't be enough and one will not have what is sufficient for life.

But there is another definition of *sufficient* for us to ponder. This meaning focuses on the *condition* of the person rather than the necessities for living. Of course, this is the meaning indicated by Jesus and by Paul in their several writings about living in an imperfect, insufficient world as a people who are sufficient in living their lives. In that famous passage in the Sermon on the Mount, Jesus puts this second definition into words (Matthew 6:25-34): *25 "Therefore I tell you, do not worry about your life, what you will eat or what you will drink,[a] or about your body, what you will wear. Is not life more than food and the body more than clothing? 26 Look at the birds of the air: they neither sow nor reap nor gather into barns, and yet your heavenly Father feeds them. Are you not of more value than they? 27 And which of you by worrying can add a single hour to your span of life?[b] 28 And why do you worry about clothing? Consider the lilies of the field, how they grow; they neither toil nor spin, 29 yet I tell you, even Solomon in all his glory was not clothed like one of these. 30 But if God so clothes the grass of the field, which is alive today and tomorrow is thrown into the oven, will he not much more clothe you—you of little faith?* ³¹ *Therefore do not worry, saying, 'What will we eat?' or 'What will we drink?' or 'What will we wear?'* ³² *For it is the gentiles who seek all these things, and indeed your heavenly Father knows that you need all these things.* ³³ **But seek first the kingdom of God[c] and his[d] righteousness, and all these things will be given to you as well.** ³⁴ *"So do not worry about tomorrow, for tomorrow will bring worries of its own. Today's trouble is enough for today."*

To those who define sufficiency in terms of having all they need and want for living, these words sound naïve and foolish. If Jesus's words are an invitation to sit back and let whatever happens happen, of course much of what we need and want in life would not simply come to us. If we didn't concern ourselves with these basic aspects of daily life, we would be compounding trouble upon ourselves and others. However, Jesus is doing his usual thing in teaching here, good Rabbi that he was. He exaggerates to make his point. And his point is that worry, excessive anxiety, fearful living, and focus on only the surface areas of life kills the spirit within and doesn't produce the goods we may so want. What he invites his listeners into is a consideration of the *condition* of their hearts and minds in dealing with these areas of life. Anxious hearts limit one's ability to live fully and fruitfully. Excessive concern over daily needs turns days into fateful struggles with the demons of fear and doubt. Empty hearts and minds are never satisfied and the resultant anxiety colors life in darker shades. And, to boot, such worry seldom is satisfied thus rendering the desire for sufficiency to be insufficient.

In considering the condition of one's heart and mind, one is invited to shed an outward focus as the place to begin and to replace it with attention to the "still small voice" speaking within in the words of Scripture as well as notions implanted by God himself. The inner voice of God, shaped by both the revelations of the Scriptures and by the soul that is open to God within, changes the focus of sufficiency from that which is on the outside of a believer to that which is on the inside. Such an inner voice strengthens a believer as one receives the presence of God into mind and heart as the condition by which one deals with daily life. Such an inner voice echoes what Paul heard as he sought to deal with his "thorn in the flesh" as he inwardly stood on the ground of faith. The words echo even today in the hearts of believers: ***"My grace is sufficient for you, for power is made perfect in weakness"*** (2 Corinthians 12:8-9). That is the sufficiency we are offered each day as God's people.

227

". . . think about these things"

Richard C. Boyd

This is a book for reflection, meditation, and devotion for Christians and others, the writings of which were born during the first two years of the COVID pandemic in America. Written by a Presbyterian clergyman with his small North Carolina congregation as well as his many friends in mind, the varied subjects are a potpourri of issues, ideas, and subjects emanating from the Scriptures and the Christian life. The title comes from Philippians 4:8 (NRSV):

Finally, beloved, whatever is true, whatever is honorable, whatever is just, whatever is pure, whatever is pleasing, whatever is commendable, if there is any excellence and if there is anything worthy of praise, think about these things.

The writer has served five Presbyterian churches during his fifty-three years of ministry. He is a graduate of Maryville College in Maryville, TN (B.A. in Philosophy and Religion), Union Presbyterian Seminary in Virginia (M.Div. in Pastoral Ministry; Th.M. in Biblical Theology) and McCormick Theological Seminary in Chicago (D. Min. in Church Revitalization). He is the father of two daughters and grandfather to three. He and his wife, Susan, live in Beaufort, NC.

CPSIA information can be obtained
at www.ICGtesting.com
Printed in the USA
BVHW031758240922
647755BV00002B/5